Microsoft® Outlook® for Mac 2011

Step by Step

Maria Langer

Published with the authorization of Microsoft Corporation by:
O'Reilly Media, Inc.
1005 Gravenstein Highway North
Sebastopol, California 95472

Copyright © 2011 Maria Langer.

Complying with all applicable copyright laws is the responsibility of the user. All rights reserved. Without limiting the rights under copyright, no part of this document may be reproduced, stored in or introduced into a retrieval system, or transmitted in any form or by any means (electronic, mechanical, photocopying, recording, or otherwise), or for any purpose, without express written permission of O'Reilly Media, Inc.

Printed and bound in the United States of America.

1 2 3 4 5 6 7 8 9   M   6 5 4 3 2 1

Microsoft Press titles may be purchased for educational, business or sales promotional use. Online editions are also available for most titles (http://my.safaribooksonline.com). For more information, contact our corporate/institutional sales department: (800) 998-9938 or corporate@oreilly.com. Visit our website at microsoftpress.oreilly.com. Send comments to mspinput@microsoft.com.

Microsoft, Microsoft Press, ActiveX, Excel, FrontPage, Internet Explorer, PowerPoint, SharePoint, Webdings, Windows, and Windows 7 are either registered trademarks or trademarks of Microsoft Corporation in the United States and/or other countries. Other product and company names mentioned herein may be the trademarks of their respective owners.

Unless otherwise noted, the example companies, organizations, products, domain names, email addresses, logos, people, places, and events depicted herein are fictitious, and no association with any real company, organization, product, domain name, email address, logo, person, place, or event is intended or should be inferred.

This book expresses the author's views and opinions. The information contained in this book is provided without any express, statutory, or implied warranties. Neither the author, O'Reilly Media, Inc., Microsoft Corporation, nor their respective resellers or distributors, will be held liable for any damages caused or alleged to be caused either directly or indirectly by such information.

Acquisitions and Development Editor: Kenyon Brown
Production Editor: Kristen Borg
Production Services: Online Training Solutions, Inc.
Technical Reviewer: Andy Ruff, Richard Kmieciak, and Albert Andersen
Indexing: Potomac Indexing, LLC
Cover: Karen Montgomery
Illustrator: Robert Romano

978-0-735-65189-0

To Chuck Joiner, with thanks.

Contents

What do you think of this book? We want to hear from you!

Microsoft is interested in hearing your feedback so we can continually improve our books and learning resources for you. To participate in a brief online survey, please visit:

> microsoft.com/learning/booksurvey

Introducing Microsoft Outlook for Mac 2011

Microsoft Outlook for Mac 2011 is an electronic communication and personal information management application that can help you take control of your email Inbox, contacts list, and calendar—all with one attractive and consistent interface. From one place, you can store, organize, manage, and retrieve many types of information. With Outlook for Mac, you can:

- Send, receive, forward, and organize email messages.
- Include images and other multimedia files as attachments to email messages you send.
- Send files created with Microsoft Office or other applications to clients, coworkers, family, or friends.
- Preview file attachments received as email attachments from others.
- Filter out junk or spam email messages.
- Schedule events, such as appointments or meetings, including recurring events.
- Invite people to meetings and keep track of their responses so that you know who will attend.
- View upcoming events and get reminders for them.
- Store contact information, including phone numbers, email addresses, Web sites, and mailing addresses, for people you know.
- Maintain and organize tasks lists.
- Store information as notes.
- Search through email messages, calendar events, contacts lists, tasks, and notes to find the information you need when you need it.

In an enterprise environment, Outlook interacts with a Microsoft Exchange Server to provide unified communications services, including real-time presence and status information, specialized functionality for internal messaging, scheduling information, and many other useful features.

New Features

Part of the Microsoft Office for Mac 2011 suite of applications, Outlook replaces Entourage 2008 with a whole new look and powerful new features. Here's a quick list of some of the ones you'll find most useful:

- The Microsoft Office ribbon puts the features and commands you use most right at the top of the Outlook window, organized by tabs.
- A unified Inbox displays all of your incoming messages together.
- Conversations make it possible to view long email threads under a single subject.
- Displaying your calendar in meeting invitations makes it easy to see, at a glance, whether you're free to attend a meeting.
- .PST import makes it easy to switch from the Windows version of Outlook to the Mac OS version.
- Mac OS X integration taps into standard Mac OS features such as Quick Look and Spotlight.
- The cleaner, more attractive interface makes it easier to work with your information.

Let's Get Started!

Outlook for Mac 2011 offers many great features to help you work smarter and more efficiently with your email, calendar, contacts, tasks, and notes. But don't just take my word for it. Dive in and see for yourself on the pages that follow.

Modifying the Display of the Ribbon

The goal of the Microsoft Office working environment is to make working with Office documents—for example, Microsoft Outlook for Mac 2011 email messages—as intuitive as possible. You work with an Office document and its contents by giving commands to the application in which the document is open. All Office for Mac 2011 applications organize commands on a horizontal bar called the ribbon, which appears across the top of each application window whether or not there is an active document.

Commands are organized on task-specific tabs of the ribbon, and in feature-specific groups on each tab. In Outlook for Mac, commands generally take the form of buttons and lists.

Throughout this book, we discuss the commands and ribbon elements associated with the Outlook feature being discussed. In this topic, we discuss the general appearance of the ribbon, things that affect its appearance, and ways of locating commands that aren't visible on compact views of the ribbon.

Dynamic Ribbon Elements

The ribbon is dynamic, meaning that the appearance of commands on the ribbon changes as the width of the ribbon changes. A command might be displayed on the ribbon in the form of a large button, a small button, a small labeled button, or a list entry. As the width of the ribbon decreases, the size, shape, and presence of buttons on the ribbon adapt to the available space.

For example, when sufficient horizontal space is available, the buttons on the Home tab of the Outlook application window are spread out and you're able to see the commands available in each group as large or wide buttons.

If you decrease the width of the ribbon, some buttons shrink and their button labels disappear.

Changing the Width of the Ribbon

The width of the ribbon is dependent on the horizontal space available to it, which depends on these two factors:

- **The width of the application window** Resizing the application window to full size provides the most space for ribbon elements. You can resize the application window by dragging the resize handle in the lower-right corner of the window.

- **Your screen resolution** Screen resolution is the size of your screen display expressed as pixels wide × pixels high. The greater the screen resolution, the greater the amount of information that will fit on one screen. Your screen resolution options are dependent on your monitor. At the time of writing, possible screen resolutions range from 800 × 600 to 2048 × 1152. In the case of the ribbon, the greater the number of pixels wide (the first number), the greater the number of buttons that can be shown on the ribbon, and the larger those buttons can be. You can change the screen resolution in the Displays preferences pane of System Preferences.

Adapting Exercise Steps

The screen images shown in the exercises in this book were captured at a screen resolution of 1024 × 768 at 72 dots per inch. If any of your settings are different, the ribbon on your screen might not look the same as the one shown in the book. Specifically, the buttons you see might be represented by larger or smaller icons than those shown, with or without button labels.

When we instruct you to give a command from the ribbon in an exercise, we do it in this format:

- On the **Home** tab, click the **Reply** button.

If the command is on a menu, we give the instruction in this format:

- On the **Home** tab, click the **New** button and then, in the menu, click **Folder**.

The first time we instruct you to click a specific button in each chapter, we display an image of the button in the page margin to the left of the exercise step.

If differences between your display settings and ours cause a button on your screen to look different from the one shown in the book, you can easily adapt the steps to locate the command. First, click the specified tab. Then look for a button that features the same icon in a larger or smaller size than that shown in the book. If necessary, point to buttons to display their names in ScreenTips.

If you prefer not to have to adapt the steps, set up your screen to match ours while you read and work through the exercises in the book.

Features and Conventions of This Book

This book has been designed to lead you step by step through all the tasks you're most likely to want to perform in Microsoft Outlook for Mac 2011. If you start at the beginning and work your way through all the exercises, you will gain enough proficiency to be able to create and work with email messages, calendar events, contact records, tasks, and notes. However, each topic is self-contained. If you complete all the exercises and later need help remembering how to perform a procedure, the following features of this book will help you locate specific information:

- **Detailed table of contents** Search the listing of the topics and sidebars within each chapter.

- **Chapter thumb tabs** Easily locate the beginning of the chapter you want.

- **Topic-specific running heads** Within a chapter, quickly locate the topic you want by looking at the running heads at the top of odd-numbered pages.

- **Glossary** Look up the meaning of a word or the definition of a concept.

- **Keyboard Shortcuts** If you prefer to work from the keyboard rather than with a mouse, find keyboard shortcuts in many places throughout the book.

- **Detailed index** Look up specific tasks and features in the index, which has been carefully crafted with the reader in mind.

You can save time when reading this book by understanding how the *Step by Step* series shows exercise instructions, keys to press, buttons to click, and other information.

Convention	Meaning
SET UP	This paragraph preceding a step-by-step exercise indicates the practice files that you will use when working through the exercise. It also indicates any requirements you should attend to or actions you should take before beginning the exercise.
CLEAN UP	This paragraph following a step-by-step exercise provides instructions for saving and closing open files or programs before moving on to another topic. It also suggests ways to reverse any changes you made to your computer while working through the exercise.
1 2	Blue numbered steps guide you through hands-on exercises in each topic.
1 2	Black numbered steps guide you through procedures in sidebars and expository text.
See Also	This paragraph directs you to more information about a topic in this book or elsewhere.
Troubleshooting	This paragraph alerts you to a common problem and provides guidance for fixing it.
Tip	This paragraph provides a helpful hint or shortcut that makes working through a task easier.
Important	This paragraph points out information that you need to know to complete a procedure.
Keyboard Shortcut	This paragraph provides information about an available keyboard shortcut for the preceding task.
Command+B	A plus sign (+) between two keys means that you must press those keys at the same time. For example, "Press Command+B" means that you should hold down the Command key while you press the B key.
 Save	Pictures of buttons appear in the margin the first time the button is used in a chapter.
Black bold	In exercises that begin with SET UP information, the names of program elements, such as buttons, commands, windows, and dialog boxes, as well as files, folders, or text that you interact with in the steps, are shown in black, bold type.
Blue bold	In exercises that begin with SET UP information, text that you should type is shown in blue bold type.

Using the Practice Files

Before you can complete the exercises in this book, you need to copy the book's practice files to your computer. These practice files, and other information, can be downloaded from here:

http://oreilly.com/catalog/9780735651890/

Display the detail page in your Web browser and follow the instructions for downloading the files.

Important The Microsoft Outlook for Mac 2011 program is not available from this Web site. You should purchase and install that program before using this book.

The following table lists the practice files for this book.

Chapter	File
Chapter 3: Composing and Sending Email Messages	Images
	Antelope Canyon.jpg
	GC Clouds.jpg
	GC Trees.jpg
	Kaibab Plateau.jpg
	LCRG.jpg
	London Bridge.jpg
	LP Aerial.jpg
	San Juan Aerial.jpg
	Stucco-100.jpg
	Stucco-50.jpg
	Movies
	ExploringSedona.mp4
	Gila Monster.m4v
	GrandCanyonDayTrip.mp4
	Other Files
	Flyer.docx
	More Message Text.textClipping

Chapter	File

Chapter 3: Composing and Sending Email Messages *(continued)*	vCards
	    Ben Andrews.vcf
	    Josh Bailey.vcf
	    Kim Akers.vcf
	    Lisa Andrews.vcf
	    Maria Langer.vcf
	    Nancy Anderson.vcf

Chapter 6: Fine-Tuning Email Settings	Coho Winery.jpg Grapes.jpg

Chapter 9: Managing Contact Information	Mike Entin.jpg
	vCards
	    Ben Andrews.vcf
	    Josh Bailey.vcf
	    Kim Akers.vcf
	    Lisa Andrews.vcf
	    Maria Langer.vcf
	    Nancy Anderson.vcf

Chapter 10: Organizing Your Contacts List	Ben Andrews.vcf Josh Bailey.vcf Kim Akers.vcf Lisa Andrews.vcf Michael Entin.vcf Nancy Anderson.vcf
Chapter 11: Working with Contact Records	April Reagan.vcf Eric Gilmore.vcf Kim Akers.vcf
Chapter 12: Tracking Tasks	Report.docx

Chapter	File
Chapter 13: Taking Notes	Phone Call Note.txt
	Images
	Antelope Canyon.jpg
	GC Clouds.jpg
	GC Trees.jpg
	Kaibab Plateau.jpg
	LCRG.jpg
	London Bridge.jpg
	LP Aerial.jpg
	San Juan Aerial.jpg
Chapter 14: Using Shared Features	Message Text.txt

Getting Support and Giving Feedback

Errata

We've made every effort to ensure the accuracy of this book and its companion content. If you do find an error, please report it on our Microsoft Press site at *oreilly.com*:

1. Go to *microsoftpress.oreilly.com*.
2. In the Search box, enter the book's ISBN or title.
3. Select your book from the search results.
4. On your book's catalog page, in the list of links under the cover image click View/ Submit Errata.

You'll find additional information and services for your book on its catalog page. If you need additional support, please send an email message to Microsoft Press Book Support at *mspinput@microsoft.com*.

Please note that product support for Microsoft software is not offered through the addresses above.

Getting Help with Microsoft Outlook for Mac 2011

If your question is about Microsoft Outlook for Mac 2011, and not about the content of this Microsoft Press book, your first recourse is the Outlook for Mac 2011 Help system. You can find general or specific Help information by clicking the Help button (labeled with a question mark) located in the upper-right corner of the Outlook for Mac program window.

If your question is about Microsoft Outlook for Mac 2011 or another Microsoft software product and you cannot find the answer in the product's Help system, please search the appropriate product solution center or the Microsoft Knowledge Base at:

support.microsoft.com

You can post questions and search previously answered questions at the Microsoft Answers community-based forums at:

answers.microsoft.com

In the United States, Microsoft software product support issues not covered by the Microsoft Knowledge Base are addressed by Microsoft Product Support Services. Location-specific software support options are available from:

support.microsoft.com/gp/selfoverview/

We Want to Hear from You

At Microsoft Press, your satisfaction is our top priority, and your feedback our most valuable asset. Please tell us what you think of this book at:

www.microsoft.com/learning/booksurvey

The survey is short, and we read *every one* of your comments and ideas. Thanks in advance for your input!

Stay in Touch

Let's keep the conversation going! We're on Twitter: *http://twitter.com/MicrosoftPress*.

How to Access Your Online Edition Hosted by Safari

The voucher bound-in to the back of this book gives you access to an online edition of the book. (You can also download the online edition of the book to your own computer; see the next section.)

To access your online edition, do the following:

1. Locate your voucher inside the back cover, and scratch off the metallic foil to reveal your access code.

2. Go to http://microsoftpress.oreilly.com/safarienabled.

3. Enter your 24-character access code in the Coupon Code field under Step 1:

(Please note that the access code in this image is for illustration purposes only.)

4. Click the CONFIRM COUPON button.

   A message will appear to let you know that the code was entered correctly. If the code was not entered correctly, you will be prompted to re-enter the code.

5. In this step, you'll be asked whether you're a new or existing user of Safari Books Online. Proceed either with Step 5A or Step 5B.

   5A. If you already have a Safari account, click the EXISTING USER – SIGN IN button under Step 2.

5B. If you are a new user, click the NEW USER – FREE ACCOUNT button under Step 2.

○ You'll be taken to the "Register a New Account" page.

○ This will require filling out a registration form and accepting an End User Agreement.

○ When complete, click the CONTINUE button.

6. On the Coupon Confirmation page, click the My Safari button.

7. On the My Safari page, look at the Bookshelf area and click the title of the book you want to access.

How to Download the Online Edition to Your Computer

In addition to reading the online edition of this book, you can also download it to your computer. First, follow the steps in the preceding section. After Step 7, do the following:

1. On the page that appears after Step 7 in the previous section, click the Extras tab.

2. Find "Download the complete PDF of this book," and click the book title:

A new browser window or tab will open. Your browser will either immediately begin downloading the file or will display a dialog box you can use to instruct it to save the file in the default download location.

3. When the file has finished downloading, locate it on your hard disk—it will likely be in your Downloads folder on your Desktop—and double-click its icon to extract the PDF file from the ZIP archive.

4. Double-click the book's PDF file icon to open it in your default PDF reader application.

Note If you have a problem with your voucher or access code, please contact mspbooksupport@oreilly.com, or call 800-889-8969, where you'll reach O'Reilly Media, distributor of Microsoft Press books.

Acknowledgments

I'd like to thank the people that were instrumental in helping me create this book.

First, at O'Reilly, Kenyon Brown. Ken and I worked together in the early 1990s on one of my very first books, back when he was with another publisher. He remembered me and was kind enough to give me a try for this project. For that, I thank him.

Also, at O'Reilly and Online Training Solutions, Inc. (OTSI), a long stream of editors and production people, including Sumita Mukherji (O'Reilly), Kristen Borg (O'Reilly), Jean Trenary (OTSI), Jaime Odell (OTSI), and Kathy Krause (OTSI). These folks helped make sure the book's text was grammatically correct, met style guidelines, and looked great in print.

At Microsoft Corporation, Andy Ruff, Richard Kmieciak, and Albert Andersen. These guys helped make sure the information I provided was technically correct.

I'd also like to thank Chuck Joiner, for letting me know that Microsoft Press was looking for an Outlook book author. I owe my participation in this project to him. Thanks, Chuck.

Finally, a big thanks goes out to my husband, Michael Chilingerian, for taking my usual vented frustrations and giving his usual support.

Part 1

Start Here

Chapter at a Glance

Add Exchange and other e-mail accounts, **page 8**

Set e-mail account and server options, **page 18**

Import existing Entourage data, **page 14**

Accounts

Show All

Margiestravel
maria@margiestravel.com

Margiestravel
Exchange Account

Account description: Margiestravel

Personal information

Full name:

E-mail address: maria@margiestravel.com

Authentication

Method: User Name and Password

User name: maria_margies

Password: ••••••••

Advanced...

Enter your account information.

E-mail address: maria@lucernepublishing.com

Password: ••••••••

☐ Configure automatically

User name: maria@lucernepublishing.com

Type: IMAP

Incoming server: mail.lucernepublishing.com : 143

☐ Override default port
☐ Use SSL to connect (recommended)

Outgoing server: mail.lucernepublishing.com : 465

☑ Override default port
☑ Use SSL to connect (recommended)

Import

Begin Import

What do you want to import?

○ Outlook Data File (.pst or .olm)
◉ Entourage information from an archive or earlier version
○ Information from another application
○ Contacts or messages from a text file
○ Holidays

Click the right arrow to continue.

◁ 1 ▷

1 Getting Started Using Outlook

In this chapter, you will learn how to

✔ Set up email accounts in Outlook.

✔ Add an Exchange account.

✔ Add an email account.

✔ Import Entourage data into Outlook.

✔ Troubleshoot connection problems.

✔ Set additional email account options.

Welcome to Microsoft Outlook for Mac 2011, Microsoft's replacement for the Microsoft Entourage application found in previous versions of Microsoft Office for Mac OS. Outlook for Mac offers Mac OS users a brand new interface for working with email, calendar events, tasks, and contacts. Its feature set is more in line with Outlook for Windows, making it easier for users who frequently use both computer platforms.

The very first step to using Outlook is to set up at least one email account. After Outlook is configured for email, you can begin using it to exchange email with others, schedule events on your calendar, track tasks, and manage your contacts.

If you've been using Entourage, you can jump start your setup process with Outlook by importing your existing Entourage data into Outlook. All of your email accounts, contacts, and calendar data will be copied to Outlook automatically so you can get right to work.

In this chapter, you'll add your email account(s) to Outlook or, if you've been using Entourage, you'll import existing data into Outlook.

> **Practice Files** No practice files are needed for this chapter. For more information about practice file requirements, see "Using the Practice Files" at the beginning of this book.

Setting Up Email Accounts in Outlook

Before you can use Outlook, you must set up at least one email account. Outlook supports many different kinds of email accounts, including:

● **Microsoft Exchange** You can configure Outlook to connect with an Exchange account hosted on Microsoft Exchange Server 2010, Microsoft Exchange Server 2007, or Microsoft Exchange Server 2003. For an Exchange account, messages are stored both on the Exchange Server and in a data file on your computer. Outlook keeps the two databases of messages synchronized when you connect so you can work with existing items and create new items when you're offline.

● *IMAP* This account type, which stands for *Internet Message Access Protocol*, downloads messages from the mail server and stores copies of them on your computer. When Outlook connects, it synchronizes the messages on the server with those on your computer. This makes it possible to work offline and to access your email from more than one computer.

   Tip Apple's MobileMe email accounts use IMAP and are supported by Outlook.

● *POP* This account type, which stands for *Post Office Protocol*, downloads messages from the mail server and stores copies of them on your computer. It automatically deletes the original messages from the server according to time-based or action-based settings you specify. For example, you can set your POP account to delete messages more than a week old or messages that you delete from your computer.

Hotmail, Gmail, and More

Outlook also supports popular Web-based email services such as Microsoft Hotmail, Google Gmail, and AOL mail. In most cases, Outlook can automatically configure itself for these accounts with only the email address and password for each account, making them very easy to set up. By adding these accounts to Outlook, you can manage all of your email in one place.

When you first start Outlook, a Welcome To Outlook For Mac window offers two options:

● **Add Account** This option enables you to add a Microsoft Exchange account or an IMAP, POP, or other type of email account to Outlook.

● **Import** This option enables you to import existing data from Entourage or another email application into Outlook.

Tip If you're upgrading from Entourage 2004 or Entourage 2008, use the Import option to get started using Outlook quickly.

You can add any number of email accounts to Outlook during initial setup or any time afterward. If you have multiple email accounts, you'll find Outlook a great tool for centralizing all of your email activities.

In the following exercises, you'll add a variety of email account types to Outlook. You'll also learn how you can import existing email account information from your old Entourage setup so you can start using Outlook quickly, without losing access to existing email messages and other Entourage data.

In this exercise, you will launch Outlook and use the Welcome window or menu commands to set Outlook as your default email application and to begin the process of adding or importing an email account.

SET UP Microsoft Outlook for Mac must be properly installed on your computer to complete this exercise. No additional files are needed.

Microsoft
Outlook
Application Icon

1. In the **Dock**, click the **Microsoft Outlook** icon.

> **Tip** If the Outlook icon does not appear in the Dock, you can find it in the Microsoft Office 2011 folder inside the Applications folder. Double-click that Microsoft Outlook icon.

2. What happens next depends on whether this is the first time you've opened Outlook.

    ○ If this is the first time you've opened Outlook and no email account has been configured, the Welcome To Outlook For Mac window appears.

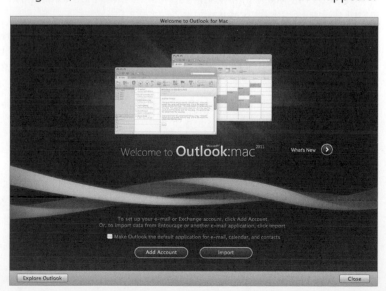

○ To set Outlook as your default email application, select the **Make Outlook the default application for e-mail, calendar, and contacts** check box.

○ To begin the process of adding a new account, click the **Add Account** button. In the **Accounts** window that appears, click either the **Exchange Account** or **E-mail Account** button to specify the type of account you want to create.

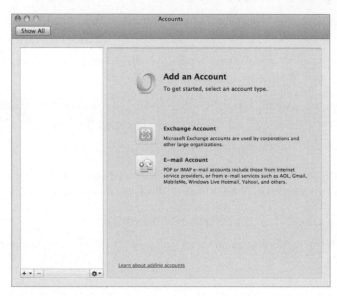

○ To begin the process of importing existing Entourage data into Outlook, click the **Import** button.

Tip To see what's new in Outlook, click the What's New button in the Welcome To Outlook For Mac window. The top half of the window changes to offer brief descriptions of six new Outlook features.

Tip To learn more about Outlook, click the Explore Outlook button to launch your default Web browser and view information about Microsoft Office 2011 on the Microsoft Mactopia Web site. When you're finished, quit your browser application to return to the Welcome To Outlook For Mac window.

○ If Outlook has already been opened or set up with at least one email account, Outlook displays the Inbox.

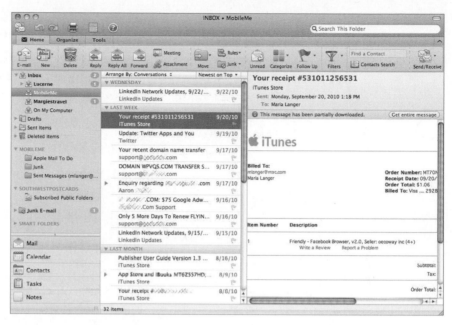

See Also For a complete description of the Outlook interface, see Chapter 2, "Introducing the Outlook Interface."

General

○ To set Outlook as your default email application, on the **Outlook** menu, click **Preferences** to display the **Outlook Preferences** window, and then click the **General** button to display **General** preferences. Click the **Make Default** button.

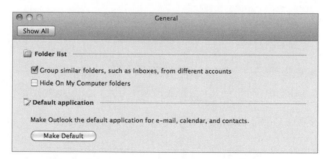

Click the window's close button to dismiss it.

○ To begin the process of importing existing Entourage data into Outlook, on the **File** menu, click **Import**.

○ To begin the process of adding an email account, on the **Tools** menu, click **Accounts** to display the **Accounts** window.

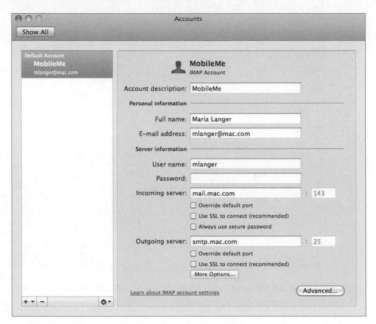

On the **+** menu at the bottom of the list of accounts, click **Exchange** or **E-mail**.

3. Continue following instructions in one of the following sections to add a new email account or to import existing Entourage data into Outlook.

 CLEAN UP Leave Outlook open if you are continuing to the next exercise.

Adding an Exchange Account

In this exercise, you'll add an Exchange account to Outlook.

SET UP You need your Exchange account user name and password to complete this exercise. In addition, if your Exchange account is hosted by a third-party service provider, you may also need to know the names and authentication requirements of your incoming and outgoing servers. This information is available from your email service provider.

1. When you tell Outlook you want to add an Exchange account, it displays a dialog sheet that prompts you for your Exchange account information.

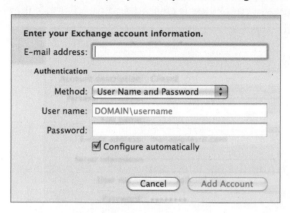

2. In the **E-mail address** field, enter your complete Exchange email address.

3. On the **Method** pop-up menu beneath **Authentication**, click the authentication method you will use with the Exchange account: **User Name and Password** or **Kerberos**.

4. What happens next depends on the authentication method you selected.

    ○ If you clicked **User Name and Password**, enter this information in the **User name** and **Password** fields.

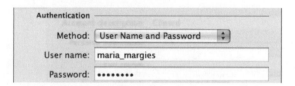

    ○ If you clicked **Kerberos**, in the **Kerberos ID** pop-up menu, select or create an ID to use for authentication.

5. To instruct Outlook to attempt to configure the account automatically, make sure the **Configure automatically** check box is selected.

6. Click **Add Account**.

    Outlook connects to the Internet and attempts to detect the Exchange server. If it succeeds and completes the setup, you can skip the remaining steps.

If Outlook cannot automatically configure the account, a message appears in the bottom of the configuration dialog sheet telling you that Autodiscover failed. The Configure Automatically check box is cleared and the dialog sheet expands to include a Server field.

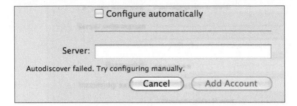

7. In the **Server** field, enter the complete name of the Exchange server.

8. Click **Add Account**.

   The account is added to the Accounts window with the settings you specified.

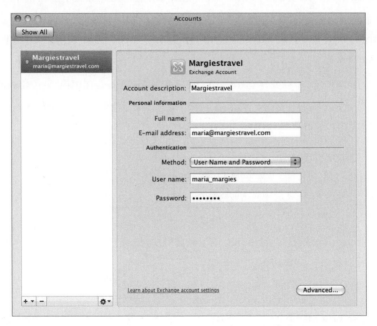

✖ **CLEAN UP** Leave Outlook open if you are continuing to the next exercise.

Adding an Email Account

In this exercise, you'll add an email account to Outlook.

 SET UP You need your email account user name and password to complete this exercise. In addition, you may also need to know the names and authentication requirements of your incoming and outgoing servers. This information is available from your email service provider.

1. When you tell Outlook you want to add an email account, it displays a dialog sheet that prompts you for your email address and password.

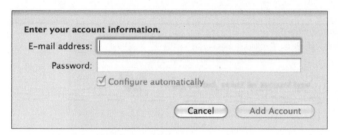

2. In the **E-mail address** field, enter your full email address.

   One of two things happens.

   ○ If your email account is with an online service such as MobileMe (formerly .Mac), Hotmail, or Gmail, the Configure Automatically check box becomes active and is selected.

   When you enter your password and click the Add Account button, your account is automatically configured and added. You can skip the remaining steps.

○ If your email account is on your own server or with an Internet service provider (ISP) unknown to Outlook, the dialog sheet expands to display additional fields.

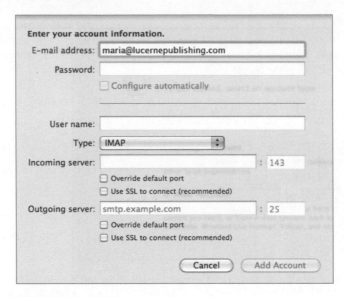

Follow the remaining steps.

3. In the **Password** field, enter your email account password.

4. In the **User name** field, enter your email account user name.

5. On the **Type** pop-up menu, click the type of account: **IMAP** or **POP**.

6. In the **Incoming server** field, enter the complete address of your incoming mail server.

7. If your email connection instructions indicate that you should use a different port than what is indicated beside the **Incoming server** field, select the **Override default port** check box and enter the correct port number.

8. If you want to use SSL to connect to the incoming mail server, select the **Use SSL to connect** check box.

9. In the **Outgoing Server** field, enter the complete address of your outgoing mail server.

10. If your email connection instructions indicate that you should use a different port than what is indicated beside the **Outgoing server** field, select the **Override default port** check box and enter the correct port number.

11. If you want to use SSL to connect to the outgoing mail server, select the **Use SSL to connect** check box.

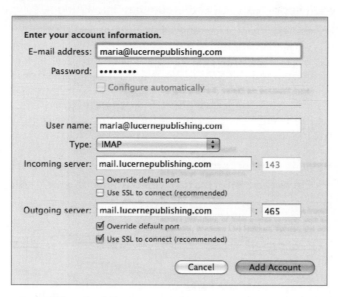

12. Click **Add Account**.

The account is added to the Accounts window with the settings you specified.

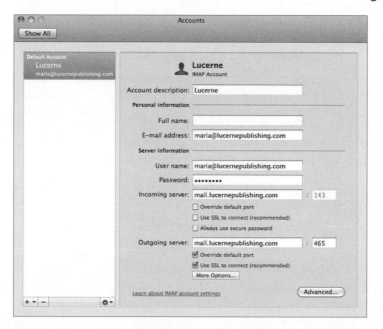

CLEAN UP Leave Outlook open if you are continuing to the next exercise.

Importing Entourage Data into Outlook

In this exercise, you'll import existing Entourage data into Outlook so you can start using Outlook without losing access to your email, calendar, and contacts.

SET UP These instructions assume that you have installed Outlook on the same computer on which you used Entourage. Your Entourage data should be stored in your Office 2008 Identities folder inside the Microsoft User Data folder. If you haven't already done so, either click the Import button in the Welcome To Outlook For Mac window, or on the File menu, click Import as instructed in the section titled "Setting Up Email Accounts in Outlook" at the beginning of this chapter.

1. When you begin the import process, the Begin Import pane of the Import wizard appears. Click **Entourage information from an archive or earlier version**.

TIP You can follow these same basic steps to import data from other applications, including Outlook for Windows and Apple Mail. Just be sure to choose the appropriate type of data in the Begin Import pane of the Import wizard.

2. Click the right arrow button.

3. In the **Choose an Application** pane, select the version of Entourage you used before upgrading to Outlook.

4. Click the right arrow button.

5. In the **Import Items** pane, select the items you want to import.

Tip By default, all items on the Import Items page of the wizard are selected, but you can click an item to clear it and exclude it from your Outlook configuration.

6. Click the right arrow button.

7. In the **Select an Identity** pane, select one of the identities in the list.

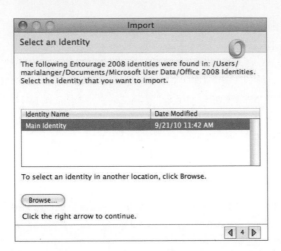

Tip In most cases, only one identity will be listed and it will be automatically selected. If the identity you want to use is not listed, click the Browse button and use the dialog box that appears to locate and choose the identity folder you want to import.

8. Click the right arrow button.

9. If a warning dialog box appears, telling you that Outlook does not support synchronization with all versions of Exchange server, click **OK**.

10. Wait while Outlook imports your Entourage data. Its progress appears in the Import window as it works.

   When it's done, the Import Complete pane appears.

11. Click **Finish**.

   The Outlook Inbox appears.

 CLEAN UP Leave Outlook open if you are continuing to exercises in the next chapter.

Troubleshooting Connection Problems

The automatic configuration feature of Outlook makes setting up Exchange and other email accounts easy—when it works. Unfortunately, not all accounts can be configured automatically. If automatic configuration fails or is simply not an available option, you need to make sure you have the correct configuration information from your account administrator or host to set up your account.

Setting Up Exchange Accounts

Several things could prevent Outlook from automatically configuring an Exchange account. Here are a few of the most common problems.

- You may need to enter more information about your account, including the Exchange server address. Make sure you get this information from your account administrator or host so it's available when you configure the account.

- Your basic configuration information may be redirected to another server to get settings for your account. If this happens, a dialog box may appear asking permission to allow the server to configure your settings. If you trust the server, click Allow and wait for automatic configuration to complete. Otherwise, click Deny and use manual configuration with the correct server setup to complete the configuration process.

- Outlook for Mac supports accounts managed by Exchange Server 2007 Service Pack 1 with Update Rollup 4 installed—or later versions of Exchange Server. If you're having trouble connecting to your Exchange account, check to make sure the Exchange Server on which your account resides is compatible with Outlook.

- If your Exchange account requires you to log on using an encrypted channel, you'll need to set up Exchange to connect with SSL. On the Tools menu, click Accounts to display the Accounts dialog box. Select the Exchange account and then click the Advanced button. Select the Use SSL To Connect check box and click OK.

- If your Exchange account requires a mail proxy server to connect to the Exchange server, you'll need to get proxy server information from your account administrator and then set up the proxy server in Mac OS X.

In most cases, your account administrator or host should be able to help you determine what information and settings are required to configure an Exchange account in Outlook. Consult the configuration instructions you received for your account to start the troubleshooting process.

Setting Up Other Email Accounts

If automatic configuration is not offered for your email account, you'll need server address and authentication information to complete the setup process. Specifically, you need to know the following information, which should be provided by your email service provider:

- Email address
- User name or user ID
- Account password
- Account type
- Incoming mail server address
- Incoming mail server port
- Incoming mail server authentication requirements
- Outgoing mail server address
- Outgoing mail server port
- Outgoing mail server authentication requirements

In some instances, an email account can be configured as either IMAP or POP, depending on what server address and port are entered for the setup. Similarly, some accounts can allow connections with or without SSL authentication.

Setting Additional Email Account Options

When setting up an email account, you can provide additional information, such as an identifying name for the account and the name you want to appear in the From field for email messages you send. You do this in the Account Description and Full Name fields of the Accounts pane for the account. On the Tools menu, click Accounts to display the Accounts window, and then click the name of the account you want to modify.

For POP accounts, you control how messages are retained on the server. Each time you connect to retrieve email messages, you receive a copy of the original message. The original message remains on the server for the period you specify in the Advanced Server settings. By default, messages remain on the server until you delete them on your computer, but you can set received messages to be automatically deleted from the server after one day, one week, one month, or never. On the Tools menu, click Accounts to display the Accounts window and then click the name of the account you want to modify. Click the Advanced button and then click the Server button. You can then choose an option from the Delete Copies From The Server pop-up menu.

To disable this feature entirely, clear the Leave A Copy Of Each Message On Server check box. This tells Outlook to delete messages from the server as soon as they are retrieved by Outlook.

Tip If you access your POP email account from multiple computers, leaving a copy of each message on the server makes it possible to retrieve the same messages from each computer. A better solution, however, might be an IMAP account, which can synchronize mailbox contents.

See Also The information in this chapter is enough to get you started sending and receiving email in Outlook. Chapter 6, "Fine-Tuning Email Settings," provides additional information about setting up email accounts.

Key Points

- You can configure Outlook to connect to Exchange, IMAP, and POP email accounts, including MobileMe, Hotmail, Gmail, and AOL mail accounts.

- You can add multiple email accounts to Outlook, thus centralizing all of your email activity in one location.

- Outlook can automatically configure many types of email accounts based on email address and account password.

- Email account options offer support for a wide range of server and authentication settings.

Chapter at a Glance

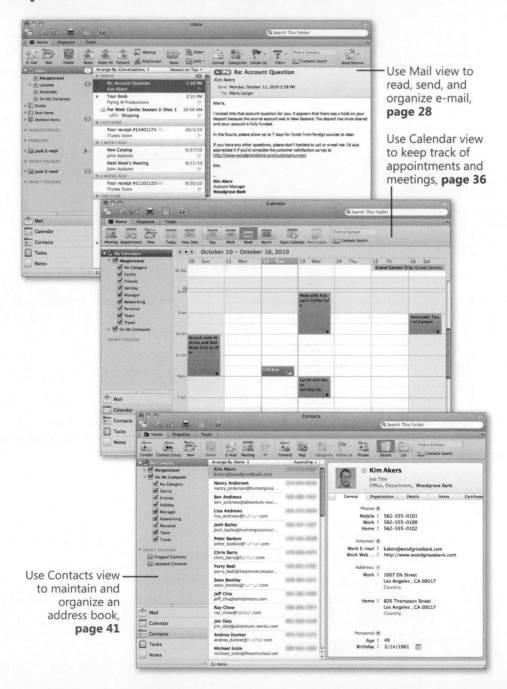

Use Mail view to read, send, and organize e-mail, **page 28**

Use Calendar view to keep track of appointments and meetings, **page 36**

Use Contacts view to maintain and organize an address book, **page 41**

2 Introducing the Outlook Interface

In this chapter, you will learn how to

✔ Explore the Outlook interface.

✔ Work with the ribbon.

✔ Work in Mail view.

✔ Work in Calendar view.

✔ Work in Contacts view.

✔ Work in Tasks view.

✔ Work in Notes view.

Microsoft Outlook for Mac 2011 organizes your information and all the tools you need to work with it by using interface elements that are familiar to Mac OS and Microsoft Office users. Email messages, contacts, and other content appear within the main Outlook for Mac window. You switch from viewing one type of information to another by clicking a button in the window's view switcher.

The Office ribbon, which varies in appearance depending on the view you're working with and the width of the window, offers access to commands and features. Within each view, the ribbon offers several task-oriented tabs of buttons and menus. You can also use familiar menu bar menus, submenus, and dialog boxes to access the commands and features you need.

In this chapter, you'll learn how the Outlook window is organized into views. You'll learn how to use commands on the ribbon and menus. You'll also explore the features within the Mail, Calendar, Contacts, Tasks, and Notes views.

> **Practice Files** No practice files are needed for this chapter. For more information about practice file requirements, see "Using the Practice Files" at the beginning of this book.

Exploring the Outlook Interface

Unlike the other components of Office, Outlook does not create a specific type of document file. Instead, it enables you to manage specific kinds of information that you use every day.

Within the Outlook application, each type of information—email, contacts, calendar events, tasks, and notes—is given its own view. This helps keep this information separate, yet together. When you work with email in the Mail view, for example, contact lists and the tools to work with them are hidden. You can still access contact information as needed, however, within the Mail view.

The Outlook interface has eight areas you use to interact with Outlook and your information.

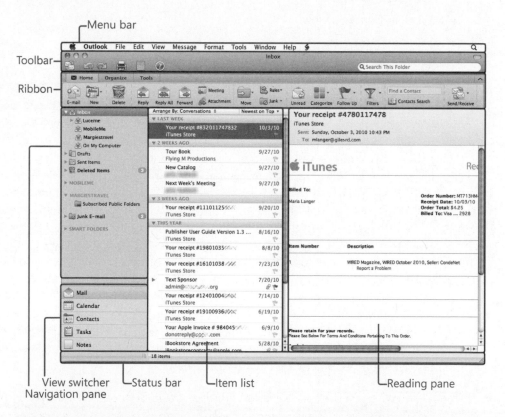

Troubleshooting The appearance of the Outlook window varies depending on the width of the window, the selected view, and any customization options that may have been set. Throughout this chapter, the screenshots represent the default settings for the Outlook interface elements.

● **Menu bar** The standard Mac OS menu bar at the top of the screen offers access to all of the Outlook commands through the use of menus, submenus, and dialog boxes. The menu bar is not part of the Outlook window but can be used with window contents.

● **Toolbar** The toolbar, which appears between the window's title bar and the Outlook ribbon, includes a handful of buttons for commands that work throughout Outlook, regardless of the view displayed.

● **Ribbon** The ribbon, which appears beneath the toolbar, offers groups of buttons and menus for working with Outlook information. Groups of buttons are organized under tabs and vary from one view to another. The ribbon offers a more efficient way to access commands than the standard menus.

> **Troubleshooting** The appearance of buttons and groups on the ribbon changes depending on the width of the window. For information about changing the appearance of the ribbon to match what you see in this book, see "Modifying the Display of the Ribbon" at the beginning of this book.

● **Navigation pane** The navigation pane, which appears on the left side of the window, offers access to groups of information. Its appearance varies depending on what view is displayed. For example, in the Mail view, it lists your Inbox, accounts, and folders for storing email. In the Contacts view, it lists contact categories and groups.

● **Item list** The item list, which appears in the center of the window, displays the contents of whatever is selected in the navigation pane. For example, if an email account is selected in the navigation pane in the Mail view, the item list displays a list of the email messages within that account's Inbox. Similarly, if a category is selected in the navigation pane of the Contacts view, the item list displays a list of contacts within that category.

● **Reading pane** The reading pane, which appears on the right side of the window, displays the content of any item selected in the item list. For example, selecting an email message in the item list of the Mail view displays the contents of that message, whereas selecting a contact name in the item list of the Contacts view displays the details about that contact.

● **View switcher** The view switcher, which appears beneath the navigation pane, has five buttons for switching among the five Outlook views. Click a button to immediately switch to that view.

● **Status bar** The status bar, which appears at the bottom of the window, displays a count of the items in the item list, as well as connection status.

Tip You can customize most elements of the Outlook interface.

Outlook contents and features are organized by view. There are five views: Mail, Calendar, Contacts, Tasks, and Notes. You work with one view at a time in the Outlook window. When a view is displayed, the ribbon displays only those buttons and menus that apply to that view.

Tip When you first start Outlook, it displays the Mail view.

You switch from one view to another by clicking one of the buttons in the view switcher area of the window. You can also use shortcut keys to switch from one view to another.

View	Keyboard Shortcut
Mail	Command+1
Calendar	Command+2
Contacts	Command+3
Tasks	Command+4
Notes	Command+5

View buttons may be large or small depending on the size of the view switcher area. You can resize the view switcher by dragging the resizing bar at the top of its pane. As you make it smaller, the bottom buttons turn into smaller icons at the bottom of the view switcher. The buttons work the same way, no matter how they appear.

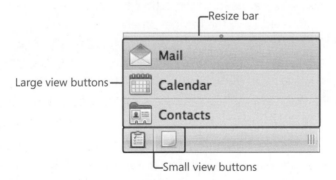

See Also We take a closer look at each view later in this chapter.

Interface: Outlook vs. Entourage

If you're upgrading to Outlook from Entourage, the interface shouldn't be all that different to you. Here's a quick rundown of some of the differences:

- Outlook offers five views; Entourage offered six views. The Project Center view available in Entourage is not available in Outlook.

- Outlook uses the label Contacts for its contact management view; Entourage used the name Address Book.

- Outlook displays view buttons in the view switcher; Entourage displayed view buttons as small icons on the toolbar.

- Outlook offers the ribbon interface for accessing most commands and features; Entourage relied on a limited number of toolbar buttons and menu commands to access features. Think of the Outlook ribbon as a supercharged Entourage toolbar. The menu is still available for accessing commands.

At first glance, the difference between Outlook and Entourage may look substantial. But look more closely and you'll see the similarities. It shouldn't take much effort to get up to speed with Outlook.

Working with the Ribbon

The ribbon, which is new in Microsoft Office for Mac, appears in all Office 2011 applications. The ribbon stretches across the top of the Outlook window, right beneath the window's title bar and toolbar.

- The ribbon has two parts: a row of tabs and a row of buttons and menus. Click a tab to display its associated buttons and menus for accessing commands.

- The three ribbon tabs remain the same in each Outlook view: Home, Organize, and Tools. The commands on each tab, however, vary depending on the currently displayed view. For example, in the Mail view, the Home tab's buttons include commands for creating new email messages, forwarding a selected message, and accessing mail rules. In Contact view, the Home tab's buttons include commands for creating a new contact and mapping a contact's address.

● Contextual ribbon tabs appear on the main Outlook window when certain items are selected. For example, if you select a meeting in the Calendar pane in Calendar view, the Meeting ribbon tab appears between the Home and Organize tabs. Clicking that tab displays options for the selected item.

● When you open an item window within Outlook, it may display its own ribbon. For example, the message window has a ribbon with two tabs, Message and Options, and the contact window has a ribbon with just one tab, Contact.

● You can minimize the ribbon so only its tabs appear. Click the button at the far right end of the ribbon. To display the ribbon again, click the button again or click the ribbon tab you want to see. If you click a currently displayed tab, you'll minimize the ribbon. You can also toggle the display of the ribbon by choosing Ribbon from the View menu or by pressing Option+Command+R.

Click here to minimize or display the ribbon.

● When you point to a button or menu on a ribbon tab, Outlook displays a ScreenTip. A *ScreenTip* is a small yellow box that contains information about the item you are pointing to.

Tip A ScreenTip is sometimes referred to as a *tooltip*.

● Buttons that include arrows are menus. There are two types of menus on the Outlook ribbon tabs:

   ○ A button with an integrated arrow displays a menu of options. You must choose an option from the menu to activate the command. An example is the New button on the Home tab in Mail view.

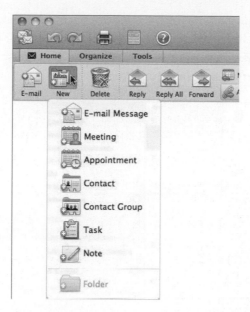

◯ A button with a separate arrow has a default option and a menu of options. The default option is normally indicated in some way in the main part of the button. Clicking the button chooses that default option. Choosing a different option from the menu not only chooses that option but sets it as the default for future use of the button. An example is the Font Color button on the Message tab of a new message window.

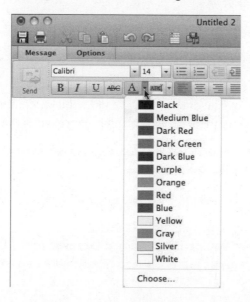

Working in Mail View

You can display Mail view by clicking the Mail button in the view switcher in the lower-left corner of the window or by pressing Command+1.

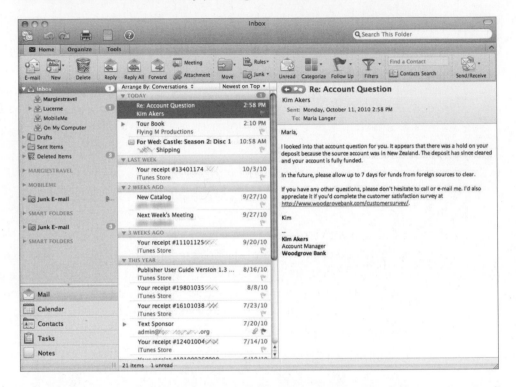

In Mail view, the navigation pane displays a number of items. Clicking an item in the navigation pane displays a list of its contents in the item list.

- **Inbox** Outlook delivers incoming email to individual accounts within the Inbox item. When you select Inbox, you see all incoming mail in the item list.

- **Drafts** When you create a new email message, Outlook stores it in the Drafts folder until it has been sent.

- **Sent Items** When an email message has been sent, it is moved to the Sent Items folder.

- **Deleted Items** When you delete an item, it is moved to the Deleted Items folder. How long an item remains in the Deleted Items folder depends on the settings for your email accounts.

See Also Email account settings are covered in detail in Chapter 6, "Fine-Tuning Email Settings."

● **Account headers** Certain types of accounts—for example, Microsoft Exchange and Apple's MobileMe accounts—have additional folders that appear under account headers in the navigation pane.

● **Junk Email** Outlook delivers messages blocked by the spam filter to this folder, where they remain until you review and delete them.

● **Smart folders** Smart folders are preconfigured as part of your Outlook installation or created by you to help manage email. These appear in a list under the Smart Folders header.

The navigation pane makes extensive use of disclosure triangles, which appear to the left of many items. Clicking a disclosure triangle displays a list of items within it in an outline view. Clicking again hides the list.

● If you have more than one email account set up in Outlook, clicking the disclosure triangle beside the Inbox, Drafts, Sent Items, Deleted Items, or Junk Email items displays a list of email accounts within that item. You can click an account to see just the items for that account, thus narrowing down the items displayed.

- You may see disclosure triangles beside the names of certain email account types, such as IMAP, under the Inbox. Clicking a disclosure triangle for an IMAP account displays the folders for that account on the server.

Again, clicking any item in the navigation pane displays a list of its contents in the item list.

Items in the navigation bar appear in bold type when they contain unread items. A white number in a blue oval indicates how many unread items there are.

The ribbon in Mail view includes three tabs:

- **Home**   This tab includes commands you need to create and manage email messages.

- **Organize**   This tab includes commands for reading, organizing, and synchronizing email messages.

- **Tools**   This tab includes commands for working with features available throughout Outlook and is identical for all views.

When you create a new email message, reply to an incoming message, or forward an incoming message to someone else, Outlook displays the message composition window. The window has its own ribbon and toolbar, separate from the ones in the main Outlook window. You can use the message composition window to create, insert, and format message content and to modify the settings for outgoing messages.

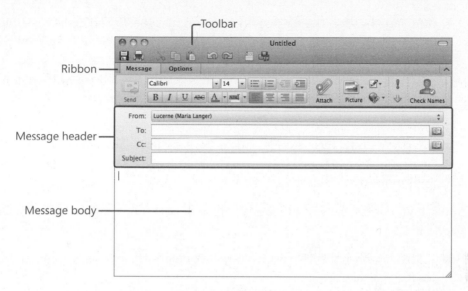

The message composition window includes the following interface elements:

● **Toolbar** The toolbar offers access to a handful of file and edit menu commands, including Save, Print, Cut, Copy, Paste, Undo, and Redo. It also includes buttons to toggle the display of the Toolbox and Media Browser for looking up information or pasting in multimedia content.

● **Ribbon** The ribbon includes two tabs:

  ○ **Message** This tab offers a number of text and paragraph formatting options and insertion commands.

  ○ **Options** This tab offers commands for setting message formatting options and accessing security and reference tools.

- **Message header** The message header includes the To and Cc fields—and, optionally, the Bcc field—for addressing the message and the Subject field for providing a message subject. If you have multiple email addresses set up in Outlook, you can also use the From field to specify which account should be used to send the message. When you attach files to the message, the attachment field appears with a list of attached files.

- **Message body** The message body is the area where you enter the content of your message. The message body can include formatted text, hyperlinks, images, movies, and sounds.

You can view incoming and other existing messages two ways from the main Outlook window:

- Click an item in the item list to view its contents in the reading pane on the left side of the window.

- Double-click an item in the item list to view its contents in a message reading window.

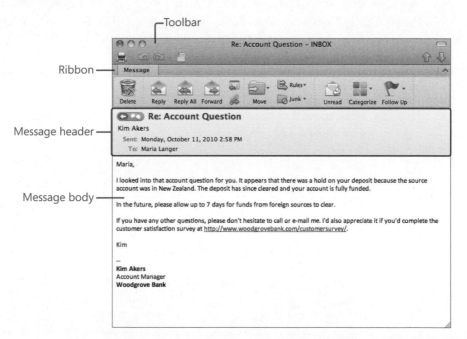

The message reading window is similar to the message composition window. It has its own toolbar and ribbon. You can use the message reading window to read, organize, and initiate actions based on the message.

The message reading window includes the following interface elements:

- **Toolbar** The toolbar offers access to just a few commands: Print, Undo, and Redo. It also includes buttons to toggle the display of the Toolbox for looking up information and Previous and Next buttons for scrolling through other messages in the list without closing the window.

- **Ribbon** The ribbon includes just one tab: Message. It includes commands to delete, reply to, forward, and move the message, as well as mark it as unread or categorize it.

- **Message header** The message header includes information about who the message is from and to, when it was sent, and its subject. Attached files are also listed in this area. In Mac OS X 10.6 Snow Leopard, you can click a Preview button to see attachments by using the Mac OS Quick Look feature. You can click the Show Conversation button beside the message subject to see a list of all messages in the conversation thread. You can also click the name of the sender to see his or her information from your Contacts.

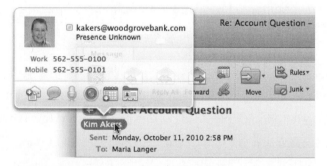

- **Message body** The message body is the area where you enter the content of your message. The message body can include formatted text, hyperlinks, images, movies, and sounds.

In this exercise, you'll take a tour of the message composition window and its interface elements. Then you'll explore how to read existing messages.

 SET UP You don't need any practice files to complete this exercise. Open Outlook and follow these steps.

1. If Mail view is not displayed, in the view switcher, click the **Mail** button.

   Keyboard Shortcut Press Command+1.

Email

2. On the ribbon's **Home** tab, click the **Email** button.

   Keyboard Shortcut Press Command+N.

An untitled message window opens with the cursor in the To box.

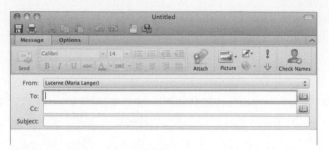

Tip Only the buttons for commands that can be performed on the currently selected message element are active.

3. Click to position the cursor in the message body. Additional commands on the ribbon become active.

4. On the toolbar and on the **Message** tab of the ribbon, review the available commands. You can use commands to edit and format text, attach files, and insert multimedia elements, links, and signatures.

5. In the message body, type **I received your voicemail message. I'll meet you on Tuesday at 10 AM as planned. See you then.**

6. Select the words *Tuesday at 10 AM*.

7. On the **Message** tab, on the **Font** menu, click **Verdana**. The selected text's font changes.

8. On the **Message** tab, click the **Bold** button. The selected text becomes bold.

9. On the **Message** tab, point to the other buttons and menus and use the ScreenTips that appear to note what they do.

10. On the **Message** tab, click **Choose** on the **Font** menu. The Fonts panel appears. You can use this standard Mac OS interface element to set font family, style, size, and color options for the selected text in the message body.

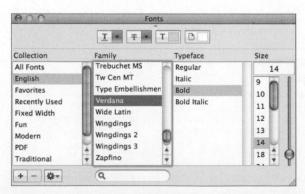

11. In the **Fonts** panel, click the close button.

12. On the **Options** tab of the ribbon, point to buttons and menus and use the ScreenTips that appear to note what they do.

Minimize

13. At the right end of the ribbon, click the **Minimize** button. The ribbon collapses so that just the two tabs show.

Undo

14. On the toolbar, click the **Undo** button twice. The bold formatting you applied to the selected text is undone.

15. On the minimized ribbon, click the **Message** tab. The ribbon expands to show Message tab options.

16. In the **Untitled** window, click the close button. Outlook displays a dialog sheet prompting you to save or discard the draft message.

17. In the dialog sheet, click **Discard Changes**. The dialog sheet and message composition window close.

18. In the navigation pane, click **Inbox**. A list of all messages in your Inbox appears in the item list.

    Tip If you have not yet used Outlook to retrieve incoming email, skip the remaining steps.

19. In the item list, click to select an email message item. The item's content appears in the reading pane.

20. In the reading pane, use the scroll bars to scroll through the content of the message.

21. In the item list, double-click the selected email message item. The item appears in a message reading window.

Reply

22. On the **Message** tab, click the **Reply** button. A message composition window appears. It is already partially filled in with the addressee, subject, and a copy of the incoming message.

23. In the window, click the close button. The window closes without prompting to save changes.

✖ **CLEAN UP** No clean-up steps are required. You are ready to continue to the next exercise.

Working in Calendar View

Calendar view appears when you click the Calendar button in the view switcher or press Command+2.

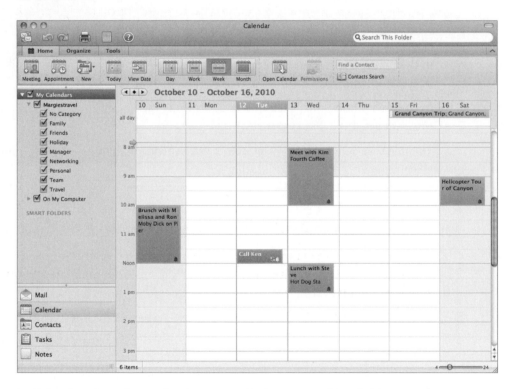

In Calendar view, the navigation pane displays a number of things:

- **Calendars** A calendar is a collection of meetings, appointments, and other calendar items stored in a specific place. In many cases, you'll have just one default Outlook calendar with items stored on your computer. But the list of calendars may also include shared calendars, Internet calendars, and SharePoint calendars you connect to.

- **Categories** Within each calendar, you should see a list of color-coded categories. You can assign categories to calendar items—and other items within Outlook—and use them to organize your data. You can hide or display a calendar's list of categories by clicking the disclosure triangle beside the calendar name.

- **Smart folders** If you have set up any smart folders, they'll appear beneath the list of calendars and categories, organized under the Smart Folders heading.

In Calendar view, the large pane of information to the right of the navigation pane is called the calendar pane. It displays calendar items for the period you select using one of the buttons on the Home ribbon. You can display the calendar by day, five-day work week, seven-day week, or month. You can also use buttons on the Home tab to view today's date or a date you specify.

The items that appear in the calendar pane depend on which calendars and categories are selected in the navigation pane. Clearing a calendar or category check box in the navigation pane hides the calendar items assigned to that calendar or category.

The ribbon in Calendar view includes four tabs:

- **Home** This tab includes commands you need to create new calendar items and set view options for the calendar pane.

- **Appointment or Appointment Series** When an item or recurring item is selected in the calendar, the Appointment or Appointment Series contextual tab appears between the Home and Organize tabs. It includes options for modifying the selected appointment's settings.

- **Organize** This tab includes commands for creating new calendars and viewing and organizing calendar items.

- **Tools** This tab includes commands for working with features available throughout Outlook and is identical for all views.

When you create or edit a calendar item, you use the meeting or appointment window. These two windows are nearly identical, but they serve different purposes.

- A *meeting* is a calendar event with invited attendees. The meeting window includes a To field you can use to address the meeting invitation to the people you want to invite. Think of a meeting as a special kind of email message. When you send the meeting invitation, the meeting is added to your calendar.

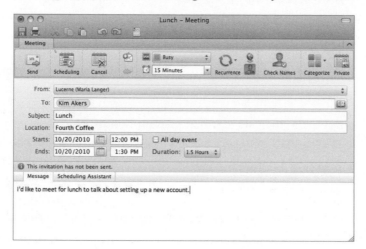

Tip If you have more than one email account set up in Outlook, a From field also appears in the meeting window. You can use the pop-up menu to choose the account you want to use to send the meeting invitation.

Tip If you have access to other users' calendars, you can use the meeting window's Scheduling Assistant, which is discussed in Chapter 7, "Scheduling Appointments and Meetings," to help you find a time when all invitees are available.

- An *appointment* is a calendar event that does not have specific invitees. Because of this, it lacks the To field you would use to send the invitation. Instead, you just click the Save & Close button to add the appointment to your calendar.

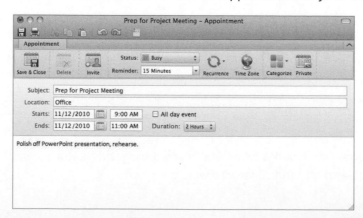

Both the meeting and appointment windows have their own tab that includes commands for setting options for the calendar item. The options vary based on the type of calendar item being created.

Tip Clicking the Invite button on the appointment window's Appointment tab changes the appointment window to a meeting window.

In this exercise, you'll explore Calendar view to look at the calendar a number of ways. You'll also take a closer look at the meeting and appointment windows to note the differences between them.

SET UP You don't need any practice files to complete this exercise. Just follow these steps.

1. If Calendar view is not displayed, in the view switcher, click the **Calendar** button.

    Keyboard Shortcut Press Command+2.

2. In the navigation pane, click the disclosure triangles to display or hide categories. Outlook is preconfigured with eight categories plus the No Category item.

    Troubleshooting If you imported existing data into Outlook, you may see different categories than those shown in this chapter.

Day

3. On the **Home** tab, click the **Day** button. Outlook switches to single day view.

4. Use the scroll bar to scroll up and down in the window. In Day, Work Week, and Week view, Outlook displays times on the left side of the calendar pane. A green arrow and line indicate the current time of day.

Work

5. On the **Home** tab, click the **Work** button. Outlook switches to Work Week view.

    Tip By default, Work Week view is five days—Monday through Friday—but you can configure the calendar feature for different work days. Chapter 8, "Managing Your Calendar," explains how.

Month

Next

6. On the **Home** tab, click the **Month** button. Outlook switches to Month view.

7. In the upper-left corner of the calendar pane, click the **Next** button several times. Each time you click, the following month is displayed.

Week

8. On the **Home** tab, click the **Week** button. Outlook switches to Week view. A week in the month you were looking at appears.

Previous

9. In the upper-left corner of the calendar pane, click the **Previous** button several times. Each time you click, the previous week is displayed.

View Date

10. On the **Home** tab, click the **View Date** button. Outlook displays a pop-up calendar with the current date selected.

11. Use navigation buttons within the calendar to display June, 2011, and click June 30. The week of June 26–July 2, 2011 appears.

Today

12. On the **Home** tab, click the **Today** button. Outlook displays the current date's week with the current day selected.

Meeting

13. On the **Home** tab, click the **Meeting** button. Outlook opens a meeting window.

14. On the meeting window's **Meeting** tab, point to buttons and use ScreenTips to learn what each button does.

15. In the **To** field, enter the email address for someone you know. As you start typing, the Send button becomes available.

Date

16. Click the **Date** button beside the **Starts** field. A pop-up calendar window appears. You can use it to select a start date. The same calendar appears if you click the Date button beside the Ends field.

Cancel

17. On the meeting window's **Meeting** tab, click the **Cancel** button. The meeting window turns into an appointment window. The To field disappears and the window's title changes.

Invite

18. On the appointment window's **Appointment** tab, click the **Invite** button. The appointment window turns into a meeting window. A To field appears in the header.

19. Click the meeting window's close button.

20. Outlook may display a dialog sheet telling you that you have not added any attendees. Click **Discard Invitation**.

CLEAN UP If you inadvertently created a calendar event while following the last few steps, select the event in the calendar pane and press Delete. In the dialog sheet that appears, click Delete to remove it. You are now ready for the next exercise.

Working in Contacts View

Contacts view appears when you click the Contacts button in the view switcher or press Command+3.

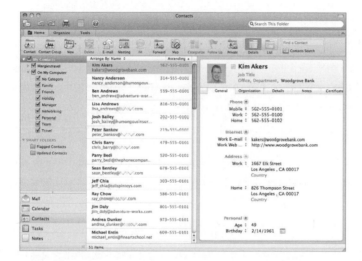

Tip In Entourage 2008 and earlier, Contacts view was called Address Book.

In Contacts view, the navigation pane displays a number of things:

- **Address books** An address book is a collection of contacts stored in a specific place. In most cases, you'll have just one default Outlook address book with contacts stored on your computer. But the list of address books may also include address books you share with others.

- **Address book folders** You can use folders to organize address book contacts. Folders you create appear in a list beneath your address books.

- **Categories** Within each address book, you should see a list of color-coded categories. You can assign categories to contacts—and other items within Outlook—and use them to organize your data. You can hide or display an address book's list of categories by clicking the disclosure triangle beside the address book name.

- **Smart folders** Smart folders appear beneath the list of address books and categories, organized under the Smart Folders heading. Outlook comes preconfigured with two smart folders for the Contacts view, but you can create others.

In Contacts view, the list pane in the middle of the window displays a list of contacts with some basic information, including the contact name, email address, and phone number. You can change the sort order of the list by choosing options from pop-up menus at the top of the list.

The contacts that appear in the item list depend on which address books and categories are selected in the navigation pane. Clearing an address book or category check box in the navigation pane hides the contacts assigned to that address book or category.

Selecting a contact in the item list displays details about that contact in the reading pane on the right side of the window. A number of tabs in that pane enable you to view a variety of stored and database-retrieved information about that contact.

In Contacts view, the ribbon has three tabs:

- **Home** This tab includes commands you need to create new contacts and contact groups, send email messages or schedule meetings for a contact, and perform other tasks with the selected contacts.

- **Organize** This tab includes commands for creating new address books and viewing and organizing contacts and the Contacts view window.

- **Tools** This tab includes commands for working with features available throughout Outlook and is identical for all views.

When you create or edit a contact, you use the contact record window. This window appears when you double-click an existing contact in the item list or click the Contact button on the Home tab.

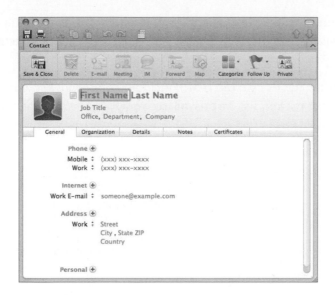

The contact record window has fields for specific types of information:

● When you create a contact record, you fill in as many fields as you have information for.

● You can use the menu buttons beside field names to change them as necessary. For example, if you want to enter a home phone number rather than a work phone number, you can click the arrows beside Work under Phone to choose a different phone number field name.

● You can click + buttons near certain field types to add additional fields. For example, if you need to add a fax phone number for a contact, you can click the + button beside Phone to add another field.

Tabs within the contact record window enable you to view or enter data in various panes: General (the primary pane where most information appears), Organization, Details, Notes, and Certificates.

The contact record window has its own tab, which includes commands for working with the contact's records. Most buttons will be unavailable (gray) on the contact record window for a new, unsaved contact.

In this exercise, you'll explore Contacts view to get familiar with its interface. You'll also take a closer look at the contact record window.

 SET UP You don't need any practice files to complete this exercise. Just follow these steps.

1. If Contacts view is not displayed, in the view switcher, click the **Contacts** button.

   Keyboard Shortcut Press Command+3.

2. In the navigation pane, click the disclosure triangles to display or hide categories. Outlook is preconfigured with eight categories plus the No Category item.

   Troubleshooting If you imported existing data into Outlook, you may see different categories than those shown in this chapter.

3. In the item list, select the name of a contact. Detailed information about that contact appears in the reading pane.

   Tip Even if you have not yet created any contacts, there should be at least one contact in the list: you.

4. In the item list, double-click the contact name you selected in the previous step. The contact record window for that contact opens.

5. Click a field in the window. An edit box appears around the field.

You can modify the field's contents. The changes are saved when you move to another field or close the window.

6. In the contact record window, click each tab to see what information is available.

   Troubleshooting The Organization and Details panes retrieve information from an LDAP server. A server must be configured with that contact listed on it for information to appear in these panes.

7. In the contact record window, click the close button. The window closes.

8. On the **Home** tab, click the **Email** button. A message composition window appears with the To field filled in. You can use this technique to send an email message from within Contacts view.

9. In the message composition window, click the close button. Then click **Discard Changes** in the dialog sheet that appears. The window closes.

10. On the **Home** tab, click the **Meeting** button. A meeting window appears with the To field filled in. You can use this technique to schedule a meeting on your calendar from within Contacts view.

11. In the meeting window, click the close button. Then click **Discard Invitation** in the dialog sheet that appears. The window closes.

Contact

12. On the **Home** tab, click the **Contact** button. An untitled contact record window appears with the First Name field selected. You could fill in this window's form by entering information and pressing Tab to move from field to field.

13. In the untitled contact record window, click the close button. The window closes.

Me

14. On the **Organize** tab, click the **Me** button. Your contact record window opens. It includes information about you.

15. In your contact record window, click the close button. The window closes.

 CLEAN UP If you inadvertently created a new contact record, select the record in the item list and press Delete. In the dialog sheet that appears, click Delete to remove it. You are now ready for the next exercise.

Working in Tasks View

Tasks view appears when you click the Tasks button in the view switcher or press Command+4.

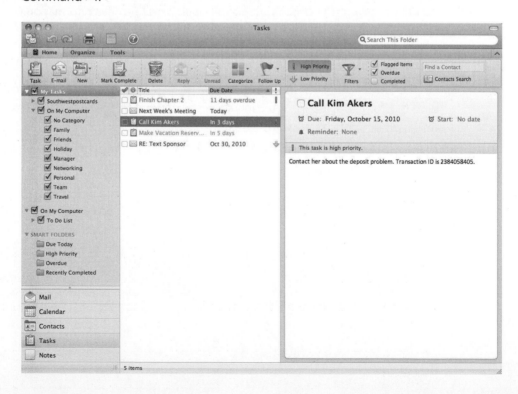

In Tasks view, the navigation pane displays a number of things:

- **Tasks lists** Tasks lists are collections of tasks stored in a specific place. In many cases, you'll have just one default Outlook tasks list with tasks stored on your computer. But the navigation pane may also include tasks lists from an Exchange account.

- **Categories** Within each tasks list, you should see a list of color-coded categories. You can assign categories to tasks—and other items within Outlook—and use them to organize your data. You can hide or display a tasks list's categories by clicking the disclosure triangle beside the tasks list name.

- **Smart folders** Smart folders appear beneath the tasks lists and their category lists, organized under the Smart Folders heading. Outlook comes preconfigured with four smart folders for tasks, but you can create others.

In Tasks view, the list pane in the middle of the window displays a list of tasks with due dates and priorities. You can change the sort order of the list by clicking a column heading. A check box in the first column makes it easy to mark a task as completed.

The second column displays an icon that indicates the source of the task. Tasks can be created in the Tasks view, by clicking the Follow Up flag for an item in any Outlook view, or by using the Flag For Follow Up command in Microsoft Word.

See Also Flagging items for follow up is covered in Chapter 12, "Tracking Tasks."

The tasks that appear in the item list depend on which task lists and categories are selected in the navigation pane. Clearing a tasks list or category check box in the navigation pane hides the tasks assigned to that task list or category.

Selecting a task in the item list displays details about that task in the reading pane on the right side of the window.

In Tasks view, the ribbon has three tabs:

- **Home** This tab includes commands you need to create new tasks and other Outlook items and work with existing tasks.

- **Organize** This tab includes commands for organizing and setting view options for tasks.

- **Tools** This tab includes commands for working with features available throughout Outlook and is identical for all views.

When you create or edit a task within Tasks view, you use the task window. This appears when you double-click an existing task in the item list or click the Task button on the Home tab.

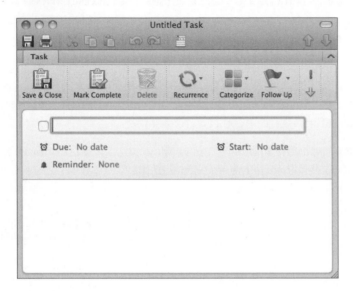

The task window has its own tab, which includes commands for setting task options. You can also set task options for due date, reminder, and start date in the header part of the task window.

In this exercise, you'll explore Tasks view to get a feel for its interface. You'll also take a closer look at the task window.

 SET UP You don't need any practice files to complete this exercise. Just follow these steps.

1. If Tasks view is not displayed, in the view switcher, click the **Tasks** button.

   Keyboard Shortcut Press Command+4.

2. In the navigation pane, click the disclosure triangles to display or hide categories. Outlook is preconfigured with eight categories plus the No Category item.

   Troubleshooting If you imported existing data into Outlook, you may see different categories than those shown in this chapter.

Task

3. On the **Home** tab, click the **Task** button. An untitled task window appears with the cursor in the task name field.

4. In the task name field, enter **Call Joe**. The title bar displays the task name you just typed.

5. Beside the **Due** field, click the words **No date**. A pop-up calendar appears.

6. On the calendar, click tomorrow's date. The date is entered into the Due field.

7. On the **Task** tab, click the **Save & Close** button. The task is added to the task list.

8. In the view switcher, click **Mail**. Outlook switches to Mail view.

9. In the item list, click to select any email message.

Save & Close

Follow Up

10. On the **Home** tab, click the **Follow Up** button. A flag appears beneath the message header in the reading pane.

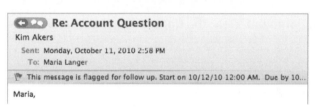

```
◀ ●● Re: Account Question
Kim Akers
 Sent: Monday, October 11, 2010 2:58 PM
  To: Maria Langer
🏳 This message is flagged for follow up. Start on 10/12/10 12:00 AM. Due by 10…

Maria,
```

11. In the view switcher, click **Tasks**. Outlook switches to Tasks view. The email message you just flagged appears in the item list as a task.

12. In the item list, double-click the task you created from an email message. The email message opens in a message reading window. Even though you are in Tasks view, you can work with this email message like any other email message.

13. In the message reading window, click the close button. The window closes.

14. On the **Home** tab, click the **Follow Up** arrow (not the button). A menu of options appears.

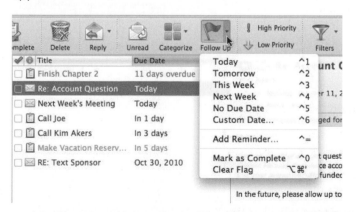

15. On the **Follow Up** menu, click **Clear Flag**. The flag is removed from the message and it disappears from the item list.

16. In the item list, select the check box to the left of the **Call Joe** task. This marks the task as completed. The item should disappear from view.

Troubleshooting If marking the task as completed does not cause it to disappear, the Completed check box on the Home tab is likely already selected. If so, you can skip the next step.

17. On the **Home** tab, select the **Completed** check box. The Call Joe task reappears with a gray background and a check mark in its check box.

18. In the item list, click the **Call Joe** task to select it.

Delete

19. On the **Home** tab, click the **Delete** button. A confirmation dialog sheet appears.

20. In the dialog sheet, click **Delete**. The task is removed.

 **CLEAN UP** On the Home tab, clear the Completed check box. You are now ready for the next exercise.

Working in Notes View

Notes view appears when you click the Notes button in the view switcher or press Command+5.

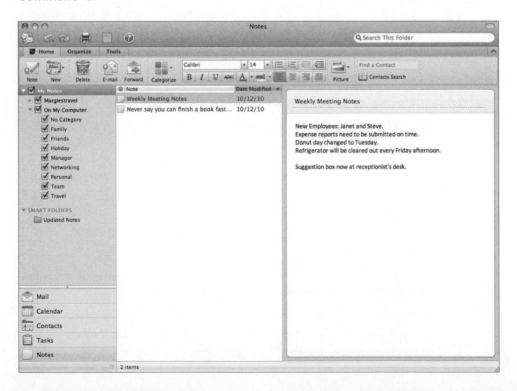

In Notes view, the navigation pane displays a number of things:

- **Notes lists** Notes lists are collections of notes stored in a specific place. In many cases, you'll have just one default Outlook notes list with notes stored on your computer. But the navigation pane may also include notes lists from an Exchange account.

- **Categories** Within each notes list, you should see a list of color-coded categories. You can assign categories to notes—and other items within Outlook—and use them to organize your data. You can hide or display a notes list's categories by clicking the disclosure triangle beside the notes list name.

- **Smart folders** Smart folders appear beneath the notes lists and their category lists, organized under the Smart Folders heading. Outlook comes preconfigured with just one smart folder for notes, but you can create others.

In Notes view, the list pane in the middle of the window displays a list of notes with modification dates. You can change the sort order of the list by clicking a column heading.

The notes that appear in the item list depend on which notes lists and categories are selected in the navigation pane. Clearing a notes list or category check box in the navigation pane hides the notes assigned to that notes list or category.

Selecting a note in the item list displays the contents of the note in the reading pane on the right side of the window.

In Notes view, the ribbon has three tabs:

- **Home** The Home tab includes commands you need to create and work with notes. It also includes text formatting commands you can use when the reading pane is active.

- **Organize** This tab includes commands for organizing and setting view options for notes.

- **Tools** This tab includes commands for working with features available throughout Outlook and is identical for all views.

When you create a note within Notes view, you use the note window. This appears when you double-click an existing note or click the Note button on the Home tab.

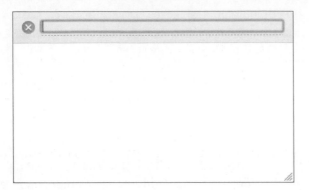

The note window has just two fields: a name field inside the yellow box and a content field. There is no ribbon.

In this exercise, you'll take a closer look at Notes view and see how you can create and delete a note.

 SET UP You don't need any practice files to complete this exercise. Just follow these steps.

1. If Notes view is not displayed, in the view switcher, click the **Notes** button.

   Keyboard Shortcut Press Command+5.

Note

2. On the **Home** tab, click the **Note** button. A new note window appears. The cursor is in the note name field.

3. Type **Outlook Notes**.

4. Press Tab. The cursor moves to the content field.

5. Type **I can use the Notes feature of Outlook to store notes and other reminders.**

6. Press Command+S to save the note. It appears in the item list with the name *Outlook Notes*.

7. In the note window, click the close button to close the note.

8. In the item list, click the note you just created. Its content appears in the reading pane.

9. In the reading pane, select the word *Notes* in the content of the message.

10. On the **Home** tab, click the **Bold** button. The selected text turns bold. You can format a note's text in the reading pane of Notes view when the note is selected in the item list.

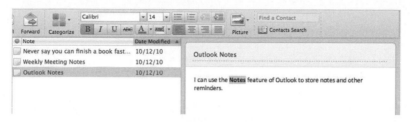

11. On the **Home** tab, click the **Delete** button. A confirmation dialog sheet appears.

12. In the dialog sheet, click **Delete**. The note is deleted.

CLEAN UP No clean-up steps are required. Leave Outlook open if you are continuing to exercises in the next chapter.

Key Points

- Outlook features are accessible though five different views: Mail, Calendar, Contacts, Tasks, and Notes.

- Although each view is designed to work with a specific kind of data, you can access certain types of Outlook data from any view.

- Outlook views share standard interface elements, including a toolbar, ribbon, and multi-pane window.

- Outlook uses task-specific windows to create and edit items such as email messages, meetings, appointments, contacts, tasks, and notes.

Part 2

Mail

Chapter at a Glance

Outlook makes it easy to address messages to contacts, **page 58**

The Message tab offers many text formatting options, **page 63**

Use the Media Browser to insert photos, audio, or movies into your e-mail messages, **page 71**

Messages are stored as drafts until they are sent, **page 76**

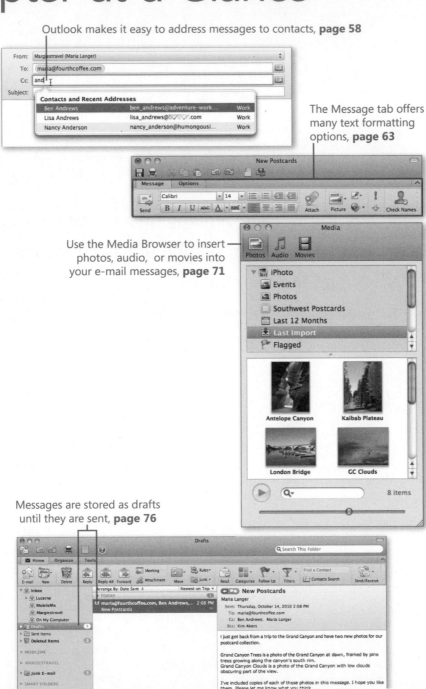

3 Composing and Sending Email Messages

In this chapter, you will learn how to

- ✔ Create messages.
- ✔ Format message text.
- ✔ Insert media in messages.
- ✔ Attach files to messages.
- ✔ Change message settings.
- ✔ Send messages.

Although Microsoft Outlook for Mac 2011 includes views for managing appointments, meetings, contacts, tasks, and notes, it's most often used for sending and receiving email in Mail view. *Email*, which is short for *electronic mail*, has all but replaced old-fashioned printed and mailed letters for most business and personal communication. It's much faster and cheaper to send email messages, so sending paper-based or so-called *snail mail* is becoming a thing of the past. In a world where many people are becoming concerned about conserving resources, email, which is not usually printed, saves paper (and money spent on paper) and prevents waste. Whether you need to communicate about business or personal matters, email simply makes sense.

Email, however, can go beyond simple text communication. You can format your messages so they look good and are easier to read. You can include clickable hyperlinks to make it easy for recipients to go directly to Internet content you specify. You can also include images or attach other computer files.

Tip In this chapter and throughout this book, we often refer to email messages as simply *messages*. When discussing other types of messages—for example, *instant messages* or *text messages*—we use those full terms.

For example, you might compose a message to a client about a job proposal and attach a copy of the proposal as a Microsoft Word or Adobe PDF file for the client to review. You might also attach images of what your product looks like to help your client visualize what you're writing about. A link to the product page on your company's Web site would be a handy way to provide access to more information. Email makes all this easy.

You can also set options for email messages that are just not possible with paper-based mail. For example, you can set a message as high priority so the recipient knows it's important. If a message has sensitive content, you can encrypt it. And if you want the recipient to be certain that the message came from you, you can digitally sign it.

See Also For more information about security features for email, see the section titled "Securing Your Email" in Chapter 6, "Fine-Tuning Email Settings."

In this chapter, you will use Mail view within Outlook for Mac to create, address, and compose messages. You will also include a custom signature, format message text, embed images, and attach files. Finally, you will set basic options for your message and send it on its way.

Important You'll use the messages you create in this chapter as practice files for exercises in later chapters of this book.

> **Practice Files** Before you can complete the exercises in this chapter, you need to copy the book's practice files to your computer. The practice files you'll use to complete the exercises in this chapter are in the Chapter03 practice file folder. A complete list of practice files is provided in "Using the Practice Files" at the beginning of this book.

Creating Messages

Creating an email message is a relatively straightforward process. You begin by displaying a message composition window and then provide the recipient addresses, subject, and content of the message.

If you have more than one email account configured in Outlook, a From pop-up menu appears in the message header. This menu includes all of the email accounts configured in Outlook and determines the return address for the message.

Tip If you use one email account far more often than others, you might want to specify that account as the default account for sending messages. You can set your default email account in Outlook preferences, as discussed in Chapter 6.

Outlook offers three different fields for addressing a message. You can find them in the message header of the message composition window:

- **To** Enter the email address of the primary recipient in this field.

  The primary recipient is the person or persons you expect to respond to the message.

- **Cc** Enter the email addresses for additional recipients to receive a copy of the message.

  Cc stands for *carbon copy*. In the days before copy machines, typists would use carbon paper to make copies of documents as they typed them. The term *cc* is from that era; a carbon copy would go to each of the Cc recipients. In Outlook, a list of these recipients appears in this field for all recipients to see.

- **Bcc** Enter the email addresses for additional recipients to receive a copy of the message without others knowing they received it.

  Bcc stands for *blind carbon copy*. This field works very much like the Cc field, but Bcc recipients are hidden in the recipients' copy of the message.

  Tip By default, the Bcc field does not appear in the message form. To display it, on the Options tab of the message composition window, click the Bcc button.

You must have at least one email address in at least one of these fields. (You cannot send an email message without a recipient!) You can have any number of recipients in each field.

There are several different ways to enter a recipient's email address in Outlook:

- Type the complete email address into the field.

  Tip To type more than one email address in an address field, separate each address with a semicolon (;).

- Type part of a previously used address into the field. Outlook displays a list of matches as you type. You can then click the address you want to enter it into the field.

- Click the Contacts Search button on the right side of the address field and, in the Contacts Search pane that appears, search your Outlook contacts for the recipient. In the list of search results, click the To, Cc, or Bcc button to assign that recipient to an address field.

See Also You can learn more about working with the Outlook Contact features in Chapter 9, "Managing Contact Information."

You enter the content of your message in the message body. This part of the window works like a little word processor with word wrap and formatting capabilities. You can enter as much text as you like in the message body. You can even paste in content from another document. You can also embed images right within the message body or attach files to the message.

See Also Formatting text, embedding images, and attaching files are covered later in this chapter, in the sections titled "Formatting Message Text," "Inserting Media in Messages," and "Attaching Files to Messages."

When you create a message, you have the option of sending it to its recipients or saving it as a draft. Saving it as a draft is a way to put it aside and finish it later if you get interrupted while composing the message or if you need additional information you have to wait to get. Draft messages are saved into the Drafts folder, which is listed in the navigation pane. You can open a draft message at any time to complete and send it—or to delete it if you change your mind about sending it.

In this exercise, you'll open a message composition window and fill in the message header with recipients and a subject. You'll then enter a brief message in the message body. You'll finish up by saving the message as a draft that you can finish in a later exercise.

SET UP You need the six vCard files located in the Chapter03/vCards folder and the More Message Text text clipping file in the Chapter03/Other Files folder to complete this exercise. Drag the vCard files into the Contact View window to add them to your address book. In the Outlook view switcher, click the Mail button to switch to Mail view. Then follow these steps.

Email

1. On the **Home** tab, click the **Email** button.

   Keyboard Shortcut Press Command+N.

   An empty message composition window opens.

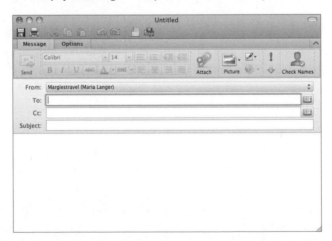

2. If the message header includes a **From** field, click it to display its pop-up menu. Then click the email account you want to use to send the message.

3. In the **To** field, type **maria@fourthcoffee.com**.

4. Press Tab to move to the **Cc** field.

5. Type **and**. Outlook attempts to match what you typed with your contacts and displays results in the Contacts And Recent Addresses menu.

6. Click **Ben Andrews**. His name is entered into the Cc field.

7. In the **Cc** field after Ben's name, type your email address.

8. Press Tab. If your name and email address is in your contacts list, your email address is replaced with your name. Otherwise, it appears as an email address.

Bcc

9. In the **Options** tab of the message composition window, click the **Bcc** button. A Bcc field appears in the message header beneath the Cc field. It appears for just this message.

    See Also You can set Outlook preferences so the Bcc field appears in all message composition windows. The section titled "Setting Reading and Composing Options" in Chapter 6 explains how.

Contacts Search

10. On the right end of the **Bcc** field, click the **Contacts Search** button. The Contacts Search pane appears.

11. In the search field at the top of the **Contacts Search** pane, type **Kim**. Kim Akers's name appears in the list.

12. Click the **Bcc** button in Kim's record to add her name to the **Bcc** field.

13. In the **Subject** field, enter **New Postcards**.

14. In the message body, type **I just got back from a trip to the Grand Canyon and have two new photos to add to our postcard collection.** Press Return twice and then type **Grand Canyon Trees is a photo of the Grand Canyon**.

As you can see, you enter text into the message composition window's message body the same way you'd enter text into Word or any other word processor.

Because you're not reading this book to get typing practice, copy and paste the remaining message text from a text clipping.

15. In the **Finder**, double-click the **More Message Text** file to open it in a text clipping window.

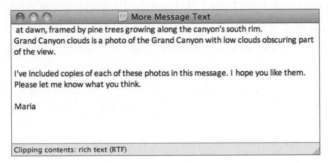

16. Press Command+A to select all text in the text clipping. Then press Command+C to copy it to the **Clipboard**. Switch back to the message composition window. Make sure the cursor is blinking after the word *Canyon*. Then press Command+V to paste the text in.

As you can imagine, you can do the same thing with existing text in any kind of document to paste it from that document into a message.

17. Examine the title bar of the message composition window.

The name of the window is now New Postcards. The subject of a message appears on the title bar unless the Subject field is empty.

A dark red dot appears in the close button. This indicates that the message contains unsaved changes.

18. Click the close button. A dialog sheet appears, warning that you are closing a message that hasn't been sent.

19. Click **Save as Draft**. The message is saved and the window closes.

20. In the navigation pane, click **Drafts**. The draft message you just saved appears in the item list.

21. In the item list, select the draft message you just created. Its content appears in the reading pane.

CLEAN UP No clean-up steps are required. You are ready to continue to the next exercise.

Formatting Message Text

Outlook offers two options when it comes to text formatting:

- *Plain Text* is just that—plain text. No formatting options are available. All text appears in 12-point Consolas font in the message composition window. How it appears in a recipient's email client software depends on how his or her software is configured.

- *HTML* is formatted text that uses *hypertext markup language*—the same formatting technique used for most Web pages. HTML gives you control over many aspects of a message's formatting. Best of all, it's understood by almost all email client software, so there's a good chance that the formatting you include in your messages will be seen by the messages' recipients.

By default, Outlook is set up to create new messages in HTML format. You can switch to plain text on a message-by-message basis. If you always want to use plain text for the messages you write, you can set Outlook preferences to use plain text as the default for all new messages.

See Also You can learn how to set the default formatting option for new messages in the section titled "Setting Reading and Composing Options" in Chapter 6.

If you use HTML formatting for the messages you write, Outlook offers a wide range of formatting options for your message text:

● Change the font, font size, and color of text.

● Apply font styles such as bold, italic, underline, and strikethrough.

● Highlight text characters.

● Create bulleted or numbered lists.

● Adjust indentation.

● Set paragraph alignment.

● Set a background color or picture.

● Format text as a clickable hyperlink.

You apply formatting to message text in Outlook the same way you might apply formatting in Word or another word processor: select the text you want to format and then apply formatting. You can see the results immediately. If you don't like what you see, you can use the Undo command to undo a formatting change.

In Outlook, you can apply formatting using five different interface elements:

● **Message tab** This tab on the ribbon in the message composition window includes buttons and menus you can use to apply basic character and paragraph formatting to selected text.

● **Options tab** This tab on the ribbon in the message composition window includes options for changing the background color or background picture of a message.

- **Fonts panel** The Mac OS X Fonts panel offers a standard interface for setting font formatting options. You can display the Fonts panel by clicking Choose at the bottom of the Font menu on the Message tab.

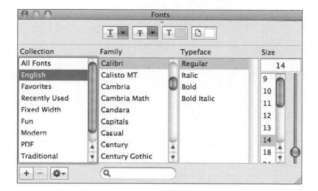

  Important With the Fonts panel, you can apply any font installed on your computer to selected message text. If the font you apply is not installed on the message recipient's computer, he or she will not see the message formatted as you intended.

- **Format menu** Using the commands on this menu's submenus, you can apply all kinds of formatting to selected text in a message.

● **Keyboard shortcuts** Many formatting options have keyboard shortcuts. Here's a table for reference.

Command	Keyboard Shortcut
Bold	Command+B
Italic	Command+I
Underline	Command+U
Strikethrough	Shift+Command+X
Increase Font Size	Shift+Command+=
Decrease Font Size	Command+- (Minus)
Left Align	Shift+Command+[
Centered	Shift+Command+\
Right Aligned	Shift+Command+]
Increase Indent	Command+]
Decrease Indent	Command+[
Hyperlink	Control+Command+K

In this exercise, you'll open the New Postcards message you created in the previous exercise and format the text. You'll also experiment with background colors and pictures.

SET UP You need the Stucco-50 and Stucco-100 images in the Chapter03/Images folder to complete this exercise.

1. In the navigation pane, click **Drafts**.

2. In the item list, double-click the **New Postcards** message to opens it in a message composition window.

3. On the **Options** tab, click the **Format** button. A confirmation dialog sheet appears, asking if you're sure you want to turn off HTML formatting.

Format

Are you sure you want to turn off HTML formatting?

If you change the message format, Outlook will remove all text formatting, such as bold and italic, as well as font and background colors and multimedia elements. This action cannot be undone.

☐ Don't show this message again

Cancel   Yes

4. Click **Yes**. The document's text changes to 12-point Consolas font.

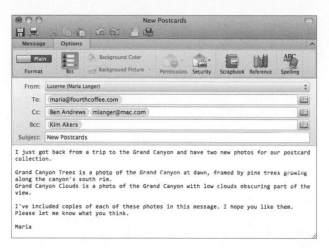

5. With the cursor anywhere in the message body, examine the **Message** tab. All formatting options are unavailable (gray). You cannot use the ribbon commands to format plain text.

6. Click the **Format** menu to display it. Almost all options are unavailable. You cannot use menus to format plain text.

7. On the **Options** tab, click the **Format** button. The message window switches back to HTML mode. The text returns to 14-point Calibri font. You can now format it again.

8. Select all the text in the message body.

9. On the **Message** tab, click the **Font** arrow to display the menu.

10. Click **Verdana**. The Verdana font is applied to all selected text.

11. On the **Message** tab, click the **Font Size** arrow to display the menu.

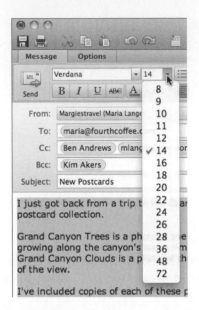

12. Click **12**. The font size of all selected text is reduced to 12 points.

    Tip Another way to set the font size is to type a value in the Font Size box instead of choosing from the menu, and then press Return.

13. Select the words *Grand Canyon Trees* at the beginning of the second paragraph.

Bold

14. On the **Message** tab, click the **Bold** button. The selected text turns bold.

Font Color

15. On the **Message** tab, click the **Font Color** arrow to display the menu.

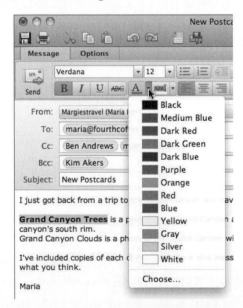

16. Click **Dark Green**. The dark green color is applied to the selected text, and the color on the Font Color button becomes dark green. You have not only applied the color but you have set the default color for the button.

17. Select the words *Grand Canyon Clouds* at the beginning of the third paragraph.

18. On the **Message** tab, click the **Bold** button. The selected text turns bold.

19. On the **Message** tab, click the **Font Color** button. The dark green color is applied to the selected text.

Bulleted List

20. Select the two paragraphs beginning with the bold words *Grand Canyon*. On the **Message** tab, click the **Bulleted List** button. The two paragraphs become indented bullet items.

Tip If a third bullet appears at an empty paragraph after the list, click to the right of it and click the Bulleted List button to reset that paragraph without bullets.

21. Select the name *Maria* at the end of the message.

22. On the **Message** tab, click the **Font** arrow to display the menu, and then click **Choose**. The Fonts panel appears.

23. In the **Family** scrolling list, click **Lucida Calligraphy**. The font applied to the selected text changes.

24. In the **Size** box, enter **14**. The font size of the selected text changes.

25. On the **Fonts** panel title bar, click the close button to close it.

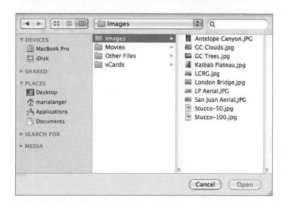

Background Picture

26. On the **Options** tab, click the **Background Picture** arrow, and then click **Choose** from the menu that appears. A standard **Open** dialog sheet appears. Use it to navigate to the **Chapter03/Images** folder.

27. Click the **Stucco-100** image file, and then click **Open**. The image is placed in the background of the message. Unfortunately, because the image is so dark, the text is difficult to read.

28. On the **Options** tab, click the **Background Picture** arrow, and then click **Choose**. The Open dialog sheet that appears should point to the Images folder inside the Chapter03 folder.

29. Click the **Stucco-50** image file, and then click **Open**. The image replaces the original image. Because it's a lighter color, the text is legible.

30. On the **Options** tab, click the **Background Picture** arrow, and then click **Remove**. The image is removed from the background.

Background
Color

31. On the **Options** tab, click the **Background Color** button. A standard Mac OS Colors panel appears.

32. In the **Colors** panel, use one of the color pickers to select a light color. The color is immediately applied to the background of the message, so you can see how it will look before you make a final decision.

33. On the **Colors** panel title bar, click the close button to close it.

34. Select the words *Grand Canyon* in the first paragraph.

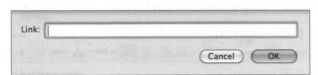
Insert a
Hyperlink

35. On the **Message** tab, click the **Insert a Hyperlink** button. A dialog sheet with a Link field appears.

36. In the **Link** field, type **http://www.nps.gov/grca**, and then click **OK**. The selected text turns into a blue, underlined hyperlink, similar to what you might find on a Web page. Clicking this text opens web page of the URL you typed.

Save

37. On the message composition window toolbar, click the **Save** button or press Command+S to save changes to the message.

 CLEAN UP No clean-up steps are required. You are ready to continue to the next exercise.

Inserting Media in Messages

With Outlook, you can insert images, sounds, and movies into messages. You can do this in one of four ways:

- **Media Browser** You can use this feature to select a photo from your iPhoto library, an audio file from your iTunes library, or a movie from your Movies folder or iTunes library. This integration with Mac OS and popular Apple applications makes it easy to find and insert the media you want.

    Important You must have Apple's iPhoto application, which is part of the iLife suite of products, installed on your computer to use the Photo Browser to insert images in your email messages.

- **Picture From File** This command displays a standard Open dialog sheet that you can use to locate, select, and open an image file to insert.

- **Copy and Paste** As you might expect, you can copy and paste an image from another application into an Outlook message body. This is a handy technique when the image is already open on your computer.

- **Drag and drop** Outlook supports drag-and-drop copying from the Finder. Just drag the icon for the media file you want to include from a Finder window into the message body to copy the file to the message.

Important You can only insert media into an HTML format message. HTML format is discussed in the section titled "Formatting Message Text" earlier in this chapter. If you want to include media files in a plain message, they must be attached. Attaching files is covered in the section "Attaching Files to Messages" later in this chapter.

When you insert a picture, the image appears embedded in the message body instead of as an attachment. Sounds and movies appear as attachments. If the message recipient has an email application that supports media in HTML messages, all media may appear in the body of the message, and sounds and movies can be played from within the message.

Inserting Media: Outlook vs. Entourage

If you're upgrading from Microsoft Entourage to Outlook, you may notice that Outlook handles multimedia elements differently. In Entourage, inserted pictures, sounds, and movies appeared *inline*, within the message body. In Outlook, only pictures appear within the message body; other multimedia appears as an attachment.

Microsoft made this change when it rewrote the message authoring code for Outlook 2011 to be more consistent with the way attachments are handled within other email applications. Keep in mind, however, that if the recipient's email application supports media in HTML messages—as Apple Mail does—the media might appear within the message, even if it is attached.

Tip It's a good idea to make sure that recipients can view or play back multimedia format files you share with them. Although each computer supports different file formats, the most commonly supported formats include JPEG, GIF, and PNG for images; MP3 for sound; and MPEG or QuickTime for movies.

In this exercise, you'll use three different techniques to insert a number of multimedia elements into the draft message you created earlier in this chapter.

 SET UP If you have iPhoto installed, you need the photo files located in the Chapter03/Images folder to complete some of this exercise. Drag all but the Stucco photos onto the iPhoto icon to copy them into iPhoto. If you have iTunes installed, you need the three movie files located in the Chapter03/Movies folder to complete some of this exercise. Drag the movie files onto the iTunes icon to copy them into iTunes. Quit both iPhoto and iTunes. Drag the Gila Monster movie to the Movies folder in your Home folder. Make sure you have access to the Chapter03 files from the Finder. Open the draft message you worked on in the previous exercise if it is not already open.

1. Click after *Maria* in the last paragraph of the message and press Return twice.

2. On the **Message** tab, click the **Picture** button to display the menu.

Picture

Photos

3. Click **Photo Browser** to open the **Media Browser**. If necessary, click the **Photos** button.

   If you have iPhoto installed, the top half of the Media Browser is populated with your iPhoto library information. (If you don't have iPhoto installed, skip to step 6.)

4. Click **Last Import** to display the photos you imported for this exercise.

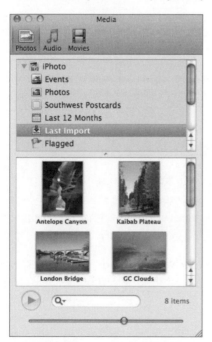

   Important The image files may appear in a different order than what is shown here.

5. Drag the **GC Clouds** photo from the **Media Browser** to the space at the end of the message body. The photo is pasted into the message body.

6. On the **Media Browser** title bar, click the close button.

7. Make sure the cursor is just to the right of the inserted image. Then, on the **Message** tab, click the **Picture** button to display its menu again.

8. Click **Picture from File**. A standard Open dialog sheet appears.

9. Navigate to the **Chapter03/Images** folder, click **GC Trees.jpg**, and then click **Open**. The image is inserted into the message beneath the other image. (If you don't have iPhoto installed, you can repeat this process to insert the GC Clouds image.)

Media Browser

10. On the message composition window toolbar, click the **Media Browser** button. The Media Browser opens again.

Movies

11. In the **Media Browser**, click the **Movies** button. The top half of the Media Browser displays the Movies folder and, if you have iTunes installed, an iTunes icon.

12. Click either **Movies** or **iTunes** to display movies in the bottom half of the window.

13. Drag the **Gila Monster** movie from the **Media Browser** to the message body. The movie appears as an attachment in the message header.

14. On the message composition window toolbar, click the **Save** button or press Command+S to save changes to the message.

✖ CLEAN UP No clean-up steps are required. You are ready to continue to the next exercise.

Attaching Files to Messages

You can attach any kind of file to an email message to send it to a message recipient. This enables you to collaborate with coworkers on the creation of Microsoft Office documents, taking full advantage of its powerful commenting and change-tracking features. It also makes it possible to share any kind of file with someone else.

In addition to using the Media Browser to attach sounds and movies, which was covered in the previous section of this chapter, Outlook offers two ways to attach a file to a message:

● **Attach command** This button or command displays a standard Open dialog sheet that you can use to locate, select, and open the files you want to attach. This makes it possible to attach any file you can access from your computer.

● **Drag and drop** With Outlook, you can drag file icons from the Finder into a message window. If the file is not an image file, it is automatically attached.

You can attach files to any message, whether it's in HTML or plain text format. Attachments are added to the attachments list in the message header.

If you change your mind about an attachment, you can easily remove it before sending the message by simply selecting it and pressing Delete. The attachment is removed from the message but is not removed from its source location on disk.

File Attachment Considerations

You should keep in mind a few important things when attaching files to share with message recipients:

- Attaching a file does not guarantee that the recipient will be able to open it. When attaching a document created with a specific application, you may want to ask the message recipient whether he or she has software that can open it before attaching and sending it. If there's any doubt about document compatibility, you might consider saving the document as a PDF—just remember that all editing capabilities will likely be lost.

- Consider file size when attaching any file—including the multimedia elements discussed in the previous section. Some email accounts have restrictions on incoming message sizes or mailbox size. If, for example, you attempt to send 8 MB of attached files to an email account that can accept only 5 MB, that message will not be received. It's often more practical to use FTP or some other file transfer option when sharing very large files.

- When attaching multiple files to an email message, you may want to use the built-in Mac OS compression feature to compress or "zip" the files into one archive. Not only will this make the total file size smaller, but it will keep the files together in one neat package.

In this exercise, you'll attach a Word document to the draft message you've been working on throughout this chapter. You'll also remove an attachment so it is not sent with the message.

 SET UP You need the Flyer document located in the Chapter03/Other Files folder to complete this exercise. Make sure you have access to the Chapter03 files. Open the draft message you worked on in the previous exercise if it is not already open.

Attach

1. On the **Message** tab, click the **Attach** button. In the **Open** dialog sheet that appears, navigate to the **Chapter03/Other Files** folder.

2. Click **Flyer**, and then click **Choose**. The file is added to the attachments field in the message header.

3. In the attachments field, click the **Gila Monster** movie file you attached in the previous exercise.

4. Press Delete. The attachment is removed.

5. On the message composition window toolbar, click the **Save** button or press Command+S to save changes to the message.

✕ CLEAN UP No clean-up steps are required. You are ready to continue to the next exercise.

Changing Message Settings

Before sending a message, you might want to set additional message options for it. Outlook offers a number of useful settings, such as the following:

- **Signature** This is a predefined footer for the bottom of the message. Normally, it includes the sender's name and contact information, but it can include any text you like. Signatures are optional, but you can set up Outlook so it automatically appends a signature to every message you write.

  See Also Creating and managing signatures is covered in detail in the section titled "Working with Signatures" in Chapter 6.

- **Security** These features enable you to digitally sign or encrypt a message. This helps protect the message from unauthorized access. By default, new messages are neither digitally signed nor encrypted.

  See Also Security features for email messages are covered in the section titled "Securing Your Email" in Chapter 6.

- **Priority** This setting offers one way to tell the message recipient how important the message is. By default, each message is set for normal priority, but you can also set it for high or low priority.

It's important to note that all of the message settings discussed in this part of the chapter are completely optional. You might never use any of them. Or you might focus on those you find most useful. Explore them to see which ones can help you work better with Outlook.

In this exercise, you'll insert a signature and set the priority for the draft message you've been working with throughout this chapter.

SET UP You don't need any practice files to complete this exercise. Open the draft message you worked on in the previous exercise if it is not already open.

1. If necessary, click to position the cursor at the very end of the message body, right after the second image, and then press Return twice. This inserts two empty paragraphs at the end of the message.

Signatures

2. On the **Message** tab, click the **Signatures** button to display the menu. This menu includes the Edit Signatures command, as well as at least one signature.

3. Click **Standard**. The standard signature is inserted at the cursor.

   Important If you have not yet configured a signature, the Standard signature may appear as just two dashes. You can customize the Standard signature or create other signatures that will appear in the Signatures menu. Chapter 6 explains how.

   Tip You can modify or delete an inserted signature just like any other message body text.

High Priority

4. On the **Message** tab, click the **High Priority** button. The button turns dark gray to indicate that it is selected.

   Tip You can set a message to normal priority by clicking the selected priority button again to deselect it.

5. On the message composition window toolbar, click the **Save** button or press Command+S to save changes to the message.

6. On the message composition window's title bar, click the close button. The window closes.

7. In the navigation bar, click **Drafts**, and then click the **New Postcards** message you've been working with. You should see several things:

   ○ In the item list, icons for attachments and high priority appear beneath the message time.

   ○ In the reading pane, the message header includes attachment information.

   ○ Beneath the message header, a note indicates that the message is high priority.

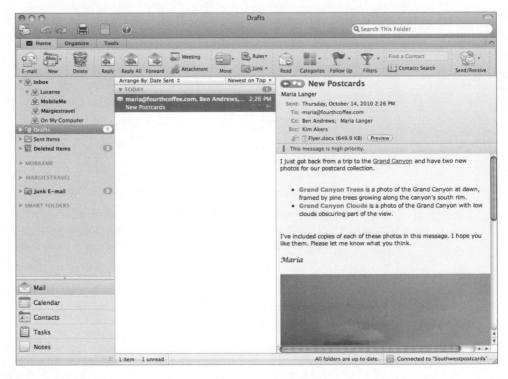

CLEAN UP No clean-up steps are required. You are ready to continue to the next exercise.

Sending Messages

When your message has been addressed, composed, formatted, and fine-tuned as desired, it's ready to send. Just click the Send button, and the message is sent to its recipients.

There are a few additional things to consider when sending an email message:

- If you don't have an Internet connection, you cannot send the message. Instead, when you click the Send button, Outlook places the message in an Outbox that appears right above the view switcher. The message remains there until you are connected to the Internet and it can be sent.

> **Tip** If you plan on working with Outlook for an extended period of time while offline, choose Work Offline from the Outlook menu. This will avoid any error messages that might appear when Outlook tries to connect to the Internet. When Internet access is available, be sure to choose Work Offline from the Outlook menu to disable this feature. Outlook should immediately connect to the Internet to send and receive messages.

- Email travels quickly, but it won't be received by the recipient until he or she checks email. So although a recipient sitting at his or her computer might receive a message from you almost immediately after you send it, a recipient on vacation without Internet connectivity might not receive your message until he or she returns a week or more later. Many people don't check work-related email accounts during off-work hours or personal email accounts while at work. Be patient if you don't get an immediate response.

- Spam filters on the recipient's email server or within the recipient's email client software could also prevent your message from reaching the recipient—or simply delay it until the recipient checks his or her Junk E-mail or Spam folder. Spam filters look for words and patterns within a message to identify potential spam content; no spam filter is perfect. Spam filters don't normally notify senders when messages are marked as spam, so you might never know your recipient didn't get the message you sent.

● If the email address you send a message to is incorrect, the message should *bounce* back with some sort of notification. This could be immediate if the information after the @ symbol is correct, or it could be several days later if the part after the @ symbol is wrong. Keep this in mind the first time you contact someone by email; if the message bounces back, chances are that you entered the email address incorrectly in Outlook or the address is old and the email account has since been closed.

Check Names

Checking Names

The Check Names button, which appears on the Message tab, makes it possible to validate the names of message recipients before sending the message. The trouble is, this feature requires either a Microsoft Exchange account with EWS/HTTP services enabled or that an LDAP server be set up as part of your Outlook configuration. In addition, it requires that each recipient either have an account on your Exchange server or be listed in a configured LDAP server.

If you do not have an LDAP server configured, this feature will not work at all. If a recipient is not listed on a configured LDAP server, this feature will not work for that recipient.

After a message has been sent, it moves from the Drafts folder to the Sent Items folder. Once it is there, you can open it to consult it, resend it, or delete it. How long an item remains in the Sent Items folder depends on the type of account it was sent from and the settings for that account.

See Also You can learn more about working with email messages stored in Outlook in Chapter 5, "Organizing Your Inbox," and about account settings in Chapter 6.

In this exercise, we'll take a last look at the draft message we've been working on throughout this chapter before sending it out to its recipients.

SET UP You don't need any practice files to complete this exercise.

1. In **Mail** view, in the navigation pane, click **Drafts,** and then double-click the **New Postcards** message. The message opens in a message composition window.

2. Note that although the email message includes four recipients, only one of them—you in the Cc field—is valid. If you send the message with all recipients, you'll likely get three error messages. If you prefer not to see these error messages, select the invalid addresses (maria@fourthcoffee.com, Ben Andrews, and Kim Akers) one at a time and press Delete to remove them. Be sure to retain at least one email address.

> **Tip** If you're curious about what happens when you send email to invalid addresses, you can leave all recipients in the message header. Shortly after sending the message you should begin to get "Undelivered Mail" messages.

Send

3. On the **Message** tab, click the **Send** button. The message window closes and the message is sent.

✖ CLEAN UP No clean-up steps are required. Leave Outlook open if you are continuing to exercises in the next chapter.

Key Points

- You create email messages in a message composition window.

- You can use the Contacts Search feature of Outlook to address messages to recipients.

- A message can include plain or formatted text, images, and other attached files.

- You can save a message as a draft so you can finish it at a later time if you need to.

- You can insert a preconfigured signature at the end of your messages and set message priority before sending.

- You need to be connected to the Internet to send a message; if you're not connected, Outlook will save the message in an Outbox until you are connected and the message can be sent.

Chapter at a Glance

Read incoming messages
in Mail view, **page 87**

Use menu commands to work
with file attachments, **page 93**

Follow message conversations,
page 87

4 Reading and Responding to Email Messages

In this chapter, you will learn how to

✔ Retrieve messages.

✔ Read messages.

✔ Work with email attachments.

✔ View message sender information.

✔ Reply to messages.

✔ Forward messages.

✔ Print messages.

✔ Automatically reply to messages.

✔ Schedule meetings from messages.

While you're sending email out to coworkers, business associates, friends, and family members, chances are they're sending email to you. You can use Microsoft Outlook for Mac 2011 to read and respond to all of your email.

Tip Outlook for Mac supports multiple email accounts, so you can to set up all of your business and personal accounts within Outlook to read your email all in one place.

As discussed in Chapter 3, "Composing and Sending Email Messages," Outlook supports plain text and HTML-based email formatting, so messages should appear within Outlook the way senders formatted them. Outlook also supports embedded images and attached files.

When you read an email message, you can reply to it or forward it to someone else's email account. You can also use it to create a new meeting on your calendar.

See Also You can learn more about organizing email messages in Chapter 5, "Organizing Your Inbox."

This chapter explains how to use Mail view within Outlook to retrieve, read, reply to, and forward messages. It also shows you how to use Mac OS X's Quick Look feature to view attachments without opening them, how to save attachments to your disk, and how to print messages. Finally, it explains how replying to a meeting request in an email message can automatically schedule a meeting in Outlook's Calendar view.

> **Practice Files** No practice files are needed for this chapter. You can complete exercises with items in your Inbox as well as items created for this and other chapters. For more information about practice file requirements, see "Using the Practice Files" at the beginning of this book.

Retrieving Messages

Although email is a lot quicker than its postal service counterpart, the two do have one thing in common: you must retrieve your mail to work with it. At a post office, that means a trip to your mailbox or post office box. Within Outlook, that means telling Outlook to connect to the server to retrieve incoming email messages.

By default, Outlook is configured to check for email every 10 minutes when it's running and connected to the Internet. When it connects, it does a few things, depending on the type of accounts you have set up:

- Sends any outgoing messages in the Outbox.

- Retrieves any incoming messages and places them in the Inbox.

- Synchronizes folders for Exchange and IMAP (including MobileMe) email accounts to account for deleted or moved messages.

- Sends the server information about retrieved or deleted messages for POP accounts. (What happens on the server depends on POP account settings.)

- Plays one of two alert sounds to notify you that it has checked for or received new mail. The sound for received mail is louder and more noticeable than the sound when there's no new mail.

See Also Adjusting the Send & Receive All schedule in Outlook is covered in the section titled "Scheduling Actions" in Chapter 6, "Fine-Tuning Email Settings." Server settings for POP accounts are covered in the section titled "Setting Additional Email Account Options" in Chapter 1, "Getting Started Using Outlook."

You can tell Outlook to check for messages any time you like. Simply click the Send/ Receive button on the Home tab or press Command+K. Outlook goes online to perform its usual tasks. The status bar at the bottom of the Outlook window reports what it's doing as it works.

You can also display the Progress window to monitor activity. Choose Progress from the Window menu or press Command+7 to display it.

If Outlook encounters any errors while checking for mail, it alerts you with an error sound and a message box.

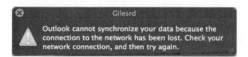

It also displays a yellow alert icon in the lower-right corner of the Outlook window. Clicking that icon, choosing Error Log from the Window menu, or pressing Command+8 displays the error log window. You can click an error message in the window to learn more about the problem.

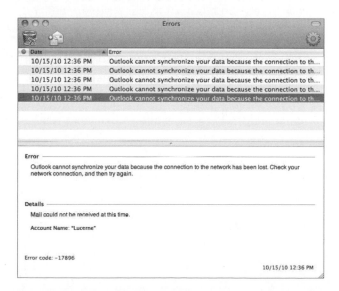

In this exercise, you'll learn how to manually check for new email and how you can moni-tor Outlook's progress.

SET UP Display the Outlook Mail view, and then follow the steps.

Send/Receive

1. On the **Home** tab, click the **Send/Receive** arrow to display the menu. The menu offers a number of commands for sending and receiving messages. A list of all the email accounts you have configured in Outlook appears at the bottom of the menu.

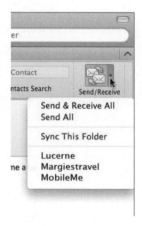

2. Click the name of one of your email accounts. Outlook goes online to check for mail for that one account. When it's done, it plays a sound.

3. Click the **Send/Receive** button. Outlook goes online to check for mail in all email accounts.

4. Before Outlook is finished checking for mail, click **Progress** on the **Window** menu or press Command+7. You can then watch the send/receive progress in the Progress window that appears. When Outlook is done checking for mail, it plays an alert sound for each account it checked.

   Tip It is not necessary to monitor the Progress window when you check for email. You might find it helpful if you think Outlook is taking longer than usual and want to see what it's doing.

CLEAN UP No clean-up steps are required. You are ready to continue to the next exercise.

Reading Messages

Incoming mail is placed in the Inbox. To view the Inbox contents, click Inbox in the navigation pane in Mail view. The items in the Inbox are listed in the item list in the middle of the window. By default, the most recent messages are on top

If you have multiple email accounts set up in Outlook, your Inbox will be split into multiple Inboxes with one for each account. To display the individual Inboxes, click the disclosure triangle beside the main Inbox in the navigation pane. The account Inboxes appear indented beneath it.

Tip If you have multiple POP accounts, they will share one Inbox called On My Computer.

The list of incoming mail in the item list varies depending on what you click in the navigation pane:

- To see a list of all incoming mail, click Inbox.
- To see a list of incoming mail for just one account, click the name of the account under Inbox.

When your Inbox—or any of its account Inboxes—contains unread messages, the Inbox name appears in bold characters with a number beside it. The number is a count of all unread messages in the Inbox. In addition, the Outlook icon in the Dock will indicate the total number of unread messages that are in your Inbox. You can identify unread messages in your Inbox by an envelope icon to the left of the bold message subject.

Outlook offers two ways to read email messages:

● **Reading pane** When you select a message in the item list, the contents of that message appear in the reading pane on the right side of the window. This is a quick way to scan incoming messages.

● **Message reading window** When you double-click a message in the item list, the message reading window opens to display the contents of the message. This is a good way to read a long or heavily formatted message.

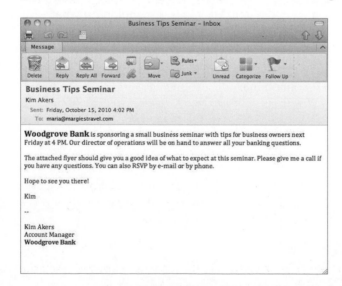

Tip If an incoming email message includes pictures, Outlook may not automatically download them. If so, it displays a message beneath the message header, explaining that the message contains pictures. Click the Download Pictures button in this area to download the images and see them in the message. You can change this behavior so Outlook automatically downloads pictures; the section titled "Setting Reading and Composing Options" in Chapter 6 explains how.

The reading pane can be configured to appear on the right, which is the default setting, or on the bottom of the Mail view window. If you prefer not to use the reading pane at all, you can hide it. The Reading Pane options are accessible from the Reading Pane menu on the Organize tab.

By default, Outlook is set up to view the Inbox item list as conversations. This groups messages with the same subject so you can easily see the exchange of messages about that subject. You can toggle conversation view on or off by clicking the Conversations button in the Organize tab.

With conversations enabled, clicking a conversation in the item list displays a list of all messages in that conversation in the reading pane—including messages you sent as part of the conversation.

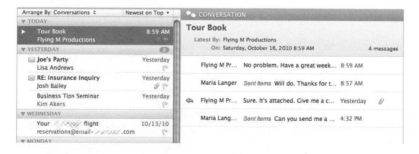

To see a list of conversation messages in the item list, click the disclosure triangle beside the message name. A list of messages appears beneath it.

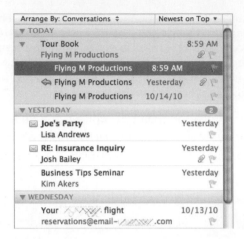

You can then click a message to read it in the reading pane or double-click a message to open it in a message reading window.

By default, a message is marked as read if you do one of two things:

- Select the message in the item list and then select another message.
- Open the message in a message reading window.

See Also You can change how Outlook determines whether a message is read by setting options in Reading preferences, which is covered in the section titled "Setting Reading and Composing Options" in Chapter 6.

When a message is marked as read, the envelope icon to the left of the message subject disappears and the subject is no longer in bold type.

A message remains in your Inbox as long as you leave it there—even if it's read. If you need to, you can mark a read message as unread or an unread message as read. You can also mark all messages in the message list as read. You do all this with the Unread and Read buttons on the Home tab and the All Read button on the Organize tab. Just select the message in the item list and click the button you want.

See Also Chapter 5 explains how to delete and move messages.

In this exercise, you'll view a list of the messages in your Inbox. If you have multiple email accounts, you'll view Inbox items individually for each account. You'll also read incoming messages in the reading pane and the message reading window. Finally, you'll see the difference in the item list when the conversations feature is enabled and disabled.

SET UP If you don't have any email messages in your Inbox after retrieving messages, take a moment to send yourself one or ask a friend to send you one. Then check for messages so the new message appears in your Inbox. The more messages you have in your Inbox, the more you can explore in this exercise.

1. In the navigation pane, click **Inbox**. The item list should display a list of all incoming email messages.

2. Note that bold messages are unread. Confirm that the number of bold messages corresponds to the number that appears to the right of **Inbox** in the navigation pane.

3. If you don't have multiple email accounts set up in Outlook, skip ahead to step 7.

4. If necessary, in the navigation pane, click the disclosure triangle beside **Inbox** to display a list of your accounts.

5. In the navigation pane, click the name of an account. The Inbox messages for just that account appear in the item list. You can repeat this step for other accounts.

6. In the navigation pane, click **Inbox** to display all Inbox messages again.

7. In the item list, click a message. The message content appears in the reading pane.

8. In the item list, double-click the same message. A message reading window opens to display the contents of the message.

9. In the message header, point to the sender name. After a moment, a window will appear with information about that sender.

10. In the message reading window's title bar, click the close button.

Conversations

11. On the **Organize** tab, confirm that the conversations feature is enabled. If it isn't, click the **Conversations** button so that it turns dark gray.

Tip You could also enable conversations by choosing Conversations from the Arrange By button's menu.

12. In the item list, select any message that displays a disclosure triangle beside it. The reading pane should fill with a list of messages in a conversation.

13. If necessary, in the item list, click the disclosure triangle beside the conversation to display the individual messages of the conversation in the item list.

14. Click a message in the conversation. Its contents appear in the reading pane.

15. Double-click the same message. A message reading window opens to display the message contents.

16. In the message reading window's title bar, click the close button.

Reading Pane

17. On the **Organize** tab, click the **Reading Pane** button to display its menu. Then click **Below**. The reading pane shifts to appear below the item list.

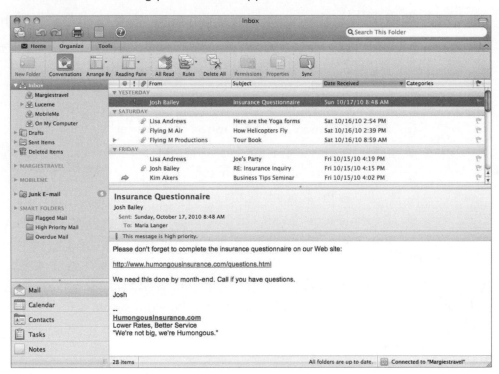

Tip If you're switching from Apple Mail to Outlook, you may find this view more familiar, because it closely matches the default layout of Apple Mail.

18. On the **Organize** tab, click the **Reading Pane** button, and then click **Hidden**. The reading pane disappears and the item list takes over the entire right side of the window. Now, the only way to read a message is to double-click it in the item list to open it in a message reading window.

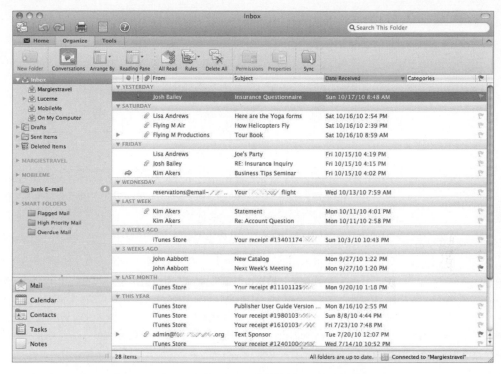

19. In the item list, select a message that you have already read.

20. On the **Home** tab, click the **Unread** button. The message subject turns bold with an envelope icon beside it again, as if it has not been read.

21. On the **Home** tab, click the **Read** button. The message is marked as read.

Read

✖ CLEAN UP On the Organize tab, click the Reading Pane button, and then click Right. You are ready to continue to the next exercise.

Working with Email Attachments

Some of the messages you receive will include file attachments. There are two ways you can tell if a message has a file attached:

- In the item list, a paper clip icon appears on the right side of any message with an attachment.

- In the reading pane or message reading window, a list of attachments appears beside a paper clip icon at the bottom of the message header.

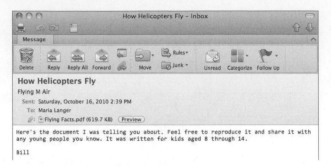

Tip If there are several attachments, only one or two might be listed in the message header, followed by a link telling you how many more there are. Click that link to see an itemized list.

You can work with attachments in a number of ways:

- **Quick Look** If your computer is running Mac OS 10.6 Snow Leopard, you can use the Mac OS Quick Look feature to see the contents of the file without opening it in another application. Simply click the Preview button that appears beside the file attachment name in the message header. A Quick Look window appears to display the document within Outlook. When you're finished previewing the document, click the Quick Look window's close button or press Esc.

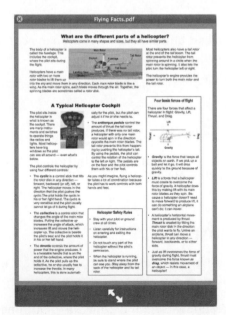

Tip You can preview document files only.

- **Open** You can also open an attachment from within Outlook. Double-click the attachment. An application that can open the attachment—if one is installed on your computer—opens and the attachment's contents appear in a document window.

Tip If an attachment is not a document, it may not open the way you expect. For example, opening an attached application file will launch that application, and opening an attached ZIP archive file will unzip the archive.

● **Save** You can also save an attachment to disk. Outlook offers two ways to do this:

  ○ Drag the attachment from the message header into a Finder window. The attachment is copied to the Finder.

  ○ Select the attachment in the message header. Then click the Message menu, click Attachments, and click Save. Use the standard Save dialog sheet that appears to name and save the attachment to disk. After the attachment is saved to disk, you can access it like any other file in the Finder or from within applications.

Tip You can chose the Save All command on the Attachments submenu under the Message menu to save all of a message's attachments to disk at once.

In this exercise, you'll preview, open, and save a message attachment.

 SET UP You need an incoming message with a file attached to complete this exercise. You should have at least one if you completed the exercises in Chapter 3. If not, send yourself a message with a file attached.

1. In the item list, locate and select a message with a paper clip icon. The message appears in the reading pane.

2. In the reading pane, click the **Preview** button beside the attachment. If you have Mac OS X 10.6 installed, a Quick Look window opens to display the contents of the file.

3. When you're finished looking at the document in Quick Look, close the **Quick Look** window.

4. In the reading pane, double-click the attachment name. A compatible application opens to display the attachment in a window.

5. When you're finished looking at the document in the application that opened it, from the application's menu, choose **Quit** or press Command+Q.

6. In the reading pane, drag the attachment from the message header to your desktop. The attachment is copied there.

✖ **CLEAN UP** Drag the attachment icon that you copied to the desktop to the Trash. You are now ready for the next exercise.

Viewing Message Sender Information

You can view information about a message sender in a window that pops up when you point to the sender's name in the reading pane or in a message reading window.

What appears in the window depends on whether the sender is in your contacts list.

● If the sender is in your contacts list, you'll see the sender's photo (if it's part of the sender's contact record) or a generic photo icon, email address, online presence (if known), and phone numbers.

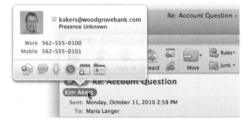

● If the sender is not in your contacts list, you'll see a generic photo icon, email address, and online presence (if known).

Either way, there will be a row of six icons at the bottom of the window:

● **Send Mail** Opens a preaddressed message composition window so you can send an email message to the sender

● **Send an Instant Message** Enables you to use Windows Live Messenger or Communicator to send an instant message to the sender

● **Call Contact** Enables you to use Windows Live Messenger or Communicator to call the sender

● **Start a Video Call** Enables you to use Windows Live Messenger or Communicator to initiate a video call to the sender

● **Schedule a Meeting** Opens a meeting window so you can schedule a meeting with the sender in your calendar

● **Open Outlook Contact** Opens a contact window so you can consult or edit contact information, or add the sender to your contacts list

> **Tip** Both you and the sender must be logged into Windows Live Messenger or Communicator to make contact with an instant message, call, or video call. If you're not logged in, the button cannot be clicked.

In this exercise, you'll examine sender information on incoming email messages and explore the options in the sender's contact card.

 SET UP In the navigation pane, click Inbox and then follow these steps.

1. In the item list, select an email message.

2. In the reading pane, point to the name of the sender in the message header. The sender's contact card appears.

3. Note the information that appears for the sender. If the sender is in your contacts list, you might see his or her photo and phone numbers.

Send Mail

4. In the contact card, click the **Send Mail** button. A message composition window, preaddressed to the sender, appears. You can use this window to compose a new message that is not a reply to the sender.

5. Close the message composition window, and then click **Discard Changes** in the dialog sheet that appears.

6. In the item list, select a different message.

7. In the reading pane, point to the name of the sender in the message header to display the contact card.

Open
Outlook Contact

8. In the contact card, click the **Open Outlook Contact** button. If the contact is in your contacts list, his or her record opens in a contact window. If the contact is not in your contacts list, Outlook creates a contact record for him or her, inserts the email address and name (if known), and displays it so you can edit it.

9. Close the contact window, and then click **Don't Save** in the dialog sheet that appears.

 CLEAN UP No clean-up steps are required. You are ready to move on to the next exercise.

Replying to Messages

When you reply to a message, you create a new message to the sender and, optionally, other recipients. You do this with the Reply and Reply All buttons on the Home tab or the message reading window's Message tab.

Although Reply and Reply All will both reply to a message, there is a significant difference between them:

- **Reply** This button addresses the reply to just the message's sender. If other recipients are included in the message's Cc field, they will not receive the reply.

- **Reply All** This button addresses the reply to the message's sender and includes other message recipients in the Cc field. You can modify the Cc field to add or remove recipients as desired.

   Tip If someone received the message through a Bcc, he or she cannot be included in a reply because the received message does not include Bcc recipients.

Reply or Reply All? Choose Wisely.

Good email etiquette suggests that you use the Reply All option only when it's necessary for *all* of the original message's recipients to see your response.

For example, suppose you're one of five recipients of a message about an upcoming trade show. The organizer wants to divvy up the booth time between all of you. You might use Reply All to indicate what days and times you'd like to be at the booth and what days you can't. This can help all of you work together to fill in the empty time slots.

Now suppose you're one of 50 recipients of a message with new rules for clearing out the office kitchen's refrigerator on Fridays. You want to reply to thank the sender for letting you know about the new policy. Is it necessary to send that thank-you reply to all 50 recipients? Probably not. After all, would you like to be included as a recipient on replies from all 50 people? Click Reply instead of Reply All.

The Subject field of a reply will include the subject of the original message preceded by *Re:*. You can modify the Subject field if you need to, but that might prevent Outlook or the recipient's email client software from recognizing it as part of a conversation.

By default, a reply will include all of the original message's text as a quote at the end of the reply. You can edit the text to remove all or part of it. Or you can select text in the original message before clicking Reply or Reply All to only include that text as a quote in the reply.

After you create a message reply, you can enter and format text, embed pictures, and attach files as with any other message you might send. When you're finished composing your reply, click the Send button on the message composition window's Message tab. The reply is sent like any other message.

Outlook indicates that a message has been replied to by placing a purple arrow to the left of the message in the item list. It also places a note and Show Reply button beneath the message header in the reading pane and message reading window that indicates when you replied to the message.

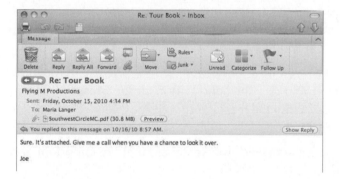

You can click the Show Reply button to open your reply in a message reading window.

In this exercise, you'll use the Reply button to create two different message replies with quoted text.

SET UP In the navigation pane, click Inbox and follow these steps.

1. In the item list, select a message you want to reply to.

Reply

2. On the **Home** tab, click the **Reply** button. Outlook opens a message composition window with the To and Subject fields filled in. The message header information and contents of the original message are copied beneath a gray line in the bottom of the message body.

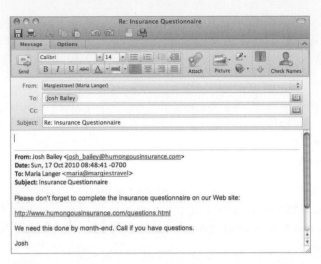

3. In the text quoted from the original message, select and delete some unnecessary text. You can pare down quoted text to keep the message brief and focus on the information you're replying to.

Send

4. To send this message, you would enter your reply at the top of the message body (above the gray line), and click the **Send** button on the **Message** tab. If you prefer not to send the reply, close the message composition window. If a dialog sheet appears, click **Discard Changes**.

5. In the reading pane, select one or two sentences that are important in the message you want to reply to.

6. On the **Home** tab, click the **Reply** button. Outlook opens a message composition window with the To and Subject fields filled in. The original message's header information and the text you selected is copied beneath a gray line in the bottom of the message body. By selecting text before clicking the Reply button, you limited what was quoted.

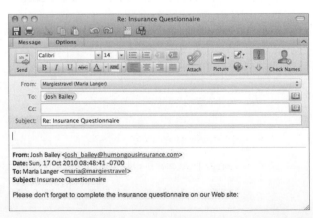

7. To send this message, enter your reply at the top of the message body, and then click the **Send** button on the **Message** tab. If you prefer not to send the reply, close the message composition window. If a dialog sheet appears, click **Discard Changes**.

 CLEAN UP No clean-up steps are required. You are ready to move on to the next exercise.

Forwarding Messages

With Outlook, you can forward a message you receive to someone else. This makes it very easy to share information you receive via email with other people.

There are two different commands for forwarding a message, both of which are available as buttons on the Home tab or message reading window's Message tab:

- **Forward** This button creates a new message that contains the contents of the original message as a quote. You can modify any part of the original message if desired to shorten it up or focus on the important part of the message. You can also select the text that you want to forward in the original message to forward just that text.

- **Attachment** This button creates a new message with the original message attached as an electronic mail (EML) format file. This is a standard email format file that can be opened by most email client programs. The entire original message is forwarded with all formatting intact.

The Subject field of a message forwarded with the Forward button will include the subject of the original message preceded by *FW:*. You can modify the Subject field if you need to.

Keep in mind that it's not uncommon to receive messages with footers that warn against forwarding a message. You should respect the wishes of the sender and not forward any message that is intended to be a private or confidential communication between you.

Outlook indicates that a message has been forwarded by placing a blue arrow to the left of the message in the item list. It also places a note beneath the message header in the reading pane and message reading window that indicates when you forwarded the message. You can click a Show Forward button to see the message you created to forward the original message in a message reading window.

In this exercise, you'll use the Forward button to create three different forwarding messages.

SET UP In the navigation pane, click Inbox, and then follow these steps.

1. In the item list, select a message you want to forward.

Forward

2. On the **Home** tab, click the **Forward** button. Outlook opens a message composition window with the Subject field filled in. The message header information and contents of the original message are copied beneath a gray line in the bottom of the message body.

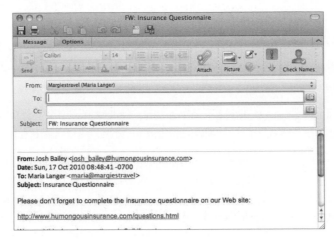

3. To send this message, you would enter one or more recipients in the **To** and **Cc** fields, type your comments at the top of the message body, and click the **Send** button on the **Message** tab. If you prefer not to forward the message, close the message composition window. If a dialog sheet appears, click **Discard Changes**.

4. In the reading pane, select some important text in the message you want to forward.

5. On the **Home** tab, click the **Forward** button. Outlook opens a message composition window with the Subject field filled in. The original message's header information and the text you selected is copied beneath a gray line in the bottom of the message body. By selecting text before clicking the Forward button, you limited what text would be forwarded from the original message.

6. To send this message, enter one or more recipients in the **To** and **Cc** fields, type your comments at the top of the message body, and click the **Send** button on the **Message** tab. If you prefer not to forward the message, close the message composition window. If a dialog sheet appears, click **Discard Changes**.

7. In the item list, select a message you want to forward.

8. On the **Home** tab, click the **Attachment** button. Outlook opens a message composition field with an .eml file attached. This file contains the complete text of the

Attachment

message you're forwarding and should be compatible with most email client software applications.

9. To send this message, enter one or more recipients in the **To** and **Cc** fields, enter a message subject in the **Subject** field, type your comments at the message body, and click the **Send** button on the **Message** tab. If you prefer not to forward the message, close the message composition window. If a dialog sheet appears, click **Discard Changes**.

 CLEAN UP No clean-up steps are required. You are ready to continue to the next exercise.

Printing Messages

Because Outlook retains all of your incoming messages until you delete them, you shouldn't need to print a message very often. If you do, however, it's easy to do.

Seriously: Do You Really Need to Print It?

Before you click that Print button, take a moment to reconsider. Do you really need to print that email message?

Years ago, when computers first began becoming common in the workplace and at home, experts predicted that computers would save paper. They were very much mistaken. Instead, businesses and individuals felt a real need to print everything that came out of their computers. Paper use actually rose.

A lot of time has gone by, and most folks have realized that they don't really need to print the content they read on their computers. It's easier and more cost-effective to forward a message or a link to a Web page than to print it and mail or hand-deliver it. Likewise, it's also quicker and more cost-effective to attach a document file—or a PDF version of it—to an email message and send it to someone than to print it and mail or hand-deliver it.

So the next time you find your mouse reaching for the Print button, take a moment to reconsider. Do you really *need* to print it?

The Print button on the toolbar in the main Outlook window or a message reading window opens a standard Print dialog sheet that you can use to print the selected message.

The Print dialog sheet has two appearances: a collapsed window with very few options and an expanded window that gives you access to all printer and Outlook options. To display the expanded view, click the disclosure triangle to the right of the Printer pop-up menu.

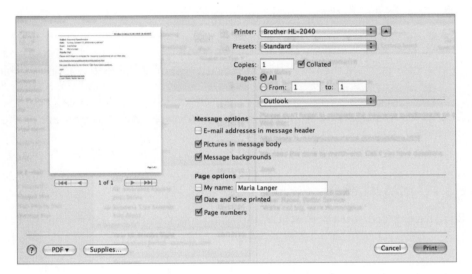

The options in the upper third of the dialog sheet are standard and work just as they do in any other application's print dialog sheet: choose a printer, use presets (when available), set the number of copies, and specify pages to be printed.

With Outlook selected from the pop-up menu beneath the standard items, the bottom part of the dialog sheet enables you to set options for the message and page:

- **Email addresses in message header** This option includes the email addresses for the To, From, and Cc fields beside the names in the message header in the printout.

- **Pictures in message body** This option includes any pictures that might be in the message body in the printout.

- **Message backgrounds** This option includes the background color or picture that might be part of the message. This option is important if the message is formatted with light text on a dark background.

- **My name** This option prints the name you enter in the box beside it in the header of the printed document.

- **Date and time printed** This option prints the print date and time in the header of the printed document.

- **Page numbers** This document prints the page number in the footer of the printed document. This is especially useful for long messages that might print on multiple pages.

The preview area on the left side of the dialog sheet shows what the message will look like when printed. You can click the arrow buttons beneath it to scroll through multiple pages if the message will print on more than one page.

When you're finished setting Outlook options, you can use buttons at the bottom of the dialog sheet to output the email message:

- **PDF** The PDF button is a menu offering several PDF output options. Of these, the ones you'll likely find most useful are Open PDF In Preview, Save As PDF, Fax PDF, and Mail PDF. These options are all standard in Mac OS X, so you can learn more about them in Mac OS Help.

- **Print** The Print button sends the document to the selected printer where it prints.

In this exercise, you'll use the Print dialog sheet to save a message as a PDF file and to print a message on your printer.

SET UP To complete this exercise, you must be connected to at least one printer and have that printer configured in Mac OS. Chances are, if you have already printed from your computer, you're all set to go.

1. In the item list, select the message you want to print.

Print

2. On the toolbar, click the **Print** button, or press Command+P. The Print dialog sheet opens. If it is not in expanded view, click the disclosure triangle to the right of the **Printer** pop-up menu.

3. Make sure **Outlook** appears on the pop-up menu beneath the standard printing options.

4. Select the **Email addresses in message header** check box. The preview area should change to show email addresses in the header area.

5. Select the **My Name** option, and make sure your name is entered beside it. The preview area should change again to show your name in the upper-left corner of the page.

6. Make sure the other check boxes are selected.

7. Click the **PDF** menu at the bottom of the dialog sheet, and then click **Open PDF in Preview**. Outlook creates a PDF of the message and displays it in a Preview application window. You could use commands under the Preview window's File menu to save or print the preview.

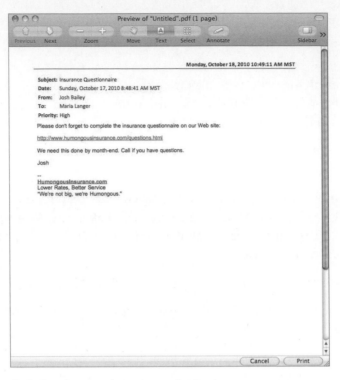

8. Quit Preview, and return to Outlook.

9. On the toolbar, click the **Print** button, or press Command+P. The Print dialog sheet opens again.

10. Set Outlook options the way you want them. Note the changes that appear in the preview area.

11. Click **Print**. The document is sent to your printer and printed.

✖ **CLEAN UP** No clean-up steps are required. You are ready to continue to the next exercise.

Automatically Replying to Messages

If you have a Microsoft Exchange account set up in Outlook, you can set it up to automatically reply to messages. This is most often used to notify people that you're away from your office and may not respond immediately to email. You set up an automatic response to email with the Out Of Office Assistant, which you display by clicking the Out Of Office button on the Tools tab.

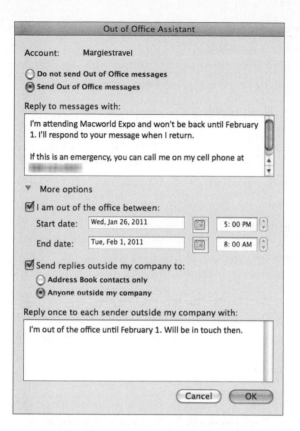

See Also You can also use the Rules feature in Outlook to automatically reply to email messages, no matter what kind of email account you have. Rules are covered in the section titled "Using Rules to Process Messages" in Chapter 6.

Using the assistant is pretty straightforward. Enable the feature by selecting the Send Out Of Office Messages option. Then set other options as desired; you may have to click the disclosure triangle beside More Options to display all available options.

- **Reply to messages with** You can enter a reply in the large field. It can be as long as you like, but the text cannot be formatted.

- **I am out of the office between** With this check box selected, you can enter a start and end date and time for the period you expect to be away.

  Tip It's a good idea to set the dates option, because it will prevent automated responses from being sent out when you return if you forget to disable the automatic reply feature.

- **Send replies outside my company to** With this check box selected, you can specify which senders should get an automated response: people in your contacts list or everyone. With this check box cleared, only senders with accounts on your company's Exchange server will get an automated response.

When you're finished setting options, click the OK button to save them.

To disable the automatic reply feature, on the Tools tab, click the Out Of Office button. Then select the Do Not Send Out Of Office Messages option in the Out Of Office Assistant dialog box, and click OK.

In this exercise, you'll use the Out Of Office Assistant to set up an automated reply to incoming mail on your Exchange account.

SET UP You must have a Microsoft Exchange account set up in Outlook to complete this exercise. If you do not have an Exchange account, this feature is not available to you.

Out of Office

1. On the **Tools** tab, click the **Out of Office** button. The Out of Office Assistant dialog box appears. If you have used this feature before, it contains the last settings you entered.

2. Select **Send Out of Office messages**.

3. In the large text box at the top, type **I am testing the automatic reply feature of my Exchange account. I will be back in 5 minutes.** Because this is just a test, we'll use this sample text in case any real messages come in. This is the message that will go to people with accounts on the same Exchange server as you.

4. If necessary, click the disclosure triangle beside **More Options** to display options at the bottom of the dialog box.

5. Select the **I am out of the office between** check box. Then enter today's date in both date boxes. Enter the current time in the top time box and the time 10 minutes or so from now in the bottom time box.

6. Select the **Send replies outside my company to** check box. Then select **Address Book contacts only**.

7. In the large text box at the bottom, type **I am temporarily out of the office. I will be back shortly.** This is the message that will go to people in your contacts list. Others will not get any message at all. If you wanted everyone to get this message, you'd select **Anyone outside my company** in step 6.

8. Click **OK** to save your settings.

9. If you have another email account that's included in your contact record, use it to send a message to your Exchange account with the subject **New Product Announcement**. When you check for mail, not only will you receive your test message, but you should receive the automatic response.

10. On the **Tools** tab, click the **Out of Office** button. The Out Of Office Assistant dialog box appears.

11. Select **Do not send Out of Office messages**. This disables automatic replies.

12. Click **OK** to save your settings.

CLEAN UP Be sure to follow steps 11 and 12 to disable the automatic replies feature. You can continue to the next exercise.

Scheduling Meetings from Messages

Sometimes you'll receive an email message and decide after reading it to schedule a meeting with the person who sent it. You can easily use an email message to add a meeting to your calendar.

See Also Adding meetings to your calendar is covered in detail in the section titled "Scheduling Meetings" in Chapter 7, "Scheduling Appointments and Meetings."

To schedule a meeting from an email message, click the Meeting button on the Home tab or the message reading window's Message tab. A new meeting window opens with the To and Subject fields filled in. You can modify those two fields if necessary to add or remove recipients or change the subject. You can then fill in the header area with the meeting location and date and time information.

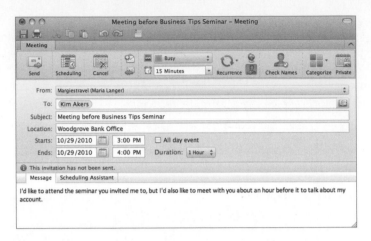

When you click Send, a few things happens:

- An calendar data (.ics) calendar format file with the meeting details is created and attached to the message.
- The message is sent to the people listed in the To field.
- A calendar item is added to your Outlook calendar for the date and time of the meeting.

As you will learn in Chapter 7, message recipients can RSVP to your meeting request by using a compatible calendar application such as Outlook or Apple iCal.

In this exercise, you'll use the Meeting button on the Home tab to create a meeting invitation.

 SET UP In the navigation pane, click Inbox, and then follow these steps.

Meeting

1. In the item list, select a message.

2. On the **Home** tab, click the **Meeting** button. Outlook opens a meeting window with the selected message's sender entered in the To field.

3. To complete the meeting invitation, you would enter location, date, and time information, as well as a message to describe what the meeting is for, and then click Send. For now, close the window. If a dialog sheet prompts you to save changes, click **Discard Invitation**.

   See Also An exercise in the section "Scheduling Meetings" in Chapter 7 will cover the details of creating and sending a meeting invitation.

 CLEAN UP No clean-up steps are required. You are ready to continue to the next chapter.

Key Points

- Outlook automatically checks for mail regularly, but you can manually check anytime you have an Internet connection.

- Outlook organizes your Inbox by account and clearly identifies unread messages.

- You can read messages in the reading pane or message reading window.

- You can view file attachments with Quick Look, open them in a compatible application, or save them to disk.

- You can reply to and forward messages.

- You can print email messages or save them as PDF files.

- If you have an Exchange account, you can set it up to automatically reply to messages while you're away.

- You can schedule a meeting based on an incoming email message.

Chapter at a Glance

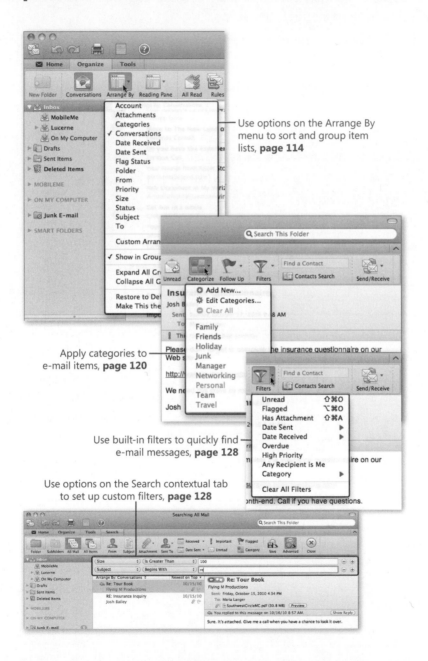

Use options on the Arrange By menu to sort and group item lists, **page 114**

Apply categories to e-mail items, **page 120**

Use built-in filters to quickly find e-mail messages, **page 128**

Use options on the Search contextual tab to set up custom filters, **page 128**

5 Organizing Your Inbox

In this chapter, you will learn how to

✔ Sort and group messages.

✔ Assign categories to messages.

✔ Organize with folders.

✔ Search for messages with filters.

✔ Use smart folders.

✔ Delete messages and folders.

If you get a lot of email—and who doesn't these days?—your Inbox can quickly become a jumbled mess of messages from a multitude of people about a wide range of topics. Finding an important message you received two or three weeks ago can be difficult when your Inbox seems to be overflowing with incoming email.

Fortunately, Microsoft Outlook for Mac 2011 offers a number of features that make it easy to take control of your Inbox. The most basic is to change the sort order of messages in the item list to view them in an order that makes sense to you. You can also group by specific message fields and sort within groups.

If you use the categories feature of Outlook for Mac, you might find it helpful to apply color-coded categories to your messages. Not only does this make certain messages stand out because of their color, but it enables you to sort and search based on category.

If you're really serious about organizing your mail, you can create custom folders and sort email messages into them. For example, suppose you're working on a project that's generating a lot of email. You might create a folder for that project and store all messages related to it in that folder. Then, when you need to find a message related to that project, you know exactly where to look for it.

When it comes to searching, Outlook offers an easy-to-use filtering feature that narrows down the display of messages in the item list by predefined criteria, such as whether the message has been read, whether it has an attachment, or how recently it was received. This can help you home in on a message or help you focus on messages that need attention. The search feature uses customizable filters to search by any message field or contents. You can save filter settings as a smart folder, making it easy to perform the search again and again.

Of course, you don't have to keep every message that comes in. You can delete messages you no longer need, removing them from your Inbox or any other folder.

In this chapter, you will learn how to do all of these things, from arranging messages in the item list and assigning categories to sorting messages into folders and creating custom searches. Using the features and techniques in this chapter will help you take—and *keep*—control of your Inbox.

> **Practice Files** No practice files are needed for this chapter. You can complete exercises with items in your Inbox as well as items created for this and other chapters. For more information about practice file requirements, see "Using the Practice Files" at the beginning of this book.

Sorting and Grouping Messages

One way to better organize your Inbox is to sort or arrange messages in the item list to display them in a way that makes more sense to you. You do this by setting Arrange By and Reading Pane options.

With the Arrange By options, you can sort the messages by any message field. You can also decide whether you want messages grouped or ungrouped and whether you want groups expanded or collapsed. Two options at the bottom of the menu enable you to restore the view to default Outlook settings or make the current settings the default settings. The Arrange By options are accessible from the Arrange By menu on the Organize tab.

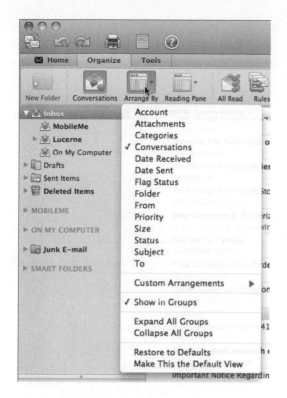

Tip The Arrange By menu includes the Conversations option discussed in the section titled "Reading Messages" in Chapter 4, "Reading and Responding to Email Messages." If you choose an option other than Conversations from the Arrange By menu, Outlook disables the conversations feature. In other words, you can't sort by a field and then view messages by conversation.

Tip Another way to set the arrangement is to use the menu in the item list column headings.

Outlook recognizes the following message fields for arranging messages:

- Account
- Attachments
- Categories
- Conversations
- Date Received
- Date Sent
- Flag Status

- Folder
- From
- Priority
- Size
- Status
- Subject
- To

You can set up custom arrangements that group and sort items exactly as you like. You do this from the Edit Custom Arrangements dialog box. This dialog box includes pop-up menus to set up grouping and sorting options:

● Group items by any message field.

● Sort groups by the group field or another field. Options vary depending on how items are grouped. You can also specify whether the groups should be sorted in ascending or descending order.

● Sort items within groups by almost any message field. The options vary depending on the group and sort group options you set. You can also specify whether the items should be sorted in ascending or descending order.

● The default display for groups can be expanded or collapsed.

After you add a custom arrangement, it appears on the Custom Arrangements submenu on the Organize tab's Arrange By menu. You can have as many custom arrangements as you like.

When the reading pane is configured to be on the bottom or hidden, the item list is wider and includes additional columns. You can easily sort the item list by clicking a column's heading. Click it again to sort by the same field in the reverse sort order. You can use options under the View menu's Columns submenu to specify which columns appear.

See Also Setting reading pane display options is covered in the section titled "Reading Messages" in Chapter 4.

In this exercise, you'll explore some of the options on the Organize tab's Arrange By menu. Then you'll set up a custom arrangement and see how easy it is to use. Finally, you'll experiment with using column headings in the reading pane to sort by a column's contents.

SET UP In the navigation pane, click Inbox. Then follow these steps.

Arrange By

1. On the **Organize** tab, click the **Arrange By** button to display a menu of options.

2. If the **Show in Groups** command does not display a check mark beside it, click it to place one there. Then display the **Arrange By** menu again.

3. Click **Date Received**. The item list is sorted and grouped by date received.

4. Repeat steps 1 and 3, but this time, click **From** on the **Arrange By** menu. The item list is sorted and grouped by sender.

5. Repeat steps 1 and 3, but this time, click **Show in Groups**. The sort order remains the same but the group heading disappears.

6. Experiment with other options on the **Arrange By** menu. Note how the sort order changes.

7. Above the item list, click the left column heading. A menu similar to the **Arrange By** menu appears.

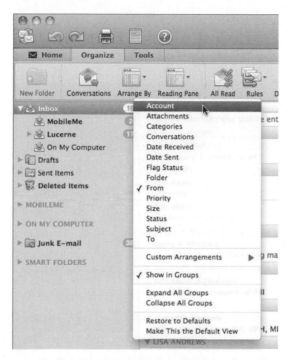

You can use this menu instead of the Arrange By menu if it's more convenient for you.

8. Click **Date Received**. The item list is sorted by date again, but without the date groups.

9. Above the item list, click the right column heading. The item list sort order reverses. Click it until it reads **Newest on Top**.

10. On the **Organize** tab, click the **Arrange By** button to display its menu again.

11. Click **Custom Arrangements**, and then click **Edit Custom Arrangements** in the submenu that appears to open the **Custom Arrangements: Mail** window. You haven't added any arrangements yet, it should be empty.

12. Click the green **New** button to open the **Edit Custom Arrangements** dialog box.

13. In the **Custom arrangement name** box, enter **Get Things Done**.

14. On the **Group items by** pop-up menu, click **Priority**. When choosing this option, the Sort Groups By option on the left automatically changes to Priority, which is the only option.

15. On the **Sort groups by** pop-up menu on the right, click **Highest priority on top**.

16. On the left **Sort items within groups by** pop-up menu, click **Received**. Then click **Newest on top** on the pop-up menu on the right.

17. On the **Default display for groups** pop-up menu, click **Expanded**.

18. Click **OK**. An item named *Get Things Done* is added to the Custom Arrangements: Mail window.

19. Click the **Custom Arrangements: Mail** window's close button to dismiss it.

20. On the **Organize** tab, click the **Arrange By** button, and then click **Custom Arrangements** to display its submenu. Get Things Done appears on the menu.

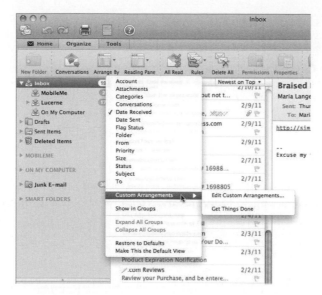

21. Click **Get Things Done**. The item list is sorted by the custom order you defined.

Reading Pane

22. On the **Organize** tab, click the **Reading Pane** button to display its menu. Then click **Hidden**. The reading pane disappears and the item list widens to take over the whole right side of the window. Additional column headings appear.

23. Click each of the column headings in the item list to see how the sort order changes. Experiment with clicking the same heading twice in a row; the first time sorts in one order; the second time sorts in reverse order.

24. Click the **View** menu, and then display the **Columns** submenu.

25. Click **Date Received**. The Date Received column disappears. You can use the Columns submenu to show or hide item list columns.

 CLEAN UP On the Organize tab, click Arrange By, and then click Restore To Defaults. In the dialog sheet that appears, click This Folder. Then on the Organize tab, click Reading Pane, and click Right. You are now ready to continue with the next exercise.

Assigning Categories to Messages

The category feature makes it possible to assign one or more color-coded categories to items throughout Outlook—including messages. When you apply a category to a message, not only do you change the color that it appears as in the item list, but you add a category tag that you can use for sorting or searching.

You apply a category to a selected message with the Categorize button on the Home tab. Select the message in the item list and then click the Categorize button to display a menu of available categories. Choose the category you want to apply, and that category tag is added to the message. The color of the message text in the item list changes to the color of the category.

You can repeat this process as much as you like to apply multiple categories to a message. To remove a category, simply click it in the menu again to clear the check mark. To clear all categories from a message, click Clear All on the Categorize menu.

Outlook comes predefined with nine categories: Family, Friends, Holiday, Junk, Manager, Networking, Personal, Team, and Travel. But you can add, remove, or modify categories if desired to better meet your needs.

See Also Adding, removing, or modifying categories is covered in detail in the section titled "Managing Categories" in Chapter 14, "Using Shared Features."

Tip You can apply categories to items throughout Outlook—including items in other mail folders. For example, you can use categories to organize and set up relationships for items in the Sent Items folder and items filed into other folders.

In this exercise, you'll apply categories to a message in your Inbox to see how its appearance changes. You'll also remove a category and clear all categories from the message.

 SET UP In the navigation pane of Mail view, click Inbox. Then follow these steps.

1. In the item list, select the first message.

2. On the **Home** tab, click the **Categorize** button to display its menu.

Categorize

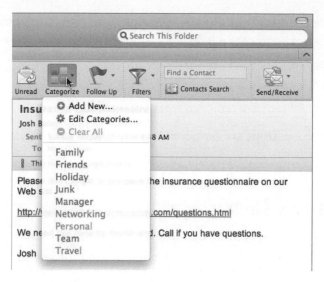

3. Click **Manager**. The Manager tag appears in the message header area of the reading pane.

4. In the item list, select a different message, and then look at the first message. The first message's subject and sender information are magenta, the color of the Manager tag.

5. In the item list, select the first message again.

6. On the **Home** tab, click the **Categorize** button, and then click **Team**. The Team tag appears in the message header of the reading pane beside the Manager tag.

7. In the item list, select a different message again and then look at the first message. Now the first message's subject and sender information are blue, the color of the Team tag. A message's color in the item list always corresponds to the last category applied to it.

8. In the item list, select the first message again.

9. On the **Home** tab, click the **Categorize** button, and then click **Team** again. The Team tag is removed from the message header of the reading pane.

10. On the **Home** tab, click the **Categorize** button again. A check mark no longer appears beside the Team category.

11. Click **Clear All**. All tags are removed from the message.

✖ CLEAN UP No clean-up steps are required. You are ready to continue to the next exercise.

Organizing with Folders

Just as you can organize files in the Finder using folders, you can organize email messages in Outlook with folders. This makes it possible to file messages based on topic, project, or other criteria.

How Outlook handles email folders depends on the type of account you are creating the folder for.

● Microsoft Exchange Server and IMAP (including MobileMe) accounts support folders on the server. When you create a folder in Outlook for an Exchange or IMAP account and then synchronize folders, Outlook copies the folder to the server. When you move messages into that folder, those messages are filed into the corresponding folder on the server. This means your Inbox is the same in Outlook as it would be when accessing your email from any other email client—including a Web-based client—or computer. This is part of what makes Exchange and IMAP so attractive to individuals who access email a variety of ways.

● POP accounts copy messages on the server to your computer and do not support synchronization. Depending on how your preferences are set, the original message may also be deleted from the server. If you create a folder in Outlook for a POP account, that folder exists only in the On My Computer Inbox within Outlook on the computer you created it in. You can still file messages into it, but the server would have no record of your efforts.

Even if you don't have a POP account, you can create folders in the On My Computer Inbox and file messages into it—including messages from server-based accounts such as IMAP and Exchange accounts. If you delete a message from its source account, it's removed from the server but the copy remains on your computer until you delete it. You might use this as a technique for archiving email messages on disk while freeing up server disk space for your email account.

Tip Your Exchange or IMAP account may already be preconfigured with folders for storing certain items. For example, an account might have its own folder for Drafts, Spam, Sent Messages, and Trash. These items may be repeated in the navigation pane under different Outlook headings. Even if folders already exist for an account, you can add more if you want to.

To create a new folder, begin by selecting the Inbox in which you want to place the folder. For example, if you wanted to add a folder to your Exchange account, you'd select that Inbox. If you wanted to add a folder on your computer, you'd select the On My Computer Inbox. Then click the New button on the Home tab and click Folder. The folder is added at the selected location. You can then rename it and begin filing items into it.

What happens when you begin dragging messages into folders depends on what you drag and where you drag it to:

- When you drag a message from an Exchange or IMAP account's Inbox to a folder in the same Inbox, the message is moved from the Inbox into the folder.

- When you drag a message from a POP account's Inbox to a folder under On My Computer, the message is moved from the POP account's Inbox into the folder under the On My Computer Inbox.

- When you drag a message from an account's Inbox to a folder in a different account's Inbox, the message is copied into the folder. That means two copies of the email message exist; you can delete either one and the other will remain.

"Inbox Zero"

The holy grail of most folks interested in managing their email is something called Inbox zero. *Inbox zero* refers to a fleeting moment when all incoming email messages are either deleted or filed into another folder, leaving zero items in the Inbox. This is the ultimate goal of many email organization efforts.

Inbox zero is possible and Outlook makes it easy to do. It's also an admirable goal for anyone who likes to be organized. The trouble is, even if you achieve Inbox zero, you're not likely to maintain it for long. As soon as new email starts arriving, you need to keep filing. It's a never-ending task.

One of the tools within Outlook that can help you achieve Inbox zero is its rules feature. Rules can be configured to automatically categorize and file incoming— and outgoing—email messages, thus taking a lot of the effort out of your hands. But be careful! You can spend almost as much time configuring rules for every possible incoming message as you would manually filing them yourself.

See Also You can learn more about setting up rules in the section titled "Using Rules to Process Messages" in Chapter 6, "Fine-Tuning Email Settings."

If you prefer not to drag, you can use the Move menu on the Home tab to move selected messages to a specific folder. This menu lists all folders you have created, along with the account each folder has been created for. If you have many folders, you can use the Choose Folder command to find the one you want. And there's even a Copy To Folder command that enables you to copy rather than move a message into a folder.

Outlook should automatically synchronize folders when you connect to send and receive email. But if you have made extensive changes to the organization of your email Inboxes, you may want to force a synchronization. To do so, in the navigation pane, click Inbox or select the Inbox folder you want to synchronize. Then, on the Organize tab, click Sync. Outlook connects and synchronizes the folder(s).

In this exercise, you'll create a new folder for one of your accounts and move items into it. You'll also create a folder in the On My Computer Inbox and copy email items into it.

SET UP If you have more than one email account set up in Outlook, in the navigation pane, click the disclosure triangle beside Inbox, if necessary, to display a list of accounts. Note that this exercise suggests specific folder names, but you can use any folder names you want and get started organizing your Inbox as you follow the steps.

1. In the navigation pane, select the account you want to create a folder for.

2. On the **Home** tab, click the **New** button to display its menu.

New

3. Click **Folder**. A new, untitled folder appears indented beneath the account name in the Inbox. An edit box appears around its name.

4. Type **Project X**, and then press Return. The folder is renamed and is automatically selected. Note that the item list is empty.

    Tip If you were unable to rename the folder before the edit box disappeared, double-click the folder name. The edit box should reappear. Type the name you want, and then press Return.

5. In the navigation pane, select the account you created the folder for. The contents of that folder appear in the item list. Note the number of items in the list by check-ing the status bar at the bottom of the Outlook window.

6. Drag the first message in the list to the **Project X** folder you created. When an oval border appears around **Project X**, release the mouse button.

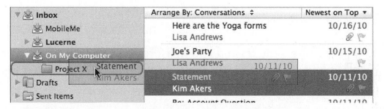

    The message is removed from the account's folder in the Inbox. The number of items in the item list should decrease by one; you can confirm this in the status bar.

7. In the navigation pane, select the **Project X** folder. The item you dragged appears in the item list. It has been moved from the Inbox into the folder.

8. In the navigation pane, select the account you created the folder for again to dis-play its contents in the item list.

9. Select an item in the item list.

Move

10. On the **Home** tab, click the **Move** button to display its menu. The name of the folder you created appears on the menu with the account it was created for in parentheses.

11. Click **Project X**. The item no longer appears in the item list.

12. In the navigation pane, click **Project X**. The item you just moved appears in the item list.

13. In the navigation pane, click **On My Computer**. (If you have only one email account configured in Outlook and it is a POP account, this is the only item that will appear under Inbox.)

14. On the **Home** tab, click the **New** button, and then click **Folder**. A new untitled folder appears under On My Computer.

15. Name the new folder **Old Mail**.

16. In the navigation pane, select the email account you worked with at the beginning of this exercise to display its contents in the item list.

17. Drag an email message from the item list to the **Old Mail** folder. If the account is not a POP account, the item is copied to the Old Mail folder, the original remains in the account's Inbox, and the number of items shown on the status bar should remain the same. If the account is a POP account, the item is moved to the Old Mail folder and the number of items should be one less.

18. In the navigation pane, select **Old Mail**. The item you dragged should appear in the item list.

19. In the navigation pane, select the email account you've been working with throughout this exercise to display its contents in the item list.

20. Select an item.

21. On the **Home** tab, click the **Move** button to display its menu. There are now two folders at the top of the menu.

22. Click **Copy to Folder**. A dialog sheet with a search box appears. You can use this search box to locate a specific folder.

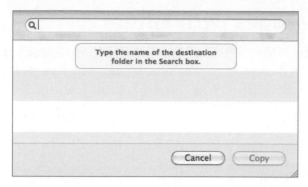

23. Type **pro**. The Project X folder appears in the list.

24. Click **Project X**, and then click **Copy**. The message remains in the Inbox for the selected account.

25. In the navigation pane, click **Project X**. A copy of the message appears there, too. The message was copied rather than moved.

26. Hold down the COMMAND key and, in the item list, click the first two items you copied to the **Project X** folder to select them both.

27. On the **Home** tab, click the **Move** button to display its menu.

28. Click **Choose Folder**. A dialog sheet like the one shown earlier appears.

29. Type **in**. A list of Inboxes appears.

30. Select the Inbox in which the messages were originally, and then click **Move**. The items are moved back to their original location. The item list for the Project X folder contains only the copied item.

    Tip You could also just drag the items back into their original location to move them back.

31. In the navigation pane, click **Inbox**.

Sync

32. On the **Organize** tab, click the **Sync** button. This synchronizes all of your Inbox folders to return messages to their original locations.

✖ **CLEAN UP** No clean-up steps are required. You'll delete the copied message and folders in an exercise later in this chapter.

Searching for Messages with Filters

One way to narrow down the contents of an Inbox or selected folder is to apply one or more of the predefined Outlook filters. The filter feature displays only those messages that match filter criterion, hiding all other messages in the folder until the filter is cleared.

Outlook comes preconfigured with nine useful filters, all of which can be found on the Home tab's Filters menu.

- **Unread** This filter displays only messages that have not yet been read or are marked as unread.

- **Flagged** This filter displays only messages that have been flagged for follow up.

- **Has Attachment** This filter displays only messages that have at least one attached file.

- **Date Sent** This filter displays messages based on the date they were sent. The filter offers three options: Today, This Week, and This Month.

- **Date Received** This filter displays messages based on the date they were received in Outlook. The filter offers three options: Today, This Week, and This Month.

- **Overdue** This filter displays only messages that are overdue for follow up.

- **High Priority** This filter displays only messages that are set as high priority.

- **Any Recipient is Me** This filter displays messages that are addressed to you. The filter is most useful in a folder that contains both received and sent messages; it will hide the sent messages unless you included yourself as a recipient when sending.

- **Category** This filter displays only messages that have been assigned to the category or categories you specify.

See Also You can learn more about unread messages in the section titled "Reading Messages" in Chapter 4; flagged messages in the section titled "Flagging Items for Follow Up" in Chapter 12, "Tracking Tasks"; attachments in the section titled "Working with Email Attachments" in Chapter 4; message priority in the section titled "Changing Message Settings" in Chapter 3, "Composing and Sending Email Messages"; and setting categories in the section titled "Assigning Categories to Messages" earlier in this chapter.

You can quickly use one of the predefined Outlook filters by choosing it from the Filters menu on the Home tab. The filter is immediately applied to the item list. If you select a second filter, Outlook displays only messages that match *both* filters, thus further narrowing down the list results.

Tip You can tell if a filter is applied by consulting the Filters button on the Home tab. If it's dark gray (unavailable) as if "pushed in," filters are applied.

When you want to view all items in the list without filters applied, you can click Clear All Filters on the Filters menu.

Outlook remembers the last filters you set. To repeat the same filter, you can click the Filter button. This restores the last used filters and applies them again.

For more powerful filtering options, you can use buttons and menus on the Search contextual tab that appears whenever filters are active or if you click in the Spotlight search box on the right end of the toolbar.

In addition to the filters already listed, the Search tab offers the following filters:

- **Location** You can use one of four buttons on this filter to search a specific location:
  - The Folder button searches the folder currently selected in the navigation pane.
  - The Subfolders button searches the folder currently selected in the navigation pane, as well as all of its subfolders.
  - The All Mail button searches all mail, including the contents of the Drafts, Sent Items, Deleted Items, and Junk Email folders. This is most useful when you're only interested in searching for email messages and don't want to see search results that include contacts, calendar items, or other Outlook data.
  - The All Items button searches globally, throughout Outlook, to include calendar items, contacts, tasks, and notes.
- **From** You can use this filter to search for items from a specific sender.

● **Subject** You can use this filter to search based on a message's subject.

● **Attachments** You can use this filter to narrow down the search by attachment size.

● **Sent To** You can use this filter to search for items sent to a specific recipient.

● **Received and Date Sent** With these filters, you can enter a specific date. Outlook will then display messages received or sent after the date you entered.

The Advanced button on the Search tab displays a filter bar under the ribbon that you can use to enter virtually any search criterion. Choose a filter from the pop-up menu on the left end of this bar and enter search criteria using options and fields that appear beside it. You can add additional filter bars to add more criteria.

To cancel a search, you can click the close button on the Search tab. This cancels search criteria and displays the full item list.

In this exercise, you'll use the Filters menu on the Home tab to set up a simple search using predefined filters. Then you'll experiment with options on the Search tab to set up a customized search using filter bars.

SET UP In the navigation pane, click Inbox. Then follow these steps.

Filters

1. On the **Home** tab, click the arrow on the **Filters** button to display a menu of options.

2. Click **Date Received,** and then click **This Month**. The item list is filtered to show only those messages that were received in Outlook this calendar month. Note that the Filters button (but not its arrow) is unavailable and the Search tab appears. This indicates that messages are being filtered.

3. On the **Home** tab, click the arrow on the **Filters** button again. This time, click **Unread**. The item list is filtered to show only messages received in Outlook this calendar month that you have not yet read. If you have read all messages, the list will be empty.

4. On the **Home** tab, click the arrow on the **Filters** button and then click **Clear All Filters**. The filters are cleared and the item list displays all items.

5. Click the **Filters** button. The item list is filtered according to the most recently set filters. Confirm this by displaying the **Filters** menu and noting which items are checked.

6. Click the **Filters** button again. The filters are cleared and the item list displays all items again.

7. On the toolbar, click in the **Spotlight** search box. The Search tab appears and becomes the active tab.

All Mail

8. On the **Search** tab, click the **All Mail** button. The button is now active and Outlook searches all mail items.

Attachment

9. On the **Search** tab, click the **Attachment** button to display its menu, and then click **Greater than 100 KB**. The item list displays messages with attachments larger than 100 KB in size. The Advanced button is active and a filter bar appears beneath the ribbon.

Subject

10. On the **Search** tab, click the **Subject** button. A Subject filter bar appears.

11. Click **Begins With** in the next pop-up menu, and then enter **re** in the text box beside it. The item list is filtered to show only items with attachments larger than 100 KB and subjects that begin with RE.

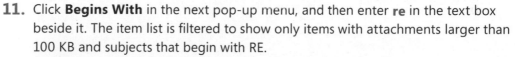
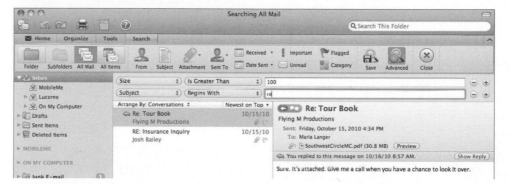

Tip If your item list is empty, that's because you don't have any messages with file attachments over 100 KB and subjects that start with *re*.

12. On the far right of the **Size** filter bar, click the – button. The Size filter disappears and the item list changes to show only items with subjects that start with *re*. The attachment criterion is removed, so items without attachments or with small attachments also appear in the list.

13. On the far right of the **Subject** filter bar, click the + button. A new filter bar appears beneath it.

14. In the new filter bar, display the first menu to see what options are available. You can use this menu to create any one of these types of filters. For now, leave it set to **Item Contains**.

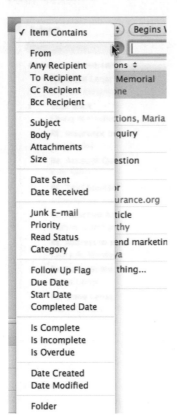

15. In the **Item Contains** filter bar text box, enter **Grand Canyon**. The item list will likely become empty because there are no mail items with a subject that starts with *re* and contain the words *Grand Canyon*.

16. Click the **–** button at the far right of the **Subject** filter bar to remove it. The item list should now show the sample message created in Chapter 3.

 **CLEAN UP** No clean-up steps are required. You will resume working with this filter set in the next exercise.

Using Smart Folders

If you find yourself using the same filters repeatedly to search Outlook mail, it's time to set up a smart folder. A smart folder is a saved collection of filters or set of search criteria. You set up filters once, then save them as a smart folder. Then, the next time you want to conduct a search, you simply open the smart folder and Outlook fills the item list with the items that match the filters associated with it.

Outlook comes preconfigured with three handy smart folders, which you can find under the Smart Folders heading in the navigation pane. If necessary, click the disclosure triangle to see them. All three of these filters are designed to help you find email messages that need attention:

- **Flagged Mail** This smart folder displays mail that has been flagged for follow up.

- **High Priority Mail** This smart folder displays mail that has been set as high priority.

- **Overdue Mail** This smart folder displays mail that is overdue for follow up.

When you create a smart folder, it appears in this list with the others.

To change the settings for a smart folder, select it to apply its filters. Then, on the Search tab, make changes as necessary. (You may have to click the Advanced button to see the filter bars.) Then click the Save button on the Search tab. Your changes become part of the smart folder's definition.

In this exercise, you'll save the filters you set up in the previous exercise as a smart folder. You'll then try each of the smart folders to see how they work.

SET UP To complete this exercise, you should have followed the instructions in the previous exercise to set up filters. You'll use those filter settings as the basis for a smart folder.

Save

1. On the **Search** tab, click the **Save** button. An untitled smart folder appears in the Smart Folders list in the navigation pane with an edit box around its name.

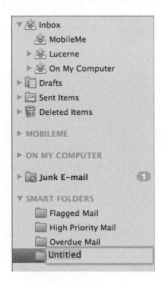

2. Type **Grand Canyon**, and then press Return. The smart folder is renamed and sorted in alphabetical order with the other smart folders.

3. In the navigation pane, click each of the smart folders, one at a time, and observe the item list. Each smart folder performs a different search.

4. Click the **Grand Canyon** smart folder.

5. On the **Search** tab, click the **Advanced** button to display the filter bar.

Advanced

6. On the right end of the **Item Contains** filter bar, click the + button. Another filter bar appears.

7. Display the first menu, and then click **Date Sent**.

8. Display the second menu, and then click **Within Last Two Months**.

9. On the **Search** tab, click the **Save** button. Your changes are saved as part of the smart folder filter settings.

CLEAN UP No clean-up steps are required. You'll delete the smart folder in the next exercise.

Deleting Messages and Folders

If you don't need to keep an email message, you can delete it. This removes it from Outlook. It may also remove it from the server, depending on the type of account and how account options are set:

- For Exchange and IMAP (including MobileMe) accounts, messages are deleted from the server when the folders are synchronized. This should happen automatically when you send and receive email, but you can force a sync by clicking the Sync button on the Organize tab.

- For POP accounts, when messages are deleted from the server depends on settings for the account. One of the options is to delete messages from the server when you delete them on your computer.

See Also You can learn more about POP email account settings in the section titled "Exploring Advanced Account Settings" in Chapter 6.

You can delete the following items from Mail view:

- Email messages in your Inbox or any of its account Inboxes, folders, and subfolders

- Email messages in the Drafts, Sent Items, and Junk Email folders

- Folders you created in Inboxes, including the On My Computer Inbox

  Important When you delete a folder, you also delete everything inside that folder.

- Smart folders

  Tip Deleting a smart folder does not delete any messages. Because smart folders are sets of search filters, when you delete a smart folder, you're deleting the search filters, not the search results.

Important You cannot delete special folders automatically created by Outlook or your email server, such as Inbox, Drafts, and Sent Items.

When you delete an email message, it is normally moved to the Deleted Items folder, where it remains until permanently deleted. When it's deleted depends on server settings (for Exchange accounts) or advanced account settings for IMAP (including MobileMe) and POP accounts. You can immediately delete any item by selecting it in the Deleted Items folder and pressing Delete. When a dialog box appears to confirm the deletion, click Delete.

In this exercise, you'll delete items you created in previous exercises in this chapter, such as deleting the copy of a message you no longer need, two folders you created, and a smart folder.

 SET UP No set-up is required for this exercise other than having Outlook started.

1. In the navigation pane, click the **Project X** folder. The first (and only) item in the item list becomes selected.

2. Press Delete. The item is immediately deleted.

3. Click the **Project X** folder again.

Delete

4. On the **Home** tab, click the **Delete** button. The folder is immediately deleted.

5. In the navigation pane, click the **Old Mail** folder. You may have to double-click it because clicking once might select the item in the item list rather than the folder. When the folder is selected, it will turn blue.

6. Press Delete. Your computer makes an alert sound; you cannot delete a folder by pressing Delete.

7. On the **Home** tab, click the **Delete** button. The folder *and the item within it* are deleted.

8. In the navigation pane, select the **Deleted Items** folder. In the item list, you should see the two messages you deleted.

9. In the navigation pane, click the disclosure triangle beside **Deleted Items** to display a list of sub-items. Do the same for the name of the account where you created the **Project X** folder and the **On My Computer** Inbox. You should see the two folders you deleted. These folders do not appear in the item list.

10. In the navigation pane, select the **Project X** folder. Make sure the folder is selected (looks blue).

11 On the **Home** tab, click the **Delete** button. A confirmation dialog sheet appears.

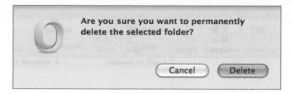

12. In the dialog sheet, click **Delete**. The folder is permanently deleted.

13. Repeat steps 10 through 12 for the **Old Mail** folder.

14. In the navigation pane, if necessary, click the disclosure triangle beside **Smart Folders** to display the list of smart folders.

15. Select **Grand Canyon**. You may have to double-click to select it; it will turn blue when it is selected.

16. On the **Home** tab, click the **Delete** button. A confirmation dialog sheet appears.

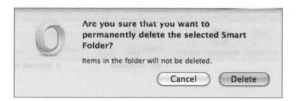

17. Click **Delete**. The smart folder is deleted. No other items are deleted.

✖ **CLEAN UP** In the navigation pane, click the disclosure triangle beside Deleted Items to hide its sub-items. You are ready to continue to the next chapter.

Key Points

- You can use options on the Arrange By menu to sort and group items in the item list.

- You can apply one or more color coded categories to email messages.

- You can organize messages by moving them into topical folders.

- You can use predefined and customizable filters to search for email messages based on message header contents or other criteria.

- You can save filter settings as smart folders to make repeating a search quick and easy.

- You can delete messages, folders, and smart folders you no longer need.

Chapter at a Glance

You can set preferences to control how
Outlook e-mail features work, **page 140**

Create formatted signatures that
you can append to the end of
e-mail messages, **page 147**

Font options control
default font settings
throughout Outlook,
page 145

Use the schedule feature
to automate tasks, **page 153**

Create rules for automatically
handling incoming e-mails,
page 160

6 Fine-Tuning Email Settings

In this chapter, you will learn how to

✔ Set reading and composing options.

✔ Define default font settings.

✔ Work with signatures.

✔ Schedule actions.

✔ Use rules to process messages.

✔ Manage mailing lists.

✔ Block spam.

✔ Secure your email.

✔ Explore advanced account settings.

How the Mail view features of Microsoft Outlook for Mac 2011 work are determined, in part, by settings that you can modify. For example, you can control when messages are marked as read, whether images are automatically downloaded in email messages, and which message format is used for new messages you create. You can specify a default font for messages and create signatures to append to the end of messages you compose. These options enable you to fine-tune Outlook for Mac so its Mail view features work the way you want them to.

You can also set up a number of more advanced email features, such as schedules and rules. You can use schedules to schedule basic tasks such as checking for new messages and emptying the Deleted Items folder. Rules enable Outlook to automatically perform tasks on email messages based on criteria and actions you specify.

If you subscribe to a mailing list, you can use the mailing list manager to set up rules for incoming and outgoing mailing list messages. Mailing list rules can prevent incoming mailing list messages from being marked as junk email and can automatically file them into a folder you specify. This can keep email list activity separate from your other email.

If junk email or *spam* is a problem for you—as it is for most people—you'll probably want to take advantage of the built-in junk email protection in Outlook. You can customize its settings to adjust the level of protection. You can also create a list of domains that are never blocked and senders who are always blocked.

Outlook also offers options for helping you secure email messages from prying eyes, including digital signing and encryption. These are part of the advanced account options in Outlook. Other advanced account options include server and folder settings. In most cases, you won't need to change these settings unless advised by your system administrator or ISP technical support staff.

In this chapter, you will look at all of these options. You'll first set basic configuration preferences for reading and writing messages and then go on to more advanced features and settings for signatures, schedules, rules, mailing lists, and junk email protection. Finally, you'll take a brief look at security and other advanced options. By the time you're finished with this chapter, you'll understand how you can make Outlook work harder to do what you need it to do.

> **Practice Files** Before you can complete the exercises in this chapter, you need to copy the book's practice files to your computer. The practice files you'll use to complete the exercises in this chapter are in the Chapter06 practice file folder. A complete list of practice files is provided in "Using the Practice Files" at the beginning of this book.

Setting Reading and Composing Options

Because most of the time that you work with Outlook Mail view will be spent reading or composing messages, you might want to set a few preferences that control certain aspects of how these features work. You do this from the Outlook Preferences window. To display this window, click Preferences on the Outlook menu. Then click the icon for the type of preference you want to set: Reading or Composing.

Reading preferences are broken down into four main sections: Mark As Read, Conversations, IMAP, and Security.

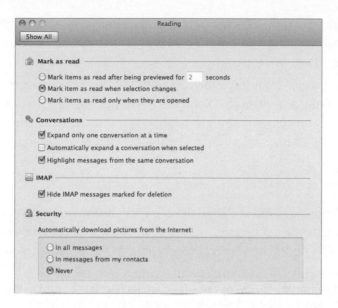

- **Mark as read** This section has three options for determining how messages you select in the item list are marked as read. Select the option for the method you prefer:

    ○ Mark items as read after being previewed for n seconds This option automatically marks a message as read if it's selected in the item list for the number of seconds you specify. By default, the seconds value is set to 2, but you can set it to anything you like.

    ○ Mark item as read when selection changes This option is the default setting. With this option selected, a selected item is marked as read as soon as you select a different item in the item list.

    ○ Mark items as read only when they are opened This option marks an item as read only if you open it in a message reading window. Simply selecting it in the item list will not mark it as read.

- **Conversations** There are three separate options here that you can enable or disable by selecting or clearing check boxes. Each deals with the conversations feature, which identifies messages with the same subject as part of a conversation.

    ○ Expand only one conversation at a time This option, which is enabled by default, will only expand one conversation to show its individual messages at a time. When you expand a different conversation, the one that was expanded collapses.

○ Automatically expand a conversation when selected This option automatically expands a conversation to show its individual messages when you select it in the item list.

○ Highlight messages from the same conversation This option, which is enabled by default, automatically highlights messages that are part of the same conversation when you select a message in the item list. This feature enables you to see related messages even when the item list is not arranged by conversation.

● **IMAP** There's only one IMAP option, which is enabled by default:

○ Hide IMAP messages marked for deletion With this option enabled, deleted IMAP messages will not appear, even if they have not yet been deleted from the server. This option only affects messages in IMAP account folders.

Tip This IMAP option applies to all IMAP accounts that are set up in Outlook. You can access additional account options for each individual account in the Accounts preferences pane for that account, as discussed later in this chapter, in the section titled "Exploring Advanced Account Settings."

● **Security** This section offers three options to determine how Outlook deals with pictures embedded in incoming messages. The idea here is to protect you from downloading images from a source that will confirm that you read the message and are a valid spam target. If images are not downloaded, you can click a button in the area below the message header to download them.

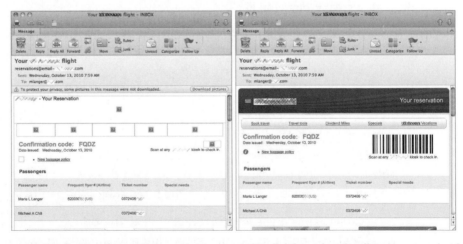

● In all messages This option automatically downloads all images embedded in all email messages.

- **In messages from my contacts** This option only downloads images embedded in messages from email addresses in your contacts list.

- **Never** This option, which is the default setting, does not automatically download any images in any messages.

See Also You can learn more about composing messages in Chapter 3, "Composing and Sending Email Messages."

Composing preferences enable you to set default options for composing messages in HTML and plain text. The options are the same in each pane of the preference window; be sure to set them in both panes if you compose both HTML and plain text messages. They're broken down into three areas: Replies and forwards, attribution of original message, and format and account.

- **Replies and forwards** There are two options here that you can enable or disable by selecting or clearing check boxes. Both concern original text in message replies or forwards.

  - **Indent each line of the original message** This option indents the original or quoted text.

  - **Place cursor before original message** This option can be disabled only if the previous option is selected. What this means is that when you reply to or forward a message, the cursor will automatically go to the beginning of the message body, with the quoted text after it. You can still manually move the cursor if you want to type elsewhere in the message body.

- **Attribution of original message** You can select one of three options for providing information about quoted text in a reply or forward.

  - **None** This option does not provide any information about the quoted text.

  - **Include From, Date, To, and Subject lines from original message** This option includes this attribution information from the original message above the quoted text.

  - **Custom attribution format** This option enables you to build your own attribution format for displaying above quoted text. You can type the static text in this option's field and use the pop-up menu at the far right end of the field to choose three variables: name, date, and address.

- **Format and account** There are five options that apply to all mail accounts. You can enable or disable them by selecting or clearing check boxes. Changing these options in the HTML pane automatically sets them the same in the Plain Text pane.

○ Compose messages in HTML by default This option turns on HTML mode for each new message you create.

○ When replying or forwarding, use the format of the original message This option switches to HTML mode or plain-text mode depending on the formatting of the message you are replying to or forwarding.

○ Reply and forward using the default email account This option always uses the default email account to reply to and forward messages.

○ Close the original message after replying or forwarding This option automatically closes the message reading window for a message when you send a reply or forward the message.

○ When sending messages, automatically Bcc [or Cc] myself This option automatically sends a copy of the messages you send to yourself. You can use a pop-up menu to determine whether the copy is sent with Bcc or Cc.

See Also You can learn more about reading messages in Chapter 3. Replying to and forwarding messages is covered in Chapter 4, "Reading and Responding to Email Messages."

In this exercise, you'll learn how to access preference settings for Reading and Composing messages.

 SET UP If Outlook is not open, open it. Then follow these steps.

1. On the **Outlook** menu, click **Preferences** or press Command+, (comma). The Outlook Preferences window opens.

2. Click the **Reading** icon to display the **Reading** preferences pane.

3. Review the available options. If you make any changes, they are automatically saved when you switch to another preferences pane or close the window.

4. Click **Show All** to display the **Outlook Preferences** window again.

5. Click **Composing** to display the **Composing** preferences pane.

6. If necessary, click **HTML**. Any changes you make to options in the top half of this preference pane affect messages composed in HTML mode only. Changes you make in the bottom half of this preference pane affect all messages you compose.

7. Click **Plain Text**. Note how the default settings in the top half of this preferences pane differ. Any changes you make to these options affect messages composed in plain text mode only.

8. Click the close button to close the **Composing** preferences pane.

CLEAN UP No clean-up steps are required. You are ready to continue to the next exercise.

Defining Default Font Settings

By default, Outlook uses 14-point Calibri font for HTML messages and 12-point Consolas font for plain text messages. But if you prefer to always use different fonts, you can change these defaults in the Fonts preference pane. Click Preferences on the Outlook menu to display the Outlook Preferences window. Then click the Fonts icon.

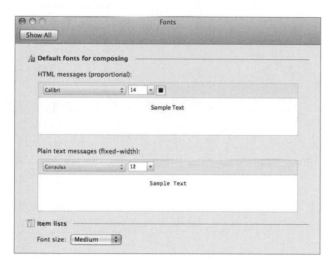

The Fonts preferences pane provides three sets of options:

- **HTML messages** This set of options controls the default font, font size, and font color for messages you compose in HTML mode. The font settings will become part of the message formatting. If message recipients have the same font installed on their computers, they will see the same font.

- **Plain text messages** This set of options controls the default font and font size for messages you compose in plain text mode. Normally, you'd set this to a fixed-width font such as Consolas, Monaco, or Courier, but you can set it to any font you like. Remember: plain text messages are unformatted. The options you set here affect how the messages look on your computer when you compose them. They do not affect how the messages will look on the recipient's computer.

- **Item lists** You can use the Font Size pop-up menu in this section to specify whether you want the size of text characters in the item list to be small, medium, or large.

Changing the default font and size for HTML or plain text messages is pretty straightforward: simply choose the font and size you want from the pop-up menus. If you want a font size that's not listed on the menu, you can enter it in the font size box.

To select a font color for HTML messages, click the color button to open the Colors panel, from which you can choose the color you want. When you're finished, you can close the Colors panel.

The two preview areas in the Fonts preferences pane show the effect of your changes on sample text. This gives you a chance to make sure you like the formatting before you close the pane.

See Also You can learn more about composing messages and the difference between HTML and plain text mode in Chapter 3.

In this exercise, you'll take a look at the Fonts preferences pane to see how you can change the font, font size, and font color for messages you compose.

 SET UP No set up is required. Just follow these steps.

1. On the **Outlook** menu, click **Preferences** or press Command+, (comma). The Outlook Preferences window opens.

2. Click the **Fonts** icon to display the **Fonts** preferences pane.

3. Click the **Font** menu under **HTML messages** to display its options. All fonts installed on your computer appear on this menu. The same is true for the Font menu under Plain Text Messages.

4. Click the **Font Size** arrow in either area. A drop-down list of standard font sizes appears. You can set the font size to anything you like by choosing from this menu or entering a value in the font box.

5. Click the color button in the **HTML messages** area. A Colors panel appears. You can use any of the color pickers to choose a default color for message text when composing in HTML mode. When you're finished with the **Colors** panel, click its close button to dismiss it.

6. Click the **Font Size** pop-up menu in the **Item lists** area to display its options.

7. Click **Small**. In the item list behind the preferences pane, you should see the font size get smaller.

8. Repeat steps 6 and 7, but this time, choose **Large**. The font characters in the item list get larger.

9. Repeat this process again to reset the font size to **Medium**.

10. Click the close button to close the **Fonts** preferences pane.

CLEAN UP No clean-up steps are necessary. You are ready to continue to the next exercise.

Working with Signatures

A signature is text that you can append to the end of an email message. It's normally used to share contact information, such as a phone number or mailing address, but it can also be used for company information, witty quotes, or privacy notices.

When you install Outlook, it comes with a preconfigured signature called *Standard* that consists of just two dashes, which is the Internet standard divider for signatures. You can modify this signature to be more useful. You can also create as many signatures as you need to sign your outgoing messages.

You create, modify, and delete signatures in the Signatures preferences pane. Click Preferences on the Outlook menu and then click Signatures in the Outlook Preferences window that appears. On the left side of the Signatures preference pane is a list of signatures. When you select a signature in the list, it displays that signature on the right, where you can edit it as necessary.

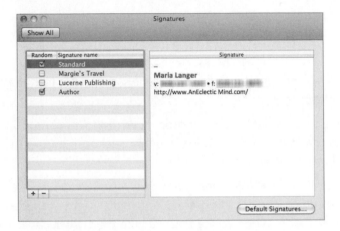

To add a signature, click the + button at the bottom of the signatures list and give the new signature a name. Then enter signature text in the edit area on the right. You can use options under the Format menu to change the font, style, size, color, and highlight of signature text. You can even paste in or drag in images such as company logos or photos. If you select the Random check box beside the signature name, the signature will be added to a pool of random signatures that Outlook can choose from.

Tip Signature text will appear formatted in HTML messages, but will appear unformatted in plain text messages.

If you have multiple signatures, you can specify which one should be used as the default signature for each of your email accounts. Just click the Default Signatures button in the Signatures preferences pane to display a dialog sheet that lets you match accounts to signatures. If you choose Random from the pop-up list, Outlook will choose one of the signatures included in the random pool of signatures.

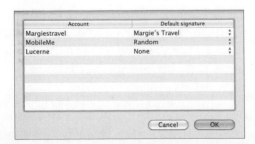

The signatures you create in the Signatures preferences pane appear on the Signatures menu of the Message tab in the message composition window. Choosing a signature from this menu inserts the signature at the cursor in the message body.

See Also You can learn more about using signatures in the messages you compose in the section titled "Changing Message Settings" in Chapter 3.

In this exercise, you'll modify the standard signature and create a new signature. You'll also set up Outlook to automatically insert a signature in the email messages you write.

 SET UP You need the *Grapes* and *Coho Winery* image files located in the Chapter06 practice file folder. Open them in an image viewing application such as Preview. Then switch back to Outlook and follow these steps.

1. On the **Outlook** menu, click **Preferences** or press Command+, (comma). The Outlook Preferences window opens.

2. Click the **Signatures** icon to display the **Signatures** preferences pane.

3. In the left side of the pane, click **Standard**. The contents of the standard signature should appear on the right side of the window.

4. Using standard text editing techniques, modify the standard signature for your own use. You might want to include your name, title, company name, phone number, Web site, or any combination of these things.

   Tip Signatures commonly begin with the pair of hyphen characters, which separate the signature text from the rest of the message. You don't, however, have to keep these characters as part of your signature.

5. Select your name in the signature.

6. Click the **Format** menu to display it. Click **Style**, and then click **Bold**.

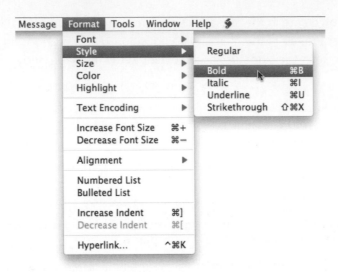

The text turns bold. You can use any options on the Format menu or its submenus to format selected text.

7. In the **Signatures** preferences pane, click the **+** button. A new untitled signature appears in the signature list and your name appears in the editing area beside it.

8. Double-click **Untitled**. An edit box appears around it.

9. Type **Coho Winery** and press Return.

10. In the editing area, click after your name and then press Return to begin a new line.

11. Type **Coho Winery** and press Return.

12. Type **123 Main Street, Quincy, WA 9848** and press Return.

13. Type **509 / 555 – 1212 • www.CohoWinery.com** and press Return.

Tip To type the bullet character between the phone number and Web address, press Option+8.

14. Switch to the **Preview** application and display the **Grapes** image file.

15. Press Command+A to select the entire image. Then press Command+C to copy the image to the **Clipboard**.

16. Switch back to Outlook.

17. With the cursor in the empty line after the phone number, press Command+V to paste in the image.

18. Select **Coho Winery** on the left side of the pane and use options on the **Format** menu's submenus to make the text bold, 18 points, and purple.

19. Repeat steps 7 through 10, but this time, name the signature **Coho Image**.

20. Switch to the **Preview** application and display the **Coho Winery** image file.

21. Press Command+A to select the entire image. Then press Command+C to copy the image to the **Clipboard**.

22. Switch back to Outlook.

23. With the cursor in the empty line after your name, press Command+V to paste in the image.

24. Select your name and use options on the **Format** menu's submenus to make the text Helvetica, bold, 18 points, and green.

25. Select the entire signature.

26. Click the **Format** menu to display it. Click **Alignment**, and then click **Centered**. The entire signature is centered.

27. In the signature list, select the check boxes for **Coho Winery** and **Coho Image**.

28. Click the **Default Signatures** button to display a dialog sheet with a list of your email accounts.

29. Under **Default Signature** for the account you use most, click **Standard** on the pop-up menu. This automatically inserts the Standard signature in a new email message you create with this account. (If you only have one email account, skip this step.)

30. Under **Default Signature** for another account, click **Random** on the pop-up menu. This automatically inserts one of the two Coho Winery signatures in a new message you create with this account.

31. Click **OK**.

32. Close the **Signatures** preferences pane.

33. In **Mail** view, press Command+N to create a new message. If the message was created with one of the two email accounts you modified, a signature should be automatically appended.

34. If you modified another email account, choose that account from the **From** pop-up menu. The signature does not change. After a signature is inserted, it can only be changed by editing or removing it.

35. Press Command+N again to create a new email message from the account you just selected. A signature should be automatically appended.

36. Select the signature in the message and press Delete to remove it.

Signatures

37. On the **Message** tab, choose a signature from the **Signatures** button's menu. The signature you chose is inserted.

38. Close all open message composition windows. Do not save changes.

39. On the **Outlook** menu, click **Preferences** or press Command+, (comma). Then click the **Signatures** icon to display the **Signatures** preferences pane.

40. Select the **Coho Winery** signature.

41. Click the – button beneath the signatures list. A confirmation dialog sheet appears.

42. Click **Delete**.

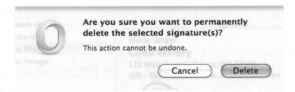

Are you sure you want to permanently delete the selected signature(s)?
This action cannot be undone.

Cancel   Delete

43. Repeat steps 40 through 42 to delete the other Coho signature.

CLEAN UP If you don't want to use the Standard signature for your email account, click Default Signatures and then change the default signature to None. Click OK to save your changes. Close the Signatures preferences pane. You are now ready to continue with the next exercise.

Scheduling Actions

By default, Outlook checks IMAP and POP accounts for new messages every 10 minutes. It does this automatically, using the scheduling feature in Outlook. You can modify this schedule and create new schedules to automate other tasks by setting options in the Schedules preferences pane. To open this preference pane, click the Schedules button on the Tools tab and then click Edit Schedules on the menu that appears. You could also open it by clicking the Schedules button in the Outlook Preferences window.

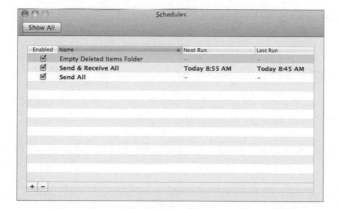

Outlook comes preconfigured with three schedules, one of which is on a timer:

- **Empty Deleted Items Folder** This schedule empties the Deleted Items folders. This task is not on a timer and must be run manually.

- **Send & Receive All** This schedule sends all outgoing messages and retrieves all incoming messages. This task is set up to run automatically every 10 minutes while Outlook is running.

- **Send All** This schedule sends all outgoing messages. This task is not on a timer and must be run manually.

You create and modify schedules in the Edit Schedule dialog box. To edit a schedule, double-click it in the Schedules preferences pane. To create a schedule, click the + button at the bottom of the schedule list in the Schedules preferences pane. Either way, you'll be working with the Edit Schedule dialog box.

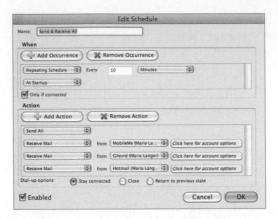

Start by entering a name in the Name box at the top of the dialog box. Then, in the When area, specify when the schedule should occur. Your options are:

- **Manually** Requires the schedule to be manually run.

- **At Startup** Automatically runs the schedule when you open Outlook.

- **On Quit** Automatically runs the schedule when you quit Outlook.

- **Timed Schedule** Enables you to set specific days of the week, hours of the day, and minutes of the hour to automatically run the schedule.

- **Repeating Schedule** Automatically runs repeatedly at the interval you specify in minutes, hours, or days.

- **Recurring** Enables you to set up a recurrence pattern for the schedule. You can set it up to be daily, weekly, monthly, or yearly and indicate start and stop times.

Tip Outlook must be running for a time-based schedule to run.

You can use the Add Occurrence button to add as many scheduling options as you like. You can also use the Remove Occurrence button to remove a selected scheduling option.

If you only want Outlook to run the schedule when you're connected to the Internet, make sure the Only If Connected check box is selected. This can help avoid error messages if Outlook is running and you do not have an active connection to the Internet.

You tell Outlook what action(s) to perform in the Action area of the dialog box. Outlook makes it possible to schedule seven different types of actions, four of which are specific to Mail view:

- **Receive Mail** Goes online to check for email in the account you specify.

- **Send All** Goes online to send all outgoing email for all accounts.

- **Run AppleScript** Runs an AppleScript script. You must have an AppleScript script or application saved on disk to use this option.

- **Delete Mail** Empties the email folder you specify.

- **Delete Junk Mail** Empties the Junk Email folders.

- **Launch Alias** Opens a file you specify.

- **Excel Auto Web Publish** Publishes a Microsoft Excel file you specify to the Web.

You can use the Add Action button to add as many actions as you like to the schedule. You can also use the Remove Action button to remove a selected action that you don't want to include.

If you have a dial-up connection to the Internet, you can select a dial-up option to determine what Outlook should do after connecting and performing the action:

- **Stay connected** Stays connected to the Internet

- **Close** Disconnects from the Internet

- **Return to previous state** Remains connected if you were already connected or disconnects if Outlook connected just to run the schedule

Finally, to make sure the schedule can be run, be sure to select the Enabled check box. When you click OK, your settings are saved.

When you create a new schedule, it's added to the Schedules menu on the Tools tab. You can manually run a schedule at any time by simply clicking its name on the menu. Or you can completely automate the task by setting it up to run at a specific time or event.

In this exercise, you'll modify two of the existing schedules to set or change automation options. You'll also create a new schedule. Along the way, you'll get a better look at how some of the more advanced scheduling features work.

SET UP No set up is required. Just follow these steps.

Schedules

1. On the **Tools** tab, click the **Schedules** button to display its menu of options.

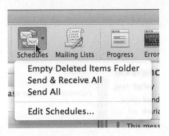

2. Click **Edit Schedules**. The Schedules preferences pane appears.

3. In the **Schedules** preferences pane, double-click **Send & Receive All** to open its **Edit Schedule** dialog box.

4. Examine the settings in the **When** area. You can see that the schedule is set to automatically occur at two times: Every 10 Minutes and At Startup.

5. Click the pop-up menu where **Minutes** is selected. You'll see that you can set the interval based on Minutes, Hours, or Days. Leave the menu set to **Minutes**.

6. Change the value in the text box from **10** to **15**. This tells Outlook to check every 15 minutes instead of every 10 minutes.

7. Examine the settings in the **Action** area. You can see that in addition to the Send All action, the schedule is also configured to Receive Mail for each of your email accounts.

8. Click **OK**. Your changes are saved.

9. In the **Schedules** preferences pane, double-click **Empty Deleted Items Folder** to open its **Edit Schedule** dialog box.

10. Examine the settings in the **When** area. This schedule is set to Manually, meaning that it will not run unless you manually run it.

11. Click the pop-up menu where **Manually** is selected to display the menu.

12. Click **Timed Schedule**. A button appears beside it.

13. Click the **Click here for timed scheduled options** button. A scheduling window appears.

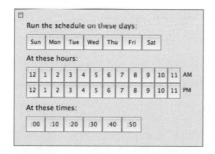

14. Click the buttons for **Mon**, **Wed**, **Fri**; click the **4** button in the **PM** row; and click the **:00** button. They all turn darker gray. The schedule is now set for Monday, Wednesday, and Friday at 4:00 PM.

15. Click the window's close button to dismiss it.

16. In the **Edit Schedule** dialog box, select the **Only if connected** check box.

17. Examine the options in the **Action** area. The schedule is set up to delete mail in the Deleted Items folder (and its subfolders) that are older than 0 days.

18. Click the pop-up menu where **Deleted Items** is selected to display its menu. Then click **Choose folder**. A Choose Folder dialog box appears. You can use this dialog box to select any Outlook folder on your computer or on the server for your Exchange account (if you have one).

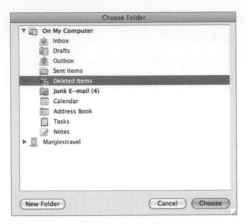

Important Use this option with care! Outlook will delete the contents of the folder you specify.

19. Click **Cancel** to dismiss the dialog box without making changes.

20. In the **Edit Schedule** dialog box, click **OK** to save your settings.

21. In the **Schedules** preferences pane, examine the **Next Run** column beside **Empty Deleted Items Folder**. It should list the date and time the schedule will run next.

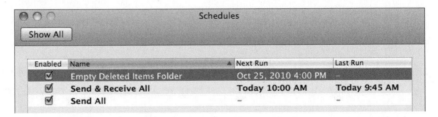

22. In the **Schedules** preferences pane, click the **+** button at the bottom of the sched-ules list. An Edit Schedule dialog box appears with some default settings.

23. In the **Name** field of the **Edit Schedule** dialog box, type **Delete Junk Email**.

24. In the **When** area, click the pop-up menu where **Manually** is selected. Then click **Recurring**.

25. Click the **Click here for recurrence options** button. The Recurring Schedule dia-log box appears.

26. In the **Recurring Schedule** dialog box, select **Weekly**. The options in the area to the right change.

27. Set options to recur every **2** weeks on **Friday**. Leave the start date to today's date, set the time to **12:00 PM** (noon), and make sure **No end date** is selected.

28. Click **OK** to save your changes.

29. In the **Action** area of the **Edit Schedule** dialog box, click the pop-up menu where **Receive Mail** is selected. Click **Delete Junk Mail**.

30. Click the pop-up menu where **Deleted Items** is selected. Then click **Choose folder**.

31. In the **Choose Folder** dialog box, select **Junk E-mail** and click **Choose**.

32. Leave the text box set to **7** days. This gives each junk email message an extra 7 days for you to review it before it's deleted.

33. Make sure the **Enabled** check box is selected.

34. Click **OK** to close the **Edit Schedule** dialog box. The new schedule is added to the list in the Schedules preferences pane.

35. On the **Tools** tab, click the **Schedules** button to display its menu. The new schedule appears there, too.

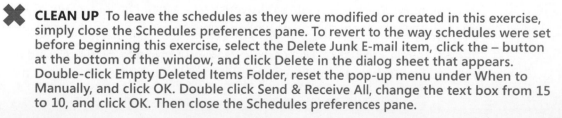

CLEAN UP To leave the schedules as they were modified or created in this exercise, simply close the Schedules preferences pane. To revert to the way schedules were set before beginning this exercise, select the Delete Junk E-mail item, click the – button at the bottom of the window, and click Delete in the dialog sheet that appears. Double-click Empty Deleted Items Folder, reset the pop-up menu under When to Manually, and click OK. Double click Send & Receive All, change the text box from 15 to 10, and click OK. Then close the Schedules preferences pane.

Using Rules to Process Messages

The rules feature of Outlook makes it possible to automatically perform actions on individual messages as they arrive in your Inbox or are sent out by you. Rules are applied to messages based on criteria you specify, such as who the message is from, what the message's subject or body contain, whether there's an attachment, or how the priority option is set. If a message matches the criteria, the actions you specify are performed on it, such as moving it to another folder, forwarding it to someone else, or saving the attachments.

Here's an example. Suppose you're working on Project X with a team of people who are included in the Project Team group you created for your contacts list. You might set up a rule that automatically moves messages from any of the Project Team members to a Project X folder you created in Mail view. Although you could also do this manually, it's a lot more efficient to let Outlook do it for you—especially if you receive dozens of new messages a day.

You create and modify Rules in Outlook in the Rules preferences pane. To open it, click the Rules button on the Home tab to display a menu of rules and then click Edit Rules. You can also open the Rules preferences pane by clicking the Rules icon in the Outlook Preferences window.

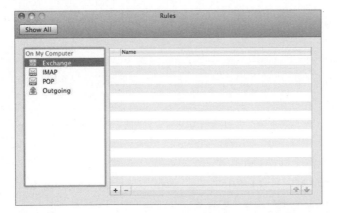

The left side of the Rules preferences pane lists the kinds of accounts you can create rules for. The items listed here depend on the types of accounts set up in Outlook on your computer. When you create a rule, you create it for a type of account or for outgoing mail. The rules for each type of account appear when that account type is selected.

To create a rule, select the type of account you want to create the rule for and then click the + button at the bottom of the rules list. To modify an existing rule, select the type of account it was created for and then double-click it in the rules list. Either way, you'll see the Edit Rule dialog box, which enables you to set rule options.

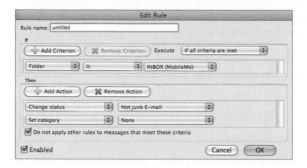

Start by entering a name for the rule in the Rule Name box. Then set up options in the If and Then areas.

You use the If area to set up search criteria for selecting which messages the rule should be applied to. Each line in the If area is another part of the criteria. The pop-up menu at the beginning of the line tells Outlook what to look at. It's very similar to setting up an advanced filter to search for items in the item list.

You can use a pop-up menu at the top of the If area to determine whether Outlook should match all criteria or any criteria and then determine whether or not the rule should be executed. You use the Add Criterion and Remove Criterion buttons to modify the list of criteria.

See Also You can learn more about using Outlook filtering features in the section titled "Searching for Messages with Filters," in Chapter 5, "Organizing Your Inbox."

You use the Then area to specify the actions Outlook should take if it gets a match. Each line in this area represents an action. You can use the Add Action and Remove Action buttons to set this up the way you like. There are 20 different actions, ranging from moving or copying the message to changing the character set or running an AppleScript.

You can select the Do Not Apply Other Rules To Messages That Meet These Criteria check box to prevent other rules from being run on messages that match the criteria you set up for this rule. This can prevent certain messages from being processed more than just once.

When you click OK, the rule is added to the Rules preferences pane, as well as to the Rules menu on the Home tab.

If you have multiple rules in the Rules preferences pane, you can set the order in which they run. This becomes important if you need rules to run in a particular order. Here's an example:

- Rule 1 searches for messages from the Project Team group members and moves it into a Project X folder.

- Rule 2 searches for messages containing the phrase "Project Z" in the Subject line or message body and moves it into a Project Z folder.

- Some members of the Project Team group are working on both projects, so their messages could match the criteria of both rules.

The solution is to run Rule 2 first and set it up so that other rules are not applied to its messages. Then the Project Z files will be properly moved into their folder and the remaining messages from the Project Team group that do not refer to Project Z will be moved into the Project X folder.

As you can imagine, this can become quite complex. You can make it easier by specifying criteria to match a narrow group of results.

Although rules run automatically when you send and receive email, you can force a rule to run at any time. Simply select its name from the Rules menu on the Home tab. This is a good way to test a rule on your existing Inbox or Sent Items content.

In this exercise, you'll create a folder called *From Contacts* in the On My Computer Inbox. You'll then create a rule that automatically copies messages from people in your contacts list to this folder as they arrive.

SET UP You need to have messages in your Inbox with at least one of them from someone in your contacts list to test the rule you're creating in this exercise. Follow these steps to create and test the rule.

1. In the navigation pane, select **On My Computer**. (You may have to click the disclosure triangle beside Inbox to see it.)

New

2. On the **Home** tab, click the **New** button, and then click **Folder**. A new untitled folder appears under On My Computer in the navigation pane.

3. In the edit box around **Untitled Folder**, type **From Contacts** and press Return.

Rules

4. On the **Home** tab, click the **Rules** button, and then click **Edit Rules**. The Rules preferences pane appears.

5. On the left side of the **Rules** preferences pane, select the type of email account you use most often.

6. At the bottom of the rules list, click the + button. The Edit Rule dialog box appears with some default settings.

7. In the **Rule Name** box of the **Edit Rule** dialog box, type **Mail from Contacts**.

8. In the **If** area, click the pop-up menu with **Folder** selected to display its options. Then click **From** in the list.

9. In the same line, click the pop-up menu in the same line with **Contains** selected to display its options. Then click **Is a Contact**.

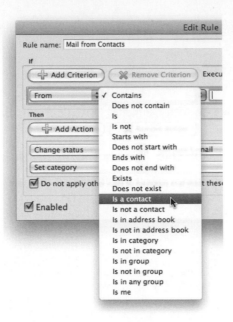

10. In the **Then** area, click the pop-up menu with **Set category** selected to display its options. Then click **Copy Message**.

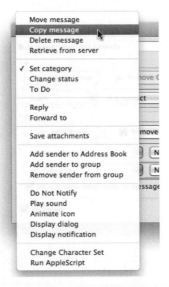

11. In the same line of the **Then** area, click the pop-up menu with **Inbox (On My Computer)** selected. Then click **Choose Folder**.

12. In the **Choose Folder** dialog box that appears, select the **From Contacts** folder you created at the beginning of this exercise. You should find it in the Inbox under On My Computer.

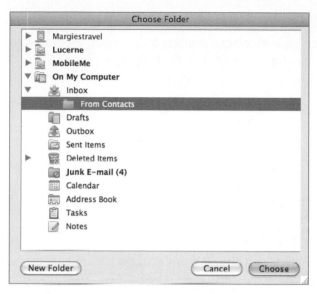

13. Click **Choose**.

14. In the **Edit Rule** dialog box, make sure the **Do not apply other rules to messages that meet these criteria** check box is selected.

15. Make sure the **Enabled** check box is selected.

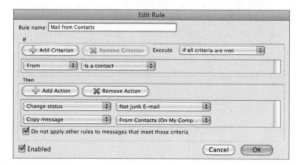

16. Click **OK**. The rule is added to the rules list in the **Rules** preferences pane.

17. Close the **Rules** preferences pane.

18. In the navigation pane, select the Inbox for an account you created the rule for. For example, if you created the rule for IMAP accounts, select an IMAP account. If you only have one account, select its Inbox.

19. On the **Home** tab, click the **Rules** button to display its menu. The rule you created should be listed at the bottom of the menu.

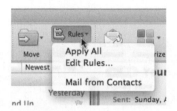

20. To test the rule, click its name. The rule is applied to the selected mailbox.

21. To see what messages matched the rule criteria, in the navigation pane, click **From Contacts**. Items matching the rule should appear in the item list.

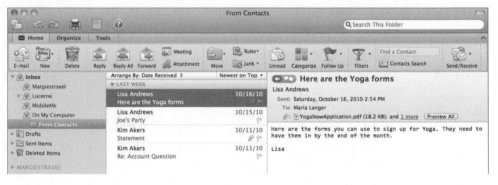

If the From Contacts folder is empty, there are no messages that match rule criteria.

Tip You can apply all rules to all Inboxes. In the navigation pane, click Inbox. Then, on the Home tab, click the Rules button, and click Apply All.

✖ **CLEAN UP** The rule you created copies rather than moves messages, so your Inbox is unaffected. To allow the rule to keep running so you can monitor its progress, do nothing. To remove the rule, on the Home tab, click the Rules button, and then click Edit Rules. In the Rules preferences pane, select the rule you created, click the – button at the bottom of the rules list, and click Delete in the dialog box that appears. Then close the Rules preferences pane. To delete the From Contacts folder, in the navigation pane, select From Contacts. (Remember, you may have to click it twice to select it; it should turn blue when selected.) On the Home tab, click the Delete button. The folder and its contents disappear. (Note that only the copies created by the rule are deleted; the original messages remain in the Inbox where they were found.)

Managing Mailing Lists

Email–based mailing lists are one way to keep up to date on topics that interest you. You and other members send messages to the mailing list and those messages are sent out to all members. The bigger and more popular a mailing list is, the more email it can generate. With a subscription to a very active mailing list, you can easily crowd out other email in your Inbox with mailing list messages.

Outlook makes it easy to keep mailing list messages separate from other email you might receive. It does this with special rules you set up with the Mailing List Manager. To get started, click the Mailing Lists button on the Tools tab. The Mailing List Manager window appears. It lists all mailing lists you've already set up rules for.

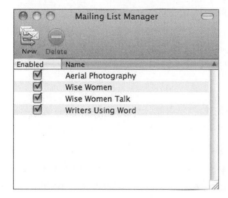

New

To add a mailing list rule, click the New button at the top of the Mailing List Manager window. To modify an existing mailing list rule, double-click it in the Mailing List Manager window. Either way, you'll see the Edit Mailing List Rule dialog box, which you can use to set options for the mailing list.

In addition to a Name box where you can enter a name for the rule, the Edit Mailing List Rule dialog box has two panes. The Mailing List pane includes basic options for setting up a mailing list rule.

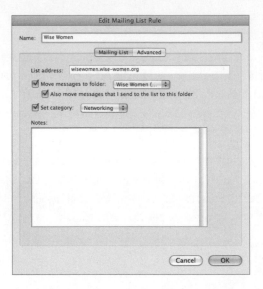

- **List address** The List address field is for the list's email address. This is the address that email for the list will come from.

- **Move messages to folder** This option enables you to set up the rule so incoming list messages are automatically moved into a folder you specify. Select the check box, then choose a folder from the pop-up menu. If the folder is not on the menu, you can select the Choose Folder option and in the Choose A Folder dialog box that appears, select or even create a new Outlook folder to store list messages. With this option enabled, you can also select the Also Move Messages That I Send To The List To This Folder check box so your outgoing messages are moved to the same folder.

- **Set category** This option enables you to set up the rule so that incoming list messages are automatically assigned the category you specify. Select the check box and then choose a category from the pop-up menu.

- **Notes** You can enter notes about the mailing list in the big Notes box. This information is not used by Outlook.

The Advanced pane enables you to set some more advanced options for the list, including other list addresses, actions for list messages, and reply options. These options control how list messages are handled by Outlook. If you're not sure how to set them, leave the default settings as is.

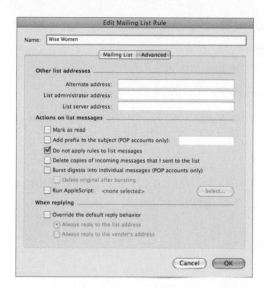

When you click OK, Outlook saves your settings. If you are creating a new mailing list rule, a dialog box appears, asking if you want to add the mailing list to your address book.

If you click Add To Address Book, Outlook may prompt you to select an address book to add it to. It then displays a contact window you can use to enter other information about the mailing list, as if it were a person. Outlook also adds the mailing list rule to the Mailing List Manager window.

See Also Adding contacts to your contacts list is covered in the section titled "Creating Contact Records" in Chapter 9, "Managing Contact Information."

In this exercise, you'll set up a mailing list rule that moves incoming list messages to a folder you specify.

SET UP You need to be subscribed to a mailing list and to have the mailing list address available to successfully complete this exercise. Then follow these steps.

Mailing Lists

1. On the **Tools** tab, click the **Mailing Lists** button. The Mailing List Manager window opens.

2. Click the **New** button to display the **Edit Mailing List Rule** dialog box.

3. In the **Name** box, enter the name of your mailing list.

4. Make sure the **Mailing List** pane is displayed. Then in the **List address** box, enter the complete email address for the mailing list.

5. Select the **Move messages to folder** option.

6. Click the pop-up menu beside that option, and then click **Choose folder**.

7. In the **Choose Folder** dialog box that appears, click **New Folder** to display the **Create New Folder** dialog box.

8. In the **Name** box of the **Create New Folder** dialog box, type **Mailing List Messages**. Then select **On My Computer**.

9. Click **OK**.

10. In the **Choose Folder** dialog box, select **Mailing List Messages**, and click **OK**.

11. In the **Edit Mailing List Rule** dialog box, select **Also move messages that I send to the list to this folder** option and make sure **Set Category** is not selected.

12. Type a brief description of the mailing list in the **Notes** box, and then click **OK**. The mailing list is added to the list in the Mailing List Manager window.

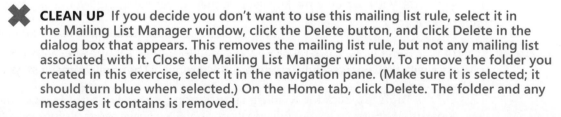

CLEAN UP If you decide you don't want to use this mailing list rule, select it in the Mailing List Manager window, click the Delete button, and click Delete in the dialog box that appears. This removes the mailing list rule, but not any mailing list associated with it. Close the Mailing List Manager window. To remove the folder you created in this exercise, select it in the navigation pane. (Make sure it is selected; it should turn blue when selected.) On the Home tab, click Delete. The folder and any messages it contains is removed.

Blocking Spam

Junk email, which is widely known as *spam*, are email messages from people you do not know that attempt to sell you products or services or get you to visit Web sites. Junk email is a real nuisance to most email users, especially when dozens of these messages can come into your Inbox every day. Fortunately, Outlook has built-in junk email protection that can help identify junk email and separate it from other Inbox items.

You can customize junk email protection options to best meet your needs. Get started by choosing Junk E-mail Protection from the Junk button's menu on the Home tab. This displays the Junk E-mail Protection dialog box, which has three panes of options:

- **Level** The Level pane enables you to set a basic level of protection. Options range from None, which offers no protection at all and relies on your email server to filter out spam, to Exclusive, which only delivers messages from email addresses in your contacts list. The default setting is low, which is a good starting point that's not likely to filter out legitimate email messages. You can also use this pane to automatically delete messages from the Junk Email folder that are older than the number of days you specify.

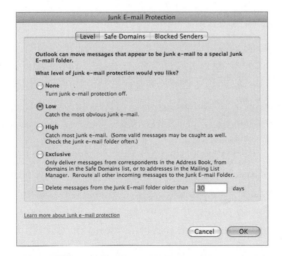

- **Safe Domains** If messages that come from certain domains should never be marked as junk email, you can add those domains to the Safe Domains pane. A domain is the part of the email address after the @, so the domain for mark@co-howinery.com would be cohowinery.com. You can list as many domains as you like, separated by commas.

- **Blocked Senders** If certain individuals or domains always send you junk email, you can enter them in the Blocked Senders pane. When messages arrive, any email from blocked addresses or domains will automatically be moved into the Junk Email folder.

When the junk email protection feature finds a message it thinks is junk, it does three things:

- It moves the message to the Junk Email folder.
- It assigns the Junk category to the message.
- It prevents embedded pictures from being downloaded. This could help prevent the sender of the message from discovering that your email address is active.

You can also mark messages as junk on the fly as you read your email. For example, suppose you're using the item list for your Inbox to read email messages. You select a message that you think is junk. While the message is selected, use options on the Junk button on the Home tab to deal with it.

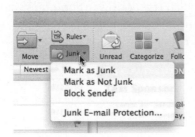

- **Mark as Junk**   Marks the message as junk and moves it into the Junk Email folder.
- **Block Sender**   Adds the sender's email address to the Blocked Senders pane of the Junk E-mail Protection dialog box. Note that this option is not always available.

If you enable junk email protection by selecting any option other than None in the Level pane of the Junk E-mail Protection dialog box, you need to periodically review the messages Outlook has moved into the Junk Email folder. Simply select the folder in the navigation pane and then use the item list to review the messages. If you find one that isn't junk, select it and choose Mark As Not Junk from the Junk menu on the Home tab.

Tip It's especially important to periodically review the contents of the Junk Email folder if you have Outlook set up to delete the contents of this folder. If you fail to check it, there's a possibility that Outlook could delete messages that aren't junk and were placed there in error.

In this exercise, you'll see how you can customize the junk email protection feature to better meet your needs.

SET UP No set up is required. Just follow these steps.

1. On the **Home** tab, click the **Junk** button to display its menu. Then click **Junk E-mail Protection**. The Junk E-mail Protection dialog box appears.

2. If necessary, click the **Level** tab in the **Junk E-mail Protection** dialog box to display its options. Then review the settings and the description for each. If Outlook has been failing to catch some junk email, you might want to increase the level of protection.

3. If you want Outlook to automatically delete junk email over a certain age, select the **Delete messages from the Junk E-mail folder older than *n* days** check box. Then enter a value in the edit box to set the maximum age of junk email.

4. Display the **Safe Domains** tab of the **Junk E-mail Protection** dialog box.

5. In the big edit box, type **microsoft.com**. This indicates that email from any address at microsoft.com is not junk.

6. Type a comma, and then type the domain name for your company. Remember the domain name is everything after the @ in an email address. This prevents email from anyone with your company's email address from being marked as junk email.

7. Display the **Blocked Senders** tab of the **Junk E-mail Protection** dialog box.

8. In the big edit box, type **contoso.com**. This automatically marks any email from an address with this domain name as junk.

9. Type a comma, and then type **sales@adatum.com**. This automatically marks any email from this specific email address as junk; email from another address at the same domain may still be delivered to your Inbox.

10. Click **OK** to save your settings.

11. In the navigation pane, select the **Junk E-mail** folder. A list of messages Outlook marked as junk appears in the item list.

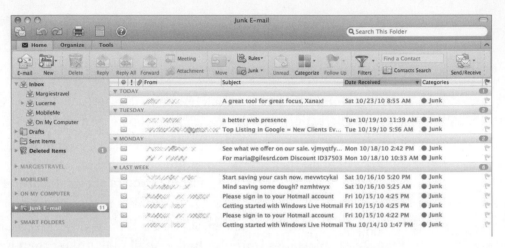

12. If you see a message that should not have been marked as junk, select it, click the **Junk** button on the **Home** tab, and click **Mark as Not Junk**. The item is moved out of the Junk Email folder and into the Inbox. You can repeat this process for every mismarked message.

13. In the navigation pane, select **Inbox**. A list of messages should appear in the item list.

14. If you see a message that should have been marked as junk, select it, click the **Junk** button on the **Home** tab, and click **Mark as Junk**. The message is moved to the Junk Email folder.

CLEAN UP No clean-up steps are required. You are ready to move on to the next exercise.

Securing Your Email

Outlook offers two ways to secure your email messages. Both are available as options on the Security button's menu on the Options tab in the message composition window.

● **Digitally Sign Message** A digital signature in an email message helps the recipient verify that the message was really sent by you and not someone pretending to be you.

● **Encrypt Message** Encryption scrambles the contents of a message so that only you and the message recipient can read it.

Both of these features have special requirements for use:

● Both you and the message recipient must have an email application that supports the S/MIME standard. Outlook does support this standard, so you can send these messages. Although all recipients should be able to read a digitally signed message, the ability to read an encrypted message depends on whether the recipient's email application supports the S/MIME standard.

● To send a digitally signed message, you must have a digital signature certificate added to your Mac's keychain. You must then link that signature to your e-mail account in the Security pane of the Advanced account settings dialog sheet.

● To send an encrypted message, you must have an encryption certificate added to your Mac's keychain. You must then link that signature to your email account in the Security pane of the Advanced account settings dialog sheet. In addition, you must also have a copy of each recipient's certificate in your Outlook contacts list, added to the Security pane of the recipient's contact window.

See Also You can learn more about security certificates in Mac OS Help. Search for "digital certificates." Adding a certificate to a contact's record is covered in the section titled "Creating Contact Records" in Chapter 9.

After the required certificate is installed in your Mac OS keychain, you can attach it to your email account in the Security pane of the Advanced settings dialog sheet. Simply choose the certificate you want to use from the two Certificate pop-up menus.

After the account is configured with the necessary certificates, you can use the Security menu options to secure your messages. The security options you choose appear beneath the header in the message composition window.

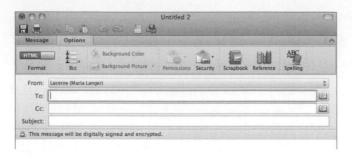

In this exercise, you'll link security certificates to one of your email accounts. You'll then activate security options for an email message you create.

 SET UP You need a digital signature certificate and encryption for one of your email accounts installed in your keychain to complete this exercise. Then follow these steps

1. On the **Outlook** menu, click **Preferences** or press Command-, (comma) to display the **Outlook Preferences** window.

2. Click **Accounts** in the **Outlook Preferences** window. The Accounts preferences pane appears.

3. On the left side of the preferences pane, select the account you have a certificate for.

4. In the lower-right corner of the window, click **Advanced**. The advanced options dialog sheet appears.

5. In the advanced options dialog sheet, click **Security** to display the **Security** options.

6. Use either or both of the **Certificate** pop-up menus to choose the certificate you want to use for this email account. The menu should include all available certificates.

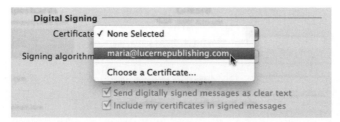

7. Set other options as desired to control digital signing and encryption options.

8. Click **OK** to save your changes.

9. Close the **Accounts** preferences pane.

Email

10. On the **Home** tab in **Mail** view, click the **Email** button to open an email composition window.

11. If you have multiple accounts, make sure the account you added the certificate(s) for is selected from the **From** pop-up menu.

Security

12. On the **Options** tab, click the **Security** button, and then select the type of security you want to add to the message. You can select both if you want to. The type of security you chose is noted beneath the message header.

13. Finish addressing and composing your message in the message composition window.

14. On the **Message** tab, click **Send**.

    If you enabled encryption and the recipient does not have a valid encryption certificate on file, a dialog box appears to warn you.

    You can click Cancel, add a certificate to the contact's record, and try sending again or send the message unencrypted.

 CLEAN UP No clean-up steps are required. You are ready to continue to the next exercise.

Exploring Advanced Account Settings

When you set up your email accounts in Outlook, Outlook applies the most commonly used account options. There are instances, however, when you might need to change advanced settings for your account. You access these settings from the Accounts preferences pane. Choose Preferences from the Outlook menu and then click the Accounts icon in the Outlook Preferences window.

The Accounts preferences pane lists all of the accounts you have set up in Outlook. In most cases, this will be just one or two accounts, but it could be more. When you select an account on the left side of the window, the basic details for the account appear on the right side.

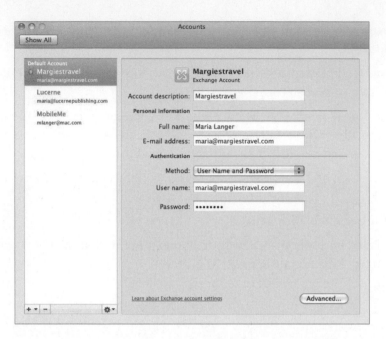

You can access advanced options for an account by clicking the Advanced button in the lower-right corner of the window when the account is selected. How the advanced options dialog sheet appears varies depending on the type of account: Exchange, IMAP (including MobileMe), or POP. It should have two or three panes of settings:

● **Server** These settings appear for Exchange, IMAP, and POP accounts. For Exchange accounts, Server settings include the Microsoft Exchange server and directory service server.

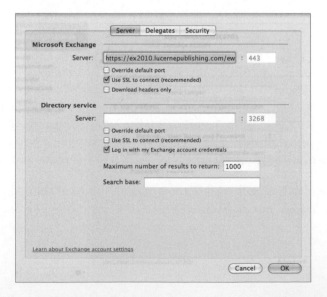

For IMAP accounts, Server settings include options for communicating with the server.

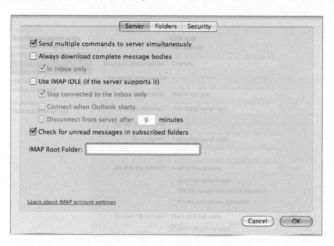

For POP accounts, Server settings include options for handling message copies on the server and deleted messages, as well as an option to download only message headers rather than entire messages.

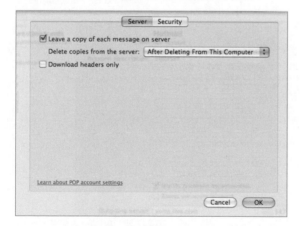

● **Delegates** Microsoft Exchange accounts have a Delegates pane, which you can use to set information about delegates on your account and your capacity as delegate on another user's account.

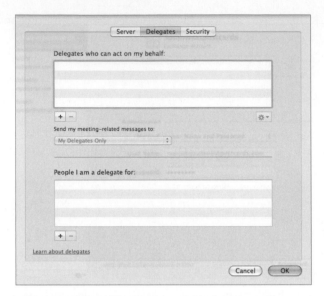

● **Folders** IMAP (including MobileMe) accounts have a Folders pane, which you can use to set options for the various folders associated with the account. Use pop-up menus to choose folders and select options for how trash should be handled.

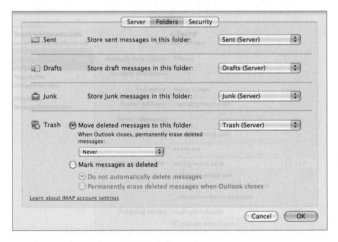

● **Security** Exchange, IMAP, and POP accounts all include the Security pane. You use this pane to link certificates with your email accounts in Outlook.

See Also To learn more about setting up certificates in Outlook, consult the section titled "Securing Your Email" earlier in this chapter.

In most cases, you will not need to change any of the settings in the advanced account options dialog sheet. In fact, changing some settings could negatively affect the operation of your account. Before making any change, especially for an Exchange account, consult your system administrator.

In this exercise, you'll open the Accounts preferences pane and explore the advanced options available for your email accounts.

 SET UP No set up is required. Just follow these steps.

1. On the **Outlook** menu, click **Preferences** or press Command-, (comma) to display the **Outlook Preferences** window.

2. Click **Accounts** in the **Outlook Preferences** window. The Accounts preferences pane appears.

3. On the left side of the window, select the account you want to explore settings for.

4. In the lower-right corner of the window, click **Advanced** to display the advanced options dialog sheet.

5. Click the buttons near the top of the dialog sheet to move from one pane of options to the next.

6. When you're finished looking at options for the account, click **OK** to dismiss the dialog sheet and save any changes you might have made.

7. Repeat steps 3 through 6 for any other accounts you want to explore settings for.

8. When you're finished, close the **Accounts** preferences pane.

 **CLEAN UP** No clean-up steps are required. You are ready to move on to exercises in the next chapter.

Key Points

- You can set options in Outlook preferences to control Reading and Composing options and set the default font for HTML and plain text messages.

- You can create multiple signatures and associate them with various email accounts.

- You can automate the completion of certain tasks by scheduling them.

- Rules make it possible to process email messages based on criteria you specify.

- The Mailing List Manager makes it easy to set up rules to separate list activity from other email.

- The built-in, customizable junk email filtering feature in Outlook keeps spam out of your Inbox.

- You can secure email messages with digital signatures and encryption.

- Every email account has a collection of advanced settings you can modify as needed.

Part 3
Calendar

Chapter at a Glance

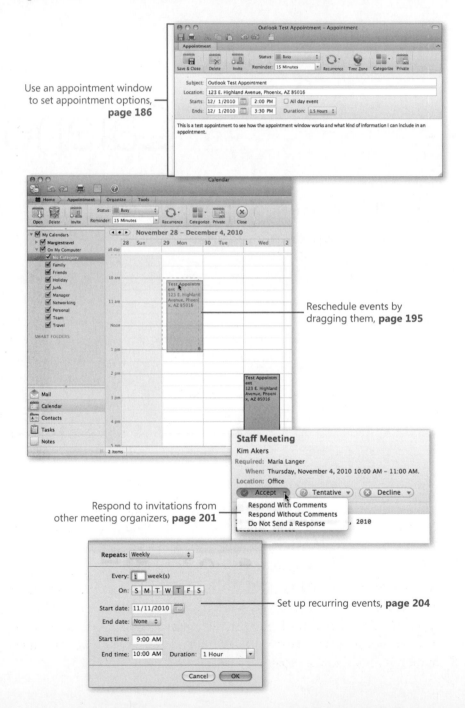

Use an appointment window to set appointment options, **page 186**

Reschedule events by dragging them, **page 195**

Respond to invitations from other meeting organizers, **page 201**

Set up recurring events, **page 204**

7 Scheduling Appointments and Meetings

In this chapter, you will learn how to

✔ Schedule appointments.

✔ Schedule meetings.

✔ Modify calendar items

✔ Respond to meeting invitations.

✔ Set event options.

Keeping track of appointments, meetings, and other date-based events can be daunting, especially if you have a busy schedule. Microsoft Outlook for Mac 2011, however, can make it easy. In the Calendar view, you can schedule all kinds of events on your personal or Microsoft Exchange Server calendar. For each event, you can include an event name, location, start and end times and dates, detailed information or notes, status, and categories. You can set reminders to alert you before an event takes place so you don't miss it. You can even set up an event to recur regularly on your calendar, like a weekly yoga session or monthly staff meeting.

Outlook for Mac distinguishes between two kinds of calendar items:

● *Appointments* are calendar items that you add to just your calendar. Although they could be meetings or other events that include other people, appointments do not include invitations. Instead, they appear only on your calendar.

● *Meetings* are calendar items that include invitees. When you schedule a meeting, you provide the email addresses of the people you want to invite. Outlook sends invitation files to each invitee. When the invitees receive the invitation, they respond; Outlook keeps track of those responses. You can also receive and reply to invitations from others; when you accept a meeting invitation, that meeting's information is added to your calendar.

In this chapter, you'll learn how to add calendar items to Outlook. You'll learn how to set options such as reminders, status, recurrence, and categories. You'll also learn how to respond to meeting requests and how to modify calendar items.

> **Practice Files** No practice files are needed for this chapter. You can complete exercises with items on your Calendar as well as items created for this and other chapters. For more information about practice file requirements, see "Using the Practice Files" at the beginning of this book.

Scheduling Appointments

An appointment is a calendar item for just you. You use appointments to schedule events that do not have invitees—for example, a lunch date with a family member, a visit to your doctor, or a pickup after your child's soccer game. In each of these examples, you're putting the event on your calendar but you are not sending an invitation to the event to someone else.

You add an appointment to your calendar with the appointment window. This window includes fields and buttons to provide information and set options for the calendar item.

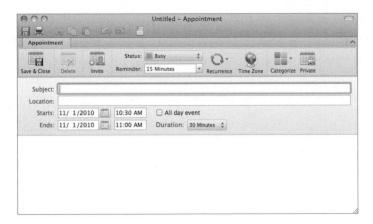

You enter information about the event into fields at the top of the window:

- **Subject** The event name or title. Examples might be *Lunch with Sally* or *Soccer Pickup*.

- **Location** The event location. This could be a general location, such as a town name, or it could be an exact location, such as a street address and suite number. Entering information in this field is not required.

● **Starts** The event start date and time. You can click the calendar icon beside the date to display a date picker; just click buttons on the calendar to find the date you want and then click it to enter it in the field.

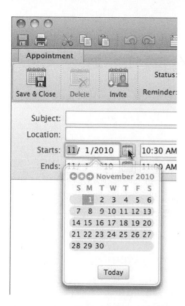

● **Ends** The event end date and time. You can click the calendar icon to enter the date with the date picker.

● **All day event** Enables you to set up the event so it lasts all day long. This might be useful to schedule a day off from work or a business trip. When you select this check box, the time fields and Duration field turn gray (are unavailable) and cannot be changed.

● **Duration** The event's duration. This is automatically calculated by Outlook based on your entries in the Starts and Ends fields, but you can change it by choosing a different duration. Making a change with this pop-up menu automatically changes the Ends time and/or date. (The All Day Event check box must be cleared to use this pop-up menu.)

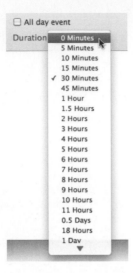

- **Time zone** When this is enabled, you can choose a time zone for the event's times. To enable this field, click the Time Zone button on the Appointment tab. It appears as a pop-up menu you can use to choose a time zone.

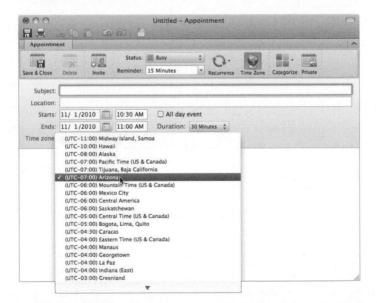

Tip Outlook gets your time zone from Mac OS X preferences. The only time you'd need to use this menu is to schedule an event using a different time zone.

- **Details** These can be entered in a large text box at the bottom of the appointment window. You might use this area to include notes or other detailed information about the appointment.

In this exercise, you'll add an appointment to your calendar.

SET UP If Outlook is not started, open it. If necessary, click the Calendar button in the View switcher. Then follow these steps.

Appointment

1. If more than one calendar is listed in the navigation pane, click **On My Computer**.

2. On the **Home** tab, click the **Appointment** button or press Command+N. An untitled appointment window opens.

   Tip Another way to create an appointment is to drag in the calendar window at the date and approximate time of the appointment. You must be in Day, Work Week, or Week view to do this. When you finish dragging, you can type in the title of the appointment. To add more details, double-click the appointment box to open an appointment window.

3. In the **Subject** field, enter Outlook Test Appointment. This text appears in the window's title bar as you type it.

4. In the **Location** field, type your home or office address.

Calendar

5. Beside the date in the **Starts** field, click the **Calendar** icon. The date picker appears.

6. In the date picker, click the right triangle beside the month name. The date picker calendar changes to display the next month.

7. In the date picker, click the first Wednesday in the month to select it. The date is entered into the Starts and Ends date fields and the date picker disappears.

8. In the **Starts** time field, enter 2:00 PM. Note that the **Ends** time field changes to 2:30 PM.

9. On the **Duration** pop-up menu, click **1.5 Hours**. The Ends time field changes to 3:30 PM.

Time Zone

10. If the **Time zone** pop-up menu is not already displayed, on the **Appointment** tab, click the **Time Zone** button.

11. On the **Time zone** pop-up menu, ensure that your time zone is already selected. If it is not, click it.

    Tip If your time zone is not selected by default, you should check Mac OS X Date & Time preferences to make sure they are set properly. You can learn more in Mac OS Help.

12. In the large text field at the bottom of the window, type **This is a test appointment to see how the appointment window works and what kind of information I can include in an appointment**. As you can see, this text field works just like an email form's message body.

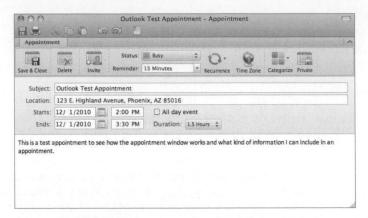

Tip If desired, you can select and format text in this field by using options on the Format menu and its submenus.

See Also You can learn more about formatting text in the section titled "Formatting Message Text" in Chapter 3, "Composing and Sending Email Messages."

13. On the **Appointment** tab, click the **Save & Close** button. The appointment is saved to your calendar and the appointment window closes.

14. In Calendar view, navigate to the date you scheduled the appointment for: the first Wednesday of next month. The appointment appears as scheduled.

CLEAN UP No clean-up steps are required. You will use the appointment you created for this exercise in another exercise in this chapter.

Scheduling Meetings

Meetings are just like appointments, but with one major difference: you must provide the email addresses for each person you want to invite to the meeting in order to schedule it. When you create a meeting, Outlook creates a special meeting file that is sent to all meeting invitees. When they open this file on their computers, they are prompted to respond to the meeting invitation. Their responses come back to you and are added to the information about the meeting.

In a way, a meeting is like a cross between an email message and an appointment. It's sent out and can be replied to like an email message, but it also adds an event to your calendar like an appointment.

You add a meeting to your calendar by using the meeting window. This window includes fields and buttons to provide information and set options for the calendar item. It has all the fields you'd find in an appointment window, plus a few others:

● **From** This field appears as a pop-up menu if you have more than one email account. Use this menu to select the account you want to use to send the meeting invitation.

● **To** This field is for a list of the meeting's invitees. You can type in multiple email addresses, separated by semicolons (;) or click the Address Book icon on the right end of the field to choose invitees from your contacts list. This works just like addressing an email message.

See Also You can learn more about addressing email messages in the section titled "Creating Messages" in Chapter 3.

● **Message** This field is for detailed information about the meeting. You might use this area for an agenda or list of topics to be covered. Or perhaps it might be a list of items to bring to the meeting. This information will be sent to all invitees.

● **Scheduling Assistant** You can use this field to find meeting times that work for all recipients. This feature requires access to the Exchange calendars for meeting invitees. As you add an invitee, his or her calendar appears in the list along with yours. You can then find dates and times when all attendees are available.

See Also You can learn more about the fields in an appointment window in the section titled "Scheduling Appointments" earlier in this chapter.

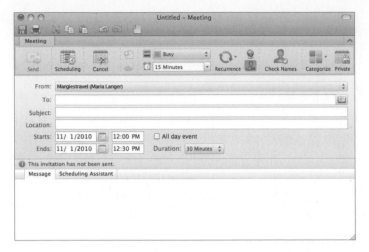

As you create an appointment, you'll see a note below the header area that says, "This invitation has not been sent." Rather than save a meeting, as you would an appointment, you send it as an invitation to each of your invitees by clicking the Send button on the Meeting tab. When you click Send, an email message is sent to each attendee. If you open the meeting window again, you'll see the note beneath the header area has changed to read, "This invitation has been sent." The event is scheduled on your calendar.

When an invitee responds to the invitation, his or her computer sends you an email message with that response, which you can see in Mail view.

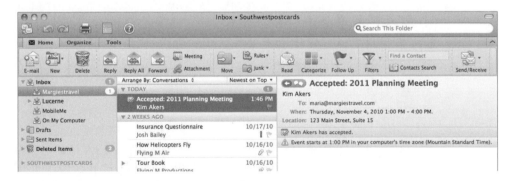

In addition, a green check mark appears beside the invitee's name in the Scheduling Assistant pane of the Meeting window.

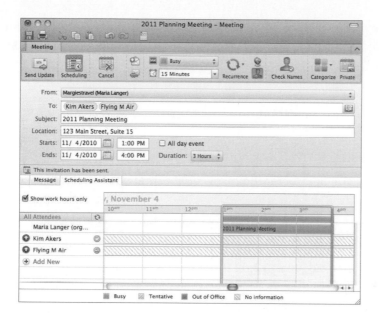

Tip The Scheduling Assistant only shows details for invitee availability for invitees who are on your Exchange server. No information will show for non-Exchange invitees.

Similarly, if an invitee declines the invitation or tentatively accepts, you're also notified by email and the invitee's response is noted in the Scheduling Assistant pane.

You can also manually set an invitee's response in the Scheduling Assistant; for example, if an invitee tells you in person or on the phone that he or she will or won't attend instead of clicking the Accept button in the email invitation, just click the icon to the right of the invitee's name, and choose a response from the pop-up menu.

In this exercise, you'll create a meeting and invite at least one friend or work associate to attend.

 SET UP To complete this exercise, you'll need to be familiar with the material in the section titled "Scheduling Appointments," earlier in this chapter. This chapter builds upon that material. You should also arrange to use the email address of a friend or coworker who uses Outlook, Entourage, or iCal to invite him or her to a test meeting; it would be a good idea for this person to be checking email regularly as you complete this exercise. In the Outlook view switcher, click the Calendar button, and then follow these steps.

1. If more than one calendar is listed in the navigation pane, select **On My Computer**.
2. On the **Home** tab, click the **Meeting** button. An untitled meeting window opens.

Meeting

3. If you have more than one email account set up in Outlook, click the **From** pop-up menu, and then click the account you want to use to send meeting invitations.

4. In the **To** field, enter the email address of the friend or coworker you want to invite to the test meeting.

5. In the **Subject** field, enter **Outlook Test Meeting**. This text appears in the window's title bar as you type it.

6. In the **Location** field, type your home or office address.

7. In the **Starts** date field, enter tomorrow's date. That date appears in the **Starts** and **Ends** date fields.

8. In the **Starts** time field, enter **10:00 AM**. Note that the Ends time field changes to 10:30 AM.

9. In the **Ends** time field, enter **12:00 PM**. The Duration pop-up menu changes to read 2 Hours.

10. If necessary, click the **Message** tab in the bottom half of the window.

11. In the large message field, type **This is a test meeting to see how Outlook's meeting feature works. Please either accept or decline this meeting invitation.**

12. In the bottom half of the window, click the **Scheduling Assistant** tab. The Scheduling Assistant lists you and the person you invited to the meeting. If you have access to the Exchange calendar for the person you invited, you may be able to see availability information.

    Tip Another way to view the Scheduling Assistant is to click the Scheduling button on the Meeting tab.

Send

13. On the **Meeting** tab, click the **Send** button. Three things happen:

    ○ A meeting invitation is sent to the email address you entered in step 4. You may hear a tone to indicate the message has been sent.

    ○ The meeting is saved to your calendar.

    ○ The meeting window closes.

14. In Calendar view, display tomorrow's date. The meeting appears as scheduled.

15. Continue working on other things. When the person you invited to the meeting responds, three things happen:

    ○ If you're working in an application other than Outlook, a dark gray notification with the message response should appear on the screen.

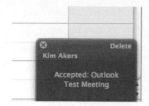

○ An email message from the person you invited appears in your Mail Inbox. You might want to read the message to see if the invitee included any comments with his or her response.

○ A green check mark appears beside the invitee's name in the Scheduling Assistant pane of the Meeting window.

✖ CLEAN UP No clean-up steps are required. You will work with this meeting again in another exercise later in this chapter.

Modifying Calendar Items

After you've created a calendar item, you can make changes to it as necessary. You start by opening the event window and making changes to its fields:

● **Subject** Change the name of the event as it appears on your calendar

● **Location** Change the location information in the appointment or meeting window

● **Starts and Ends** Change the date or time of the event and move it to a new location in your calendar.

> **TIP** You can also change a calendar item's date and time by dragging it to a new location on your calendar.

● **Duration** Change the size of the event's box in the calendar's Day, Work Week, and Week views.

● **Description or Message** Change the details that appear in the lower half of the appointment or meeting window.

What you do next depends on whether you're modifying an appointment or a meeting:

● When you make changes to an appointment, click the Save & Close button on the Appointment tab to save your changes and close the window. The changes are saved and, if they affect the appointment's date or time, the appointment is moved to the appropriate place on your calendar.

- When you make changes to a meeting, you click a Send Update button on the Meeting tab. That not only moves the meeting to the appropriate place on your calendar (if necessary), but it sends an updated invitation to all invitees. It also updates the Scheduling Assistant in the meeting window to indicate that the invitees have not responded—even if they had responded to the original invitation. Invitees will be prompted to respond to the changed meeting.

The situation is similar when you delete a calendar item. If you delete an appointment, it's simply removed from your calendar. But when you delete a meeting, you need to click a Send Cancellation button to let all the invitees know that the meeting has been canceled.

You can also turn an appointment into a meeting. You do this by clicking the Invite button on the Appointment toolbar. This turns the appointment window into a meeting window and adds From (if you have more than one email address) and To fields to the window's header. It also adds the Scheduling Assistant to the bottom of the window. When you change an appointment to a meeting, you must enter names of invitees and then send the invitation in order to save it.

For a meeting, you can modify the following options in the Scheduling Assistant pane:

- Change the importance of or remove an invitee. Each person invited to a meeting can be set as either *Required*, *Optional*, or *Resource*. By default, each one is set as Required, but you can change that setting or even remove an invitee.

- Change the response of an invitee. Although this option is set automatically by Outlook based on the response received from each invitee, you can manually change the setting. The options are as follows:

  - *No Response* means the invitee has not yet responded to the invitation.

  - *Accepted* means the invitee has responded to the invitation and plans to attend.

  - *Tentative* means the invitee has responded to the invitation and might attend.

  - *Declined* means the invitee has responded to the invitation and will not attend.

In this exercise, you'll make some changes to the appointment and meeting you created in the previous exercises in this chapter. You'll also delete both calendar items and send a cancellation notice to the meeting invitee.

SET UP This exercise works with the two calendar items created in the previous exercises. If you have not completed those exercises, do so before starting this exercise. Then make sure the Calendar button is selected in the view switcher, click the Week button on the Home tab, and follow these steps.

1. In Calendar view, navigate to the appointment you created in the exercise at the beginning of this chapter. You'll find it on the first Wednesday of next month.

2. Double-click the appointment to open it in the appointment window.

3. In the **Subject** field, delete the word *Outlook* and the space immediately after it. The name of the appointment changes in the title bar.

4. Click the **Duration** field, and then click **2 Hours**. The Ends time field changes to 4:00 PM.

Save & Close

5. On the **Appointment** tab, click the **Save & Close** button. The name of the meeting and the size of its box change in the calendar.

6. With the cursor in the middle of the appointment's box, drag into the **10 am** area on Monday of the same week. A dashed border appears where the appointment will be moved as you drag it.

When you release the mouse button, the appointment moves to the new position.

7. Double-click the appointment to open it in an appointment window. Note that the date has changed to two days earlier and the time has changed to four hours earlier in the day.

Invite

8. On the **Appointment** tab, click the **Invite** button. The appointment window changes into a meeting window. The ribbon and header options change accordingly.

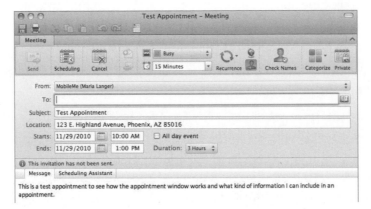

To complete the conversion to a meeting, you'd enter invitees in the To field and click the Send button. We don't need to do that.

Cancel

9. On the **Meeting** tab, click the **Cancel** button. The meeting window turns back into an appointment window. Because this was never scheduled as a meeting, the Cancel button just converts it back into an appointment and does not actually cancel the appointment.

10. On the **Appointment** tab, click the **Save & Close** button.

11. In the **Calendar** window, select the appointment.

12. Press the Delete key. A confirmation dialog sheet appears.

13. Click **Delete** in the confirmation dialog sheet. The appointment is removed from your calendar.

14. In the **Calendar** window, navigate to the meeting you created in the second exercise of this chapter. It should be scheduled on tomorrow's date.

15. Double-click the meeting to open it in a meeting window.

16. Change the start time of the meeting to **11:00 AM**. The end time changes to 1:00 PM.

17. In the **Message** field at the bottom of the window, add the following text at the end of the message: **This will be a lunch meeting.**

Scheduling

18. On the **Meeting** tab, click the **Scheduling** button. The Scheduling Assistant pane appears at the bottom of the window. Note that it shows the original meeting as well as a frame indicating where the modified meeting would appear on the day's calendar. Any check marks that may have appeared beside invitees' names are gone.

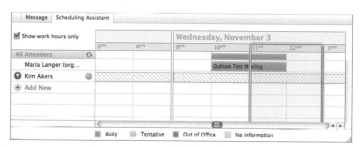

19. Click the purple arrow to the left of an invitee's name to display a menu of options.

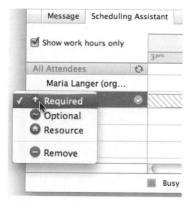

You can indicate the importance or role of an dinvitee by choosing an option. If you choose Remove, the invitee is removed from the list. For now, leave your invitee set to **Required**.

Tip The Resource option is useful in an Exchange environment when a resource such as a meeting room can be scheduled.

20. Click the gray button to the right of an invitee's name to display a menu of responses.

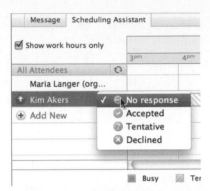

You can manually set a response for any invitee.

21. Click **Tentative**. The gray button turns to a teal button with a question mark inside it.

Send Update

22. On the **Meeting** tab, click the **Send Update** button. Your changes are applied, the **meeting** window closes, and a meeting update notice is sent to the invitee. When he or she responds, the meeting information will be updated accordingly.

23. In the **Calendar** window, double-click the meeting again to open it in a **meeting** window.

24. On the **Meeting** tab, click the **Cancel** button. The Meeting tab clears to offer only two buttons, one of which is unavailable.

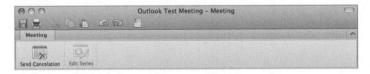

Send
Cancellation

25. On the **Meeting** tab, click the **Send Cancellation** button. Three things happen:

  ○ The meeting window closes.

  ○ The meeting is removed from your calendar.

  ○ A cancellation message is sent to your invitees.

TIP If you change your mind and decide to keep the meeting and not send a cancellation notice to all invitees, simply close the meeting window without clicking the Send Cancellation button. If prompted to save changes, click Discard Changes.

 CLEAN UP No clean-up steps are required. You are ready to continue to the next exercise.

Responding to Meeting Invitations

As you invite others to your meetings, other people may be inviting you to theirs. You'll receive their invitations in email. When you open the email message in a mail reading window, you'll find a calendar area on the right side of the window with the meeting time indicated. This calendar is handy for seeing, at a glance, whether the meeting invitation conflicts with anything else on your calendar.

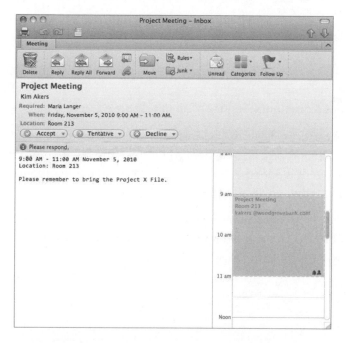

There are two ways to respond to the invitation.

● Click the Accept, Tentative, or Decline button in the message reading window to respond.

● Double-click the meeting box in the email message to open a meeting response window. This window looks and works like a regular meeting window, but it offers four buttons on the Meeting tab: Accept, Tentative, Decline, and Reply. The benefit of this window is that it enables you to add notes about the meeting when you add it to your calendar.

No matter which method you choose, each button—Accept, Tentative, or Decline—has a menu offering three options:

● **Respond With Comments** Opens a meeting response window that you can use to enter your comments. When you click Send, the comments are sent by email to the meeting organizer, along with your response.

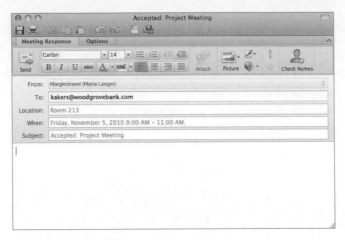

- **Respond Without Comments** Sends an email response to the meeting organizer.

- **Do Not Send a Response** Records your response in Outlook but does not send notification to the meeting organizer. Unless you inform the meeting organizer some
other way or the event is added to your Exchange calendar, the organizer has no
way of knowing whether you'll attend.

If you accept or tentatively accept a meeting invitation, Outlook adds the meeting to
your calendar—just as if you had created it yourself. If you tentatively accept, a striped
border appears on the left side of the meeting's box on your calendar.

After you respond to an invitation, you can change your mind. Just double-click the
meeting in your calendar to open it in a meeting response window. Then click the
Accept, Tentative, or Decline button to send a new response.

If you decline an invitation, it is not added to your calendar. If you decline an invitation
that you have already accepted, it is removed from your calendar.

If the meeting organizer makes changes to meeting information, he or she may send an
update. You handle the update the same as the original meeting invitation. When you
respond, the meeting information is automatically updated on your calendar.

In this exercise, you'll respond to an invitation for a meeting and include a comment. Then you'll change your mind and decline the invitation.

 SET UP To complete this exercise, ask a friend or coworker using Outlook, Entourage, or iCal to invite you to a sample meeting. You'll need to have a meeting invitation in your Mail Inbox to complete these steps.

1. In the view switcher, click **Mail**.

2. In your Inbox, locate and double-click the email message containing the meeting invitation.

3. In the message header, click the **Accept** button to display its menu.

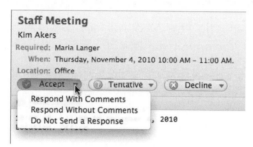

4. Click **Respond With Comments**. A meeting response window opens.

5. In the message body, type **I'm looking forward to attending**.

6. On the **Meeting Response** tab, click the **Send** button. The meeting response window closes, the response is sent to the meeting organizer, and the meeting is added to your calendar.

7. In the view switcher, click **Calendar**.

8. Navigate to the date and time of the meeting you were just invited to. The meeting should appear in a box on your calendar.

9. Double-click the meeting to open the meeting window.

Decline

10. On the **Meeting** tab, click the **Decline** button to display its menu.

11. Click **Respond Without Comments**. The meeting window closes, the event is removed from your calendar, and your updated response is sent to the meeting organizer.

✖ CLEAN UP No clean-up steps are required. You are ready to continue to the next exercise.

Setting Event Options

In addition to setting basic appointment and meeting information such as an event name, location, date, and time, you can set other options, such as the following:

- **Status** This option determines how the event will look on your shared Exchange calendar (if you have one). The options are Free, Tentative, Busy, and Out Of Office.

- **Reminder** You can use this option to set a reminder for the event. Choose an option from the pop-up menu. The times range from 0 Minutes to 2 Weeks. By default, this option is set to 15 Minutes, but you can change this default value in Calendar preferences.

    See Also The default reminder setting is covered in the section titled "Setting Calendar Options" in Chapter 8, "Managing Your Calendar."

- **Recurrence** You can use this option to set up repeating events, such as weekly meetings or monthly donut day. The recurrence feature is very flexible, making it possible to set up events to repeat based on days, weeks, months, or years.

- **Categorize** You can assign one or more categories to each event. This makes it possible to associate events with other categorized items, such as email messages and contacts.

    See Also Creating custom categories is covered in detail in the section titled "Managing Categories" in Chapter 14, "Using Shared Features."

- **Private** Clicking this button on an event's ribbon hides the event's details from others. This option works with shared Exchange calendars.

- **Request Responses** When you create a meeting, you can use this button to include a request for an RSVP. This option is turned on by default and makes it possible to include comments with the response. It also displays a prompt to send a decline message if the invitee later deletes the event from his or her calendar. Either way, the invitee will receive a message with response capabilities.

    Tip If an invitee does not respond but you have access to his or her Exchange calendar, Outlook will automatically record his or her response when you open the event on your calendar.

If you set a reminder, Outlook displays an Office Reminders window at the time you specified. For example, if you set the reminder to 15 minutes before the event (the default setting), the reminder window appears 15 minutes before the event time.

You can click the Snooze button to temporarily dismiss the reminder window for the default amount of time (5 minutes). If you click the arrow on the Snooze button, you can display a menu and choose a different length of time to temporarily dismiss the reminder window. The window will continue to reappear after the time interval you specify until you permanently dismiss it.

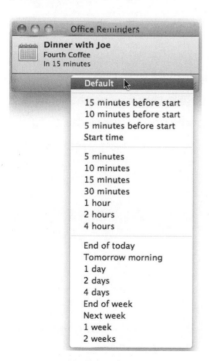

If you wanted to permanently dismiss the reminder window, you could click the Dismiss button. Clicking the triangle on the dismiss button displays a menu that includes a Dismiss All command, which dismisses all reminder windows that might be open.

In this exercise, you'll explore the other options you can set for an appointment or meeting by creating a new, recurring appointment and setting options for it.

SET UP In the view switcher, click Calendar. On the Home tab, click Month to switch to Month view. Then follow these steps.

1. Double-click the calendar box for today's date. An untitled appointment window opens.

2. In the **Subject** field, type **Staff Meeting**. The name appears in the title bar.

3. In the **Location** field, type **Room 123**.

4. In the **Starts** time field, set the time to approximately 15 minutes in the future.

5. If the **All day event** check box is selected, clear it.

6. Click the **Duration** pop-up menu to display its options, and then click **1 Hour**.

Status

7. On the **Appointment** tab, click the **Status** menu to display its options.

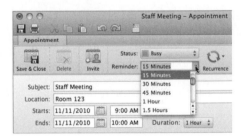

Note that you can choose any of these options to indicate your availability on an Exchange calendar. For now, leave it set to Busy.

Reminder

8. On the **Appointment** tab, click the triangle on the **Reminder** drop-down list to display its menu.

9. Click **5 Minutes**. You will probably have to scroll up to find it.

10. Click the **Recurrence** button to display its options. The wording of the options vary depending on the day of the week.

Recurrence

11. Click **Custom**. A dialog sheet for setting a custom repeating interval appears.

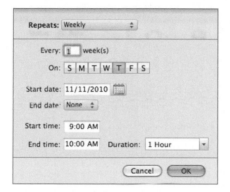

12. On the **Repeats** pop-up menu, make sure **Weekly** is selected.

13. In the **Every** box, type **2**.

14. In the **On** area, ensure that the button for the current day of the week is selected.

15. In the **End date** area, ensure that **None** is selected. This sets the appointment to be scheduled indefinitely into the future.

16. Ensure that the **Start date**, **Start time**, **End time**, and **Duration** fields are correct.

17. Click **OK**. The recurrence settings appear in the bottom of the appointment details area.

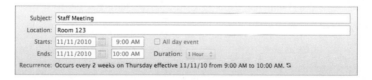

Categorize

18. On the **Appointment** tab, click the **Categorize** button to display a list of categories.

19. Click **Team**. The Team category is applied and the word *Team* appears in a blue oval in the appointment details area.

20. Repeat steps 18 and 19, but this time, click **Manager**. The Manager category is also applied and *Manager* appears in a magenta oval beside *Team*. You can apply as many categories as you like.

Private

21. On the **Appointment** tab, click the **Private** button. The button is now active and turns dark gray. If you saved the event, its details would not appear on a shared calendar.

22. Click the **Private** button again. The button is deselected and turns light gray again.

23. On the **Appointment** tab, click the **Save & Close** button. The appointment is saved to your calendar and the appointment window closes.

24. Examine your calendar for today's date. You should see the appointment you just created, colored magenta.

25. Examine the calendar for the rest of the month and the next few months. The appointment should repeat every two weeks.

26. Wait for the **Office Reminder** window for today's occurrence to open. When it does, click the arrow on the **Snooze** button and then click **10 minutes**. The reminder disappears. If it reappears again as you complete the exercise, click its **Dismiss** button to permanently dismiss it.

27. Select one of the appointments in the series, and then press Delete. A confirmation dialog sheet appears, asking if you want to delete this occurrence.

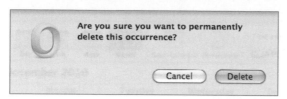

28. Click **Delete**. The selected occurrence is deleted. You can use this technique to delete a single event—for example, if a regularly scheduled meeting is canceled.

29. Double-click another one of the appointments in the series to open its appointment occurrence window.

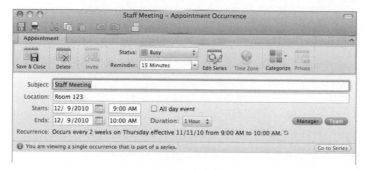

30. Change the **Starts** time field to **9:30**.

31. On the **Appointment** tab, click the **Save & Close** button. Just this one occurrence is changed.

32. Double-click the same appointment to reopen its appointment occurrence window.

Edit Series

33. On the **Appointment** tab, click the **Edit Series** button. The appointment series window appears in place of the appointment occurrence window.

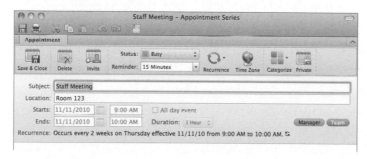

34. Click the arrows icon at the right end of the **Recurrence** line. The recurrence dialog sheet appears again.

35. Change the **Starts** time to **10:00 AM**, and then click **OK**.

36. On the **Appointment** tab, click the **Save & Close** button. All occurrences are changed to the new time.

37. Double-click any of the appointments in the series to open it.

38. On the **Appointment** tab, click the **Edit Series** button.

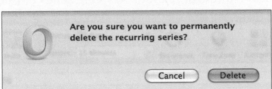
Delete

39. On the **Appointment** tab, click the **Delete** button. A confirmation dialog sheet appears, asking if you want to delete the recurring series.

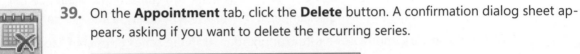

Are you sure you want to permanently delete the recurring series?

Cancel   Delete

40. Click **Delete**. All appointments in the series are removed from your calendar.

CLEAN UP No clean-up steps are required. You are ready to continue with exercises in the next chapter.

Key Points

- You can schedule appointments and meetings on your Outlook calendar.
- Meetings differ from appointments in that they include invitees.
- Outlook can automatically track responses from invitees to the meetings you organize.
- When you respond to a meeting invitation, Outlook can add the meeting to your calendar.
- You can set up appointments and meetings to recur regularly.
- The Office Reminder window can remind you about calendar items.
- When you set a calendar item as private, its details are not shared with others.

Chapter at a Glance

Set Calendar preferences to control the way the calendar feature looks and works, **page 214**

Move events from one calendar to another, **page 219**

Set permissions for another Exchange user to view your calendar, **page 224**

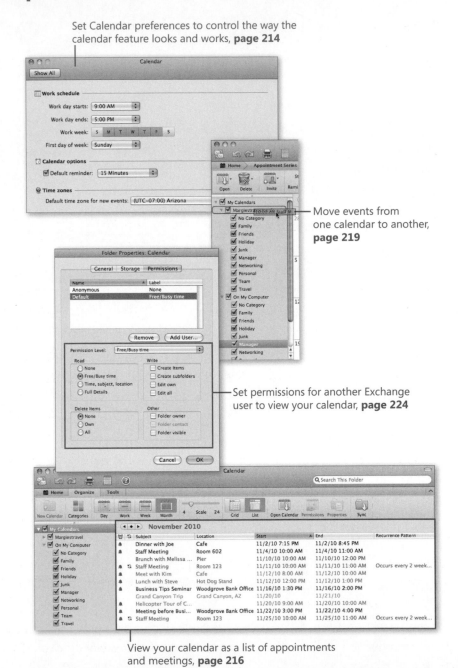

View your calendar as a list of appointments and meetings, **page 216**

8 Managing Your Calendar

In this chapter, you will learn how to

- ✔ Set calendar options.
- ✔ Work with calendar views.
- ✔ Work with multiple calendars.
- ✔ Share calendar information.
- ✔ Print calendars.

As you add events to your calendar to plan the days and weeks ahead, you may find your calendar filling up with the appointments and meetings that make up your business and personal life. Life is complicated—and busy!—these days, and using the calendar features of Microsoft Outlook for Mac 2011 is a good way to keep on top of things.

Outlook for Mac has a number of features that make managing your calendar easier. For example, it enables you to view your calendar a number of ways—by day, work week, calendar week, or month—so you can see your schedule in a way that's most meaningful to you. You can even use the My Day window to focus on the calendar items and tasks you need to do today.

If you use the category feature of Outlook, you can fine-tune the display of events to include only those categories you need to see when you need to see them. And if you're juggling more than one set of events—for example, the events of your work and family life—you can separate them by creating multiple calendars. This is especially useful if your work calendar is shared via a Microsoft Exchange Server.

If you have a Microsoft Exchange account, your Exchange calendar is visible to your co-workers and theirs are visible to you. This makes it easier to schedule meetings at times when all invitees are available.

In this chapter, you'll start by learning about Outlook Calendar preferences, which you might want to change to customize the way calendar features work for you. Then you'll learn how to work with calendar views, including the My Day window, and manage multiple calendars within Outlook. Finally, you'll learn how to share your calendar with other Exchange users and how to print it for reference when you're away from your computer.

> **Practice Files** No practice files are needed for this chapter. You can complete exercises with items on your calendar as well as items created for this and other chapters. For more information about practice file requirements, see "Using the Practice Files" at the beginning of this book.

Setting Calendar Options

Outlook Calendar preferences include a number of options that you might want to change to fine-tune the way Outlook works for you. To access these settings, open the Outlook Preferences window and then click the Calendar icon.

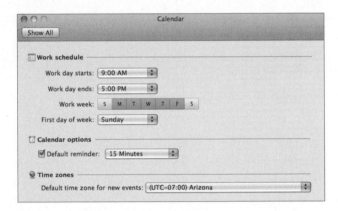

Options are broken down into three major areas:

● **Work Schedule** These options control the appearance of the day, work week, week, and month views. You can set four different work schedule options:

  ○ **Work day starts** This is the usual start time for your work day. Choose a time from the pop-up menu. In Day, Work Week, and Week view, times before this time are shaded gray. By default, this option is set for 9:00 AM.

  ○ **Work day ends** This is the usual end time for your work day. Choose a time from the pop-up menu. In Day, Work Week, and Week view, times after this time are shaded gray. By default, this option is set for 5:00 PM.

  ○ **Work week** This is a series of buttons representing the days of the week you usually work. Click a button to toggle its setting. Dark gray buttons are selected. The days you select determine which days appear in Work Week view and which days do not appear shaded gray in Week view. By default, this option is set for Monday through Friday.

○ **First day of week** This is the first day of the week as you want it to appear on your calendar. By default, this option is set to Sunday, but it can be set to any day of the week. Note that this will dramatically change the appearance of your calendar in Work Week, Week, and Month views.

● **Calendar options** This option controls the default reminder for new appointments and meetings. When the check box is selected, the default reminder time chosen from the pop-up menu is used. The options on the pop-up menu range from 0 Minutes to 2 Weeks. If you don't want reminders set by default—in other words, you want the reminder options set to None—clear the Default Reminder check box.

● **Time zones** This option enables you to set the default time zone for new events. Use the pop-up menu to choose your time zone. You can override this setting for a calendar item in an appointment or meeting window.

When you're finished checking or changing options, click the window's close button to dismiss it. Your settings are automatically saved.

In this exercise, you'll explore the Calendar preferences within Outlook and make changes to better meet your needs.

 SET UP You don't need any practice files to complete this exercise. With Outlook open and active, in the view switcher, click Calendar. Then, on the Home tab, click Week and follow these steps.

1. On the menu bar, click **Outlook**, and then click **Preferences**, or press Command+, (comma). The Outlook Preferences window opens.

2. Click the **Calendar** icon. The Calendar preferences pane appears.

3. In the **Work schedule** area, use the pop-up menu and buttons to set your usual work day start and end times, work week days, and the first day of the week. As you make changes, you may see them in the calendar window behind the Calendar preferences pane.

4. Choose your preferred default reminder time for new events from the pop-up menu under **Calendar options**. If you prefer Outlook to not automatically set a reminder, clear the **Default reminder** check box.

5. If your time zone is not correctly indicated in the pop-up menu under **Time zones**, choose it from the menu.

6. On the window's title bar, click the close button. The window closes.

Appointment

7. If you made changes to the default reminder option, on the **Home** tab, click the **Appointment** button to open an untitled appointment window. The Reminder drop-down list should indicate the default option you selected. Click the window's close button to dismiss it without creating an appointment.

✖ **CLEAN UP** No clean-up steps are required. You are ready to continue to the next exercise.

Working with Calendar Views

You can modify the overall view of your calendar to best meet your needs. In addition to switching between Day, Work Week, Week, and Month view, you can:

● Specify which categories should be displayed.

● Set the hours scale to determine how many hours fit in a window.

● Toggle between grid and list views.

If you use the category feature extensively to color-code calendar events and other Outlook items based on topic or project, you can fine-tune the display of calendar items by indicating which categories should be displayed. In the navigation pane, select or clear check boxes beside the categories. If you have multiple calendars, you'll need to do this individually for each calendar.

See Also You can learn more about assigning categories to calendar items in the section titled "Setting Event Options" in Chapter 7, "Scheduling Appointments and Meetings," and about working with categories in the section titled "Managing Categories" in Chapter 14, "Using Shared Features."

If a category check box is selected, items with that category assigned will appear on the calendar. If a category check box is cleared, items with that category assigned will not appear on the calendar. If a calendar item has more than one category assigned and at least one of those categories is selected, the item will appear on the calendar.

If you're displaying your calendar in Day, Work Week, or Week view, you can change the scale of the window's grid to display more or fewer hours of the day within the window. On the Organize tab, drag the Scale slider to the left or right. Dragging to the left shows fewer hours in the window; dragging to the right shows more hours in the window. By dragging this slider, you can view from 4 to 24 hours in the window.

No matter which calendar view you're in, you can switch from the default grid view to a list view by clicking the List button on the Organize tab. List view shows calendar items in a list, with multiple columns of information. You can sort this list by clicking a column heading: one click sorts in ascending order and a second click on the same heading sorts in descending order.

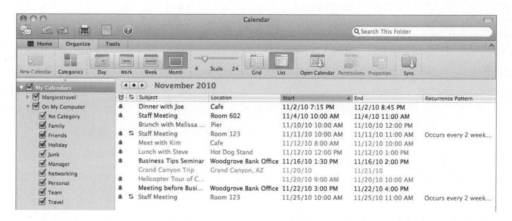

To switch back to grid view, click the Grid button on the Organize tab.

In this exercise, you'll explore options to change the view of your calendar by using the navigation bar and Organize tab.

SET UP To see these features in action, it's best to have several calendar items with a variety of different categories applied. You can use existing calendar items or create new ones following the instructions in Chapter 7. Then, in the view switcher, click Calendar and, on the Organize tab, click Month. You're now ready to follow these instructions.

1. If necessary, in the navigation pane, click the disclosure triangle beside each of your calendars to display all categories.

2. Experiment with clearing and selecting various check boxes. Note the change in your calendar.

   Tip If you clear the check box for a calendar, all of that calendar's events are hidden.

Week

3. On the **Organize** tab, click the **Week** button to switch to **Week** view.

4. On the **Organize** tab, drag the **Scale** slider to the right.

Each hour box gets smaller so more hours fit in the window.

5. Drag the **Scale** slider to the left. Each hour box gets bigger so fewer hours fit in the window.

List

6. Drag the **Scale** slider to the position you prefer.

7. On the **Organize** tab, click the **List** button. The calendar changes to list view. All calendar items for the current week appear in the list.

Next

8. At the top of the calendar area, click the **Next** button to display the following week's events.

9. On the **Organize** tab, click the **Month** button. The list now includes all calendar items for the month.

Month

10. At the top of the calendar item list, click the **Subject** heading. The list items are sorted alphabetically by subject.

11. Click the **Subject** heading again. The list is sorted alphabetically in descending order by subject.

12. At the top of the calendar item list, click the **Start** heading. The list is sorted in date order.

Grid

13. On the **Organize** tab, click the **Grid** button. The calendar returns to standard grid view.

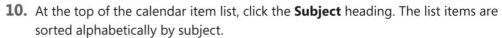 

CLEAN UP No clean-up steps are required. You are ready to continue to the next exercise.

Working with Multiple Calendars

Outlook supports multiple calendars or calendar folders. In fact, if you have an Exchange account and another type of email account, Outlook has probably already created two calendars for you. These are considered *primary* calendars because they're created automatically by Outlook as part of your email account setup.

All of your calendars are listed in the navigation pane. If you have only one calendar, its name is simply *Calendar*. If you have multiple calendars, they're listed in the navigation pane under the My Calendars heading; you can click a disclosure triangle, if necessary, to see them. When you have multiple calendars created by Outlook, they're named based on your Exchange account name or *On My Computer*.

See Also You can set options in the Categories preferences pane to specify which categories appear in the navigation pane. Consult the section titled "Managing Categories" in Chapter 14 to learn how.

If, for some reason, you want to create a new calendar, you can do so by adding a new folder to the navigation pane in Calendar view. If you have one calendar, select the Calendar heading and choose Folder from the New button on the Home tab. If you have multiple calendars, select the On My Computer heading and choose Folder from the New button on the Home tab. A new Untitled Folder appears.

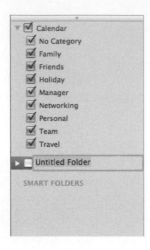
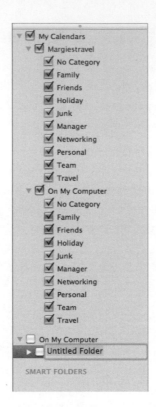

You can then type in a name for the folder to use it as a new calendar.

To delete a calendar you created, select its name and choose Delete from the Edit menu or press Command+Delete. A confirmation dialog sheet appears; you'll have to click the Delete button to remove the calendar.

Important When you delete a calendar, you delete all items on that calendar.

Tip You cannot delete a calendar created by Outlook.

Each calendar uses the same list of categories, which appear beneath the calendar name. When you add or remove categories, the categories are added to or removed from all calendars.

See Also Adding and removing categories is covered in the section titled "Managing Categories" in Chapter 14.

If you have multiple calendars, Outlook adds a new appointment or meeting to the calendar that was selected when you created the event. If you add an event to the wrong calendar, you can always move it from one calendar to another. Simply drag the event from the calendar window onto the name of the calendar you want to move it to.

When you release the mouse button, the event is moved to the calendar you dragged it to. You might find this useful if you created a work-related event on a personal calendar and need to move it to your Exchange calendar so coworkers can see it.

See Also When you open a coworker's calendar in Outlook, it also appears in the navigation pane. Sharing calendars with coworkers is covered in the section titled "Sharing Calendar Information" later in this chapter.

In this exercise, you'll create a new calendar, add two appointments to it, and then move one appointment to another calendar. You'll also delete the new calendar and its appointment.

 SET UP If Calendar view is not already showing, in the view switcher, click Calendar. On the Home tab, click Week. You can now follow these steps.

1. Start by adding a new calendar folder:

    ○ If you only have one calendar, in the navigation pane, select the **Calendar** heading.

    ○ If you have more than one calendar, in the navigation pane, select the **On My Computer** heading.

New

2. On the **Home** tab, click the **New** button to display its menu of options.

3. Click **Folder**. A new *Untitled Folder* item appears in the navigation pane.

4. While the item name is still selected, type **Home Calendar**, and press Return. The item is named *Home Calendar*.

5. In the navigation pane, click the disclosure triangle to the left of **Home Calendar** to display a list of categories within it.

6. In the navigation pane, select the **Home Calendar** check box. The check boxes for all categories beneath it also become selected.

7. In the navigation pane, select **Family** beneath **Home Calendar**.

8. On the **Home** tab, click **Appointment**. An untitled appointment window appears. The Family category is already applied to it.

Save & Close

9. Name the appointment **Dinner with Family** and set it up for later today at 7:00 P.M. Then, on the **Appointment** tab, click the **Save & Close** button to add it to your calendar.

See Also If you need help creating an appointment, consult the section titled "Scheduling Appointments" in Chapter 7.

10. In the calendar window, scroll down so you can see the new appointment on your calendar.

11. In the navigation pane, clear the check box beside the name of each of your other calendars. All events should disappear except the one on your new calendar.

12. In the navigation pane, select **Home Calendar**.

13. Create another new appointment. This time, schedule it for Friday at lunchtime. Name it **Lunch with Joe**. Close the appointment window. Note that it is created with No Category assigned to it.

14. Although the new appointment was created on your personal calendar, it really should belong on a work-related calendar. Drag the appointment box from the calendar window to the Networking category under another calendar in the navigation pane.

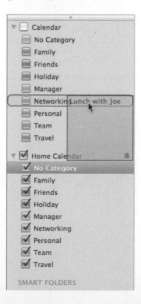

The appointment disappears.

15. In the navigation pane, select the check box beside the name of the calendar you dragged the appointment to. The appointment reappears in the same calendar location, now colored orange. Not only has it been moved to the other calendar, but that calendar's Networking category has been applied to it.

16. In the navigation pane, clear the check box beside **Home Calendar**. Only the first appointment you created for this calendar disappears.

17. Select the check box beside **Home Calendar** to display its appointment again.

18. In the navigation pane, select the **Home Calendar** heading.

19. Press Command+Delete. A confirmation dialog sheet appears.

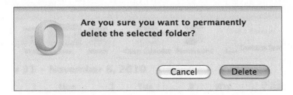

20. Click **Delete**. The Home Calendar and its appointment disappear.

 CLEAN UP Select the Lunch With Joe appointment and press Delete. Then click Delete in the confirmation dialog sheet that appears. You can now continue to the next exercise.

Sharing Calendar Information

If you have an account on a Microsoft Exchange Server, your Exchange account's calendar can be shared with other users on that server. At the same time, you may be able to access the calendars maintained by your coworkers for their accounts. This is common in a workplace that uses Exchange and related services. It makes it possible to see what your coworkers are doing so it's easier to set up meetings with them.

To share your calendar with other Exchange users, you need to set permissions for the calendar's folder. You do this with the Permissions pane of the Folder Properties dialog box. To display this dialog box, in the navigation pane, select the Exchange calendar and then click the Permissions button on the Home tab.

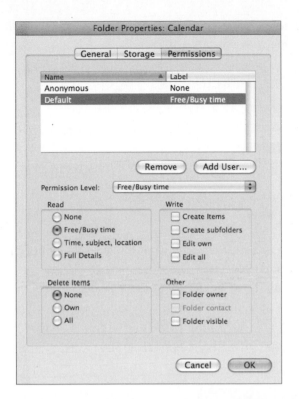

Tip How access to your calendar is allowed depends, in part, on the Exchange server settings; it may or may not allow anonymous or default users. Your network administrator should be able to tell you more.

You can use the Permissions pane to add specific individuals and groups with accounts on your Exchange server who can access your calendar. Start by clicking the Add User button in the Permissions pane to display the Select User dialog box. Enter all or part of the user's name and click Find to locate the user's account.

In the Select User dialog box, select the account you want to add, and click OK. The user is added to the Permissions pane with default settings.

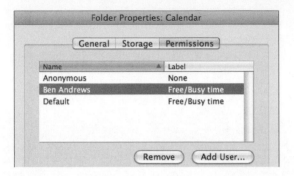

For each account you add, you can specify exactly what the account owner can do: read items, write (or change) items, or delete items. This determines the level of details that appear in the Scheduling Assistant to other Exchange users who schedule meetings. With the account selected, choose an option from the Permission Level pop-up menu. This menus offers a number of preconfigured options based on the kind of user you're adding; when you choose one of these options, the settings in the Permissions pane change accordingly.

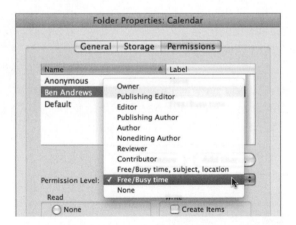

If you want the user to be able to see items on your calendar, you'll need to choose an option that enables the Folder Visible check box. Two commonly used options are:

- **Reviewer** This option enables the user to see the full details of your calendar but not make any changes to it.

- **Editor** This option enables the user to see, modify, and delete the full details of your calendar. Be sure you grant this permission to only those users you trust.

Tip If you're not sure how to set permission levels for a user on your calendar, discuss these options with your network administrator.

When you're finished setting user options, click OK to save them.

If another user has set you up to access his or her calendar, you can open the calendar in Outlook on your computer. On the Home tab, click the Open Calendar button to display the Open Other User's Folder dialog box. Type all or part of the user's name in the User box and make sure Calendar is selected from the Type pop-up menu.

When you click OK, Outlook displays the Select User dialog box to list matches to what you entered. Select the account you want to add and click Select. Outlook connects to the server to check permissions. One of two things happens:

● If the proper permissions are set up for your account, the folder appears in the navigation pane under Shared Calendars.

● If the proper permissions are not set up for your account, a dialog box tells you Outlook can't open the folder and refers you back to the calendar owner.

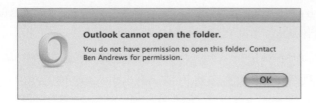

Tip In order for you to be able to see another user's calendar folder and the items within it, the user must include the Full Details and Folder Visible permissions for your account.

In this exercise, you'll set up permissions for another Exchange user to access your calendar. You'll also open another Exchange user's calendar on your computer.

 SET UP To complete this exercise, you must have a Microsoft Exchange account set up on your computer and be part of a Microsoft Exchange network with at least one other user. To open another user's calendar on your computer, that user must set up access permissions for your account. If necessary, in the view switcher, click Calendar. Then, in the navigation pane, select the name of your Exchange calendar. You can then follow these steps.

Permissions

1. On the **Home** tab, click the **Permissions** button. The Permissions pane of the Folder Properties: Calendar dialog box appears.

2. In the **Permissions** pane, click **Add User**. The Select User dialog box appears.

3. In the search box at the top of the dialog box, enter all or part of the name of another user on your Exchange server, and then click **Find**. Outlook queries the server and, in the bottom of the Select User dialog box, displays a list of accounts that match what you entered.

4. In the search results, select the name of the user you want to add permissions for, and then click **OK**. The user's name is added to the list in the Permissions pane.

5. In the **Permissions** pane, select the name of the user you just added.

6. On the **Permission Level** pop-up menu, click **Reviewer**. The Full Details and Folder Visible options become selected in the permissions detail area at the bottom of the dialog box.

7. Click **OK**. The person you added can now see the details of your calendar on his or her computer.

Open Calendar

8. On the **Home** tab, click the **Open Calendar** button. The Open Other User's Folder dialog box appears.

9. In the **User** box of the **Open Other User's Folder** dialog box, type all or part of the name of the user whose calendar you want to open.

10. Make sure **Calendar** is selected from the **Type** pop-up menu.

11. Click **OK**. Outlook queries the server and displays the Select User dialog box with a list of users that match what you typed.

12. In the **Select User** dialog box, select the name of the user whose calendar you want to open, and then click **Select**. If all permissions settings are correct, the dialog boxes should disappear and, after a moment, the user's calendar appears in the navigation pane under Shared Calendars.

13. In the navigation pane, select the check box for the user's calendar. His or her calendar events should appear on your calendar.

14. (Optional) To remove the shared calendar from Outlook, in the navigation pane, right-click the calendar name, and then click **Remove from View** on the contextual menu that appears.

The shared calendar disappears.

15. (Optional) To stop sharing your calendar, in the navigation pane, select your Exchange calendar and then, on the **Home** tab, click the **Permissions** button. In the **Permissions** pane, select the name of the user you want to stop sharing with and click **Remove**. Then click **OK**.

✖ **CLEAN UP** No clean-up steps are required. You can continue to the next exercise.

Printing Calendars

Outlook enables you to print your calendar in four different styles: Day, Work Week, Week, and Month. You can print all events on a calendar or just events tagged with the selected categories. You can even specify a start and end date for the printout, so it covers the exact period you need to print. You do all this in the Print dialog box.

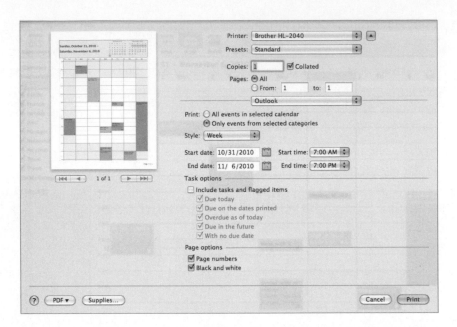

You open the Print dialog box just as you would in any other Mac OS application: by choosing Print from the File menu or by pressing Command+P. In Outlook, you can also click the print icon on the toolbar.

The Print dialog box has two different appearances: a collapsed version that shows only the Printer and Presets pop-up menus and a handful of buttons or the expanded version that shows all options, as well as a print preview. To switch from one to the other, click the disclosure triangle beside the Printer pop-up menu.

Exact printer options vary based on your printer, but the Outlook options in the lower half of the dialog box should be the same no matter what printer you have:

- **Print** You can use this option to select whether you want to print all events in the selected calendar or just those events in the selected calendar that are displayed.

- **Style** Use this pop-up menu to indicate whether you want to print a Day, Work Week, Week, or Month calendar. If you choose Month, the time options disappear.

- **Start date, Start time, End date, and End time** These options enable you to set the range of dates and times to print. Keep in mind that if you have events scheduled outside of each day's time frame, they will not appear on the printed calendar.

- **Task options** Use these options to include a list of tasks in a column on the right side of the printed page. When you select the Include Tasks And Flagged Items check box, you can toggle check boxes to determine which tasks are included.

  See Also Tasks are covered in detail in Chapter 12, "Tracking Tasks."

● **Page options**   These options determine how pages will print:

   ○ **Page numbers**   This option prints page numbers on each page. This is espe-cially important if your printout is more than one or two pages long.

   ○ **Black and white**   This option prints in shades of gray rather than color. Use this option if you don't have a color printer or would prefer not to print in color.

Tip If Outlook options are not displayed, you can show them by choosing Outlook from the pop-up menu beneath the Pages boxes near the top of the dialog box.

Each time you make a change in one of the settings, the preview area may change ac-cordingly. If your printout will be more than one page, you can use the arrow buttons beneath the preview to see what each page will look like when printed.

When you're ready to print, click the Print button at the lower-right corner of the dialog box. The document is sent to the printer.

Tip You can use options under the PDF menu at the bottom of the Print dialog box to create, email, or fax a PDF of your document. You might find this handy to share a "hard copy" of your calendar without actually printing it. You can learn more about this Mac OS X feature in Mac OS help.

In this exercise, you'll open the Print dialog box and explore some of its printing options.

SET UP In the view switcher, click Calendar. In the navigation pane, select a calendar. On the Home tab, click the Week button. Then follow these steps.

Print

1. On the toolbar, click the **Print** button. The Print dialog box appears.

2. If the dialog box does not include options and a preview area, click the disclosure triangle beside the **Printer** pop-up menu.

3. By default, Week is selected from the Style pop-up menu. That's because the cal-endar was displayed in Week view when you opened the Print dialog box. On the **Style** pop-up menu, click **Month**. Three things happen:

   ○ The preview changes to show an entire month.

   ○ The dates change to encompass the entire month.

   ○ The time pop-up menus disappear.

4. On the **Style** menu, click **Day**. The preview area shows a single day from the begin-ning of the month.

5. On the **Style** menu, click **Work Week**. The preview area shows a work week period from the beginning of the month.

6. Beneath the preview area, use the arrows to scroll through all pages of the printout.

7. In the **Start date** field, enter today's date. The preview area may change to show a different work week.

   Tip You can click the calendar icon to use a date picker to enter the date.

8. In the **End date** field, enter the date a week from today. The number of pages in the report changes to 2. When you print a Work Week or Week, entire weeks are printed.

9. On the **Start time** menu, click **10:00 AM**. The calendar grid in the preview area changes to show fewer boxes.

10. On the **End time** menu, click **9:00 PM**. The calendar grid changes again, this time to show more grid boxes.

11. Select the **Include tasks and flagged items** check box. A column with tasks appears on the right side of the preview.

12. Clear the **Page numbers** option. The page number footer disappears from the preview area.

13. Clear the **Black and white** check box. The preview appears in color.

14. (Optional) Click **Print**. The two pages of the calendar are sent to your printer and the Print dialog box disappears.

✖ **CLEAN UP** If you did not print the calendar, click the Cancel button in the Print dialog box to dismiss it without printing.

Key Points

- You can set Calendar preferences to control the appearance and operation of some calendar features.

- You can view your calendar in a number of ways.

- You can have more than one calendar.

- If you have multiple calendars, you can move calendar items between them.

- You can set permissions to share your Exchange calendar with other users on your Exchange server.

- If permissions for your Exchange account are set so you can view another user's calendar, you can open that calendar in Outlook on your computer.

- You can print your calendar in Day, Work Week, Week, or Month view.

Part 4

Contacts

Chapter at a Glance

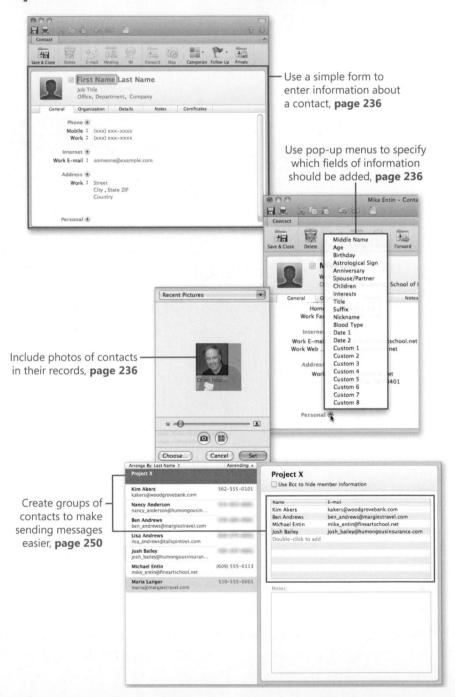

Use a simple form to enter information about a contact, **page 236**

Use pop-up menus to specify which fields of information should be added, **page 236**

Include photos of contacts in their records, **page 236**

Create groups of contacts to make sending messages easier, **page 250**

9 Managing Contact Information

In this chapter, you will learn how to

- ✔ Create contact records.
- ✔ View contact information.
- ✔ Modify and delete contact records.
- ✔ Work with contact groups.

The Contacts view in Microsoft Outlook for Mac 2011 makes it easy to maintain an address book or contacts list of all the people you know and keep in touch with. For each contact, you can maintain a wide variety of information, including name, photo, job title, company, phone numbers, Internet addresses, mailing addresses, birthday, spouse/partner name, interests, and even blood type. You can also use custom fields to track other information that is important to you, such as a contact's favorite color or restaurant. And if that isn't enough, you can use a freeform Notes field to enter any kind of information you want about a contact.

Outlook for Mac maintains all of this information in its contacts list, which you can organize by name or any other data field. It uses this information throughout the other views in Outlook, making it easy to send an email message to a contact or invite a contact to a meeting. Information can be consulted or updated at any time. You can also delete contact records for people you no longer need to keep in touch with.

If you often need to contact multiple people at once, you can create a contact group that includes all of these people. For example, suppose you're working on a project that requires you to include five specific people in all project-related email messages. You can create a group for the project and add those five people to it. Then, when you write an email message, you simply address it to the group. Outlook automatically sends the message to each person in the group.

In this chapter, we'll begin working with Contacts view to add, modify, and delete contact records and groups. Along the way, you'll learn how to view the details for your contacts.

Important You'll use the contacts you create in this chapter as practice files for exercises in later chapters of this book.

> **Practice Files** Before you can complete the exercises in this chapter, you need to copy the book's practice files to your computer. The practice files you'll use to complete the exercises in this chapter are in the Chapter09 practice files folder. A complete list of practice files is provided in "Using the Practice Files" at the beginning of this book.

Creating Contact Records

Each contact's information is stored in a separate contact record. A *record* is a collection of information about one contact. All of a contact's information should be included in the contact's single record.

Although a contact is often a person, it can also be a company. For example, you might have a contact record for the local phone company that includes its customer service phone number and your account number. It isn't necessary to identify a specific individual at a company unless you do business with a specific person there.

Each contact record includes multiple fields of information. A *field* is a specific kind of information, such as a name, phone number, or ZIP code. Outlook offers the following fields for contact records:

- **Name** Outlook includes several fields for entering the name of a contact, including:
  - ○ First Name
  - ○ Last Name
- **Job Information** Job information fields include:
  - ○ Job Title
  - ○ Office
  - ○ Department
  - ○ Company
- **Picture** You can include a photo or company icon for a contact. This image will appear for the contact in various places throughout Outlook.
- **Phone Numbers** You can record multiple phone numbers for each contact. Outlook provides the following fields for phone numbers:
  - ○ Mobile
  - ○ Work and Work 2

- ❍ Home and Home 2

- ❍ Work Fax

- ❍ Home Fax

- ❍ Page

- ❍ Primary

- ❍ Assistant

- ❍ Phone 1, Phone 2, Phone 3, and Phone 4

- ● **Internet Information** You can store multiple types of Internet information for each contact:

  - ❍ Work Email

  - ❍ Home Email

  - ❍ Other Email

  - ❍ IM Address (for instant messaging)

  - ❍ Work Web Page

  - ❍ Home Web Page

- ● **Address** Outlook supports multiple fields for Work and Home address. For each set, you have several fields:

  - ❍ Street

  - ❍ City

  - ❍ State

  - ❍ ZIP (or postal code)

  - ❍ Country

  Tip Entering complete street addresses makes it possible to map contacts using Bing.

- ● **Personal Information** You can include a number of other fields in each record as needed:

  - ❍ Middle Name (which could be used for middle initial)

  - ❍ Age (this field is automatically calculated if you enter information in the Birthday field)

  - ❍ Birthday

  - ❍ Astrological Sign

  - ❍ Anniversary

○ Spouse/Partner

○ Children

○ Interests

○ Title (such as Mrs. or Dr.)

○ Suffix (such as Jr. or III)

○ Nickname

○ Blood Type

○ Date 1 and Date 2 (for other dates you might want to store)

○ Custom 1 – 8 (for use however you see fit)

You don't have to fill in every field for a contact—in fact, you probably won't. But it's good to know that fields are available if you need them.

You create a contact record by filling in a form in the header area and General pane of a contact window. Each field includes either the field name or some guidance text to help you enter information correctly.

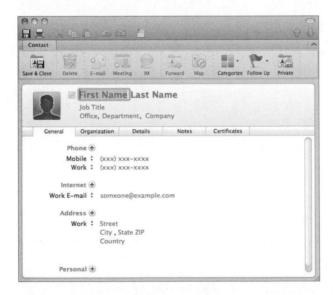

When you open the contact window, only minimum fields appear; you can use + buttons for each type of field to add more fields if you need them. If the wrong name appears beside a field, you can click the menu button beside the field name to change the name of the field. If you leave a field blank, Outlook automatically removes it from the contact record when you save it; you can always add it back if you need it later.

When you're finished entering information, click the Save & Close button on the Contact tab to save the information. The newly created contact record appears in the item list with your other contacts.

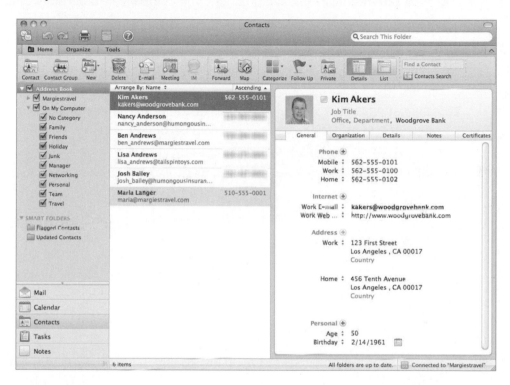

In this exercise, you'll create a new contact record that includes a variety of information about a contact.

SET UP You need access to the Mike Entin image file in the Finder to complete this exercise. This image is located in the Chapter09 practice files folder. In the view switcher within Outlook, click Contacts. Then follow these steps.

1. If you have more than one contacts list in the navigation pane, select the one you want to add the contact to.

Contact

2. On the **Home** tab, click the **Contact** button. An untitled contact window appears with its First Name field selected.

3. Type **Mike**, and press Tab. The name *Mike* appears in the title bar and the Last Name field becomes selected.

4. Type **Entin**, and press Tab. Mike's last name appears in the title bar and the Job Title field becomes selected.

5. Type **Web Designer**, and press Tab. The Office field becomes selected.

6. We don't need to enter anything in the **Office** field, so press Tab again to skip it. The Department field becomes selected.

7. Type **Communications**, and press Tab. The Company field becomes selected.

8. Type **School of Fine Arts**, and press Tab. The Mobile field under Phone becomes selected.

9. Type **(609) 555-0112**, and press Tab. The Work field under Phone becomes selected.

10. Type **6095550113**, and press Tab. Outlook reformats the phone number using the default format, and the Work E-mail field becomes selected.

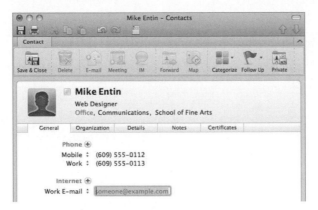

11. Click the **+** button beside **Phone** to display a menu of phone number fields.

12. Click **Work Fax**. The Work Fax field is added to the window and becomes selected.

Phone ⊕
Mobile : (609) 555-0112
Work : (609) 555-0113
Work Fax : (xxx) xxx-xxxx

13. Type **6095550114**, and press Tab. The phone number is formatted and entered into the field, and the Work E-mail field becomes selected again.

14. Click the arrow button beside the **Work** phone number field to display a menu of field names.

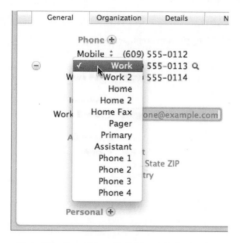

15. Click **Home**. The field is relabeled as the Home phone number field.

16. In the **Work E-mail** field, type **mike_entin@fineartschool.net**.

17. Click the + button beside **Internet** to display a menu of Internet fields.

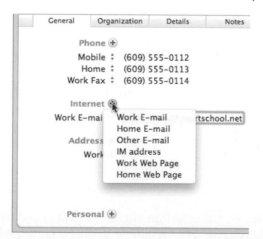

18. Click **Work Web Page**. The Work Web Page field is added to the window and becomes selected.

19. Type **www.fineartschool.net**, and press Tab. The Street field beside Work becomes selected.

20. Type the following address into the **Street**, **City**, **State**, and **ZIP** fields: **123 Main Street, Atlantic City, NJ 88401**.

21. Click the **+** button beside **Personal**. (You may have to scroll down in the window to see it.) A menu of personal information fields appears.

22. Click **Birthday** to add the **Birthday** and **Age** fields to the window.

23. In the **Birthday** field, enter your birth date. Outlook automatically enters your current age in the Age field.

Tip Although you can click the Calendar icon beside the field to use a date picker window to enter the date, you might find it quicker to simply type it.

Tip You can add a reminder to your calendar by pointing to the Birthday field and clicking the Add Reminder button. An all-day event is added to your calendar on that date, recurring every year, with a reminder 18 hours before it.

24. In the window's header area, double-click the **Picture** placeholder. A dialog sheet for setting a picture appears.

25. Click the **Choose** button and use the **Open** dialog box that appears to navigate to the **Chapter09** folder.

26. Select the **Mike Entin** image file and click **Open**. The image appears in the dialog sheet.

27. If necessary, drag the scaling slider near the bottom of the dialog sheet to change the image magnification. You can also drag the image around in the window to position it for cropping.

28. When the box surrounds the part of the image you want to include, click **Set**. The image appears in the header area of the contact window.

Save & Close

29. On the **Contact** tab, click the **Save & Close** button. The window closes and the new contact is added to your contacts list.

✖ **CLEAN UP** No clean-up steps are required. You will continue working with this contact record in other exercises throughout this chapter.

Viewing Contact Information

In Contacts view, the list view pane of the Outlook window lists all of your contacts. For each record, you'll see the contact name, email address, and phone number. You can use list view as a quick reference for each of your contacts.

There are two ways to view a contact's detailed information:

● Select the contact name in the item list and view the contact's information in the reading pane.

● Double-click a contact name in the item list and view the contact's information in the contact window.

Either method gives you access to all of a contact's information. Not only can you view the information in the contact header area, but you can also see the information in each pane of the contact window:

● **General** This pane shows the most information for a contact. It's where you enter all contact information.

● **Organization** This pane displays organizational information for a contact if that contact is listed on an LDAP server associated with a Microsoft Exchange Server account set up in Outlook.

● **Details** This pane displays additional information for a contact if that contact is listed on an LDAP server associated with an Exchange account set up in Outlook.

Important Because LDAP is generally blocked outside of firewalls, LDAP information will be disabled for Exchange users who are roaming. VPN is a common solution for this issue; consult your system administrator to learn more.

- **Notes** This pane displays any notes you may have entered for the contact. This is a free-form field where you can enter any information you like related to a contact.

- **Certificates** This pane is where you store encryption certificates you use to exchange secure email messages with a contact.

  See Also Using certificates is covered in the section titled "Securing Your Email" in Chapter 6, "Fine-Tuning Email Settings."

Adding Encryption Certificates

If you plan to exchange encrypted email with a contact, you'll need to store an encryption certificate for the contact in the Certificates pane of his or her contact record. There are two ways to do this:

- Open a message from a sender that is digitally signed. In the information area at the top of the message, click Details and then click Add Encryption Certificate To Contacts.

- If the certificate has been saved as a file on your computer, in the Certificates pane of the contact's record, click the + button. Then use the dialog box that appears to locate, open, and select the contact's certificate file.

Tip If you don't send or receive encrypted email, you don't need to worry about encryption certificates.

A list of certificates saved for a contact appears in the Certificates pane for the contact. Each certificate is associated with a specific email address, so if a person has more than one email address, he or she may have more than one encryption certificate.

In this exercise, you'll view contact records in a variety of ways to see what information appears and where it can be found.

SET UP You need to have created the Mike Entin contact record in the previous exercise to complete this exercise. If Contacts view is not displayed, in the view switcher, click Contacts. Then follow these steps.

1. In the navigation pane, make sure the **My Contacts** check box is selected and then click **My Contacts**. A list of contacts appears in the item list.

2. In the item list, select **Mike Entin**. His contact record appears in the reading pane.

3. If necessary, click the **General** tab in the reading pane to display contact information. Note that all the information you entered appears in the contact header and this tab of the contact record.

4. In the reading pane, click the **Organization** tab. An error message appears, telling you that the directory service for this contact can't be found. That's because Mike Entin has not been included in an LDAP server configured for Outlook.

5. In the reading pane, click the **Details** tab. The same error message appears, for the same reason.

6. In the reading pane, click the **Notes** tab. There are no notes for Mike Entin, so the tab is blank.

7. In the reading pane, click the **Certificates** tab. The Encryption Certificates box is empty because no certificates have been added for Mike Entin.

8. Click the **General** tab again. This is the tab of information you'll access most often.

9. In the item list, double-click the contact record for **Mike Entin**. The contact record opens in its own contact window. Note that the Contact tab near the top of the window offers options for working with that contact.

10. In the contact window, click each tab beneath the contact record header. The same information that appeared in the reading pane appears in this window.

11. In the contact window, click the **General** tab.

12. In the contact window title bar, click the close button to close the window.

✖ CLEAN UP No clean-up steps are required. You are ready to continue to the next exercise.

Modifying and Deleting Contact Records

After a contact record has been created, it can be modified to add, remove, or change contact information. This makes it possible to keep contact information up to date at all times.

If you no longer need a contact record, you can delete it from Outlook.

Tip Deleting a contact record deletes only the information in that record. It does not affect any email communications or tasks related to that contact.

You can make changes to or delete a contact record in the main Outlook window or in the contact window for that contact.

In this exercise, you'll modify a contact record to change the information it contains. You'll also see how you can delete a record that you no longer need.

SET UP You need the Mike Entin record created earlier in this chapter to complete this exercise. In the item list, make sure the Mike Entin record is selected and its General tab of options is displayed.

1. In the contact record header in the reading pane, click the word *Designer*. A selection box appears around the job title, *Web Designer*, and a blinking cursor appears within it.

2. Edit the job title to say **Web Developer**, and then press Return.

3. Under the **Phone** heading, point to **Mobile**. A – button appears to the left of the Mobile tag.

4. Click the – button. The Mobile tag and number beside it disappear.

5. Under the **Phone** heading, click **Home** to display a menu of tags to apply to that phone number.

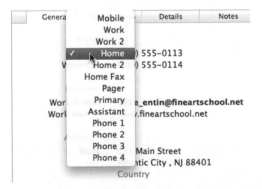

6. Click **Work**. The Work tag now appears beside that phone number.

7. In the item list, double-click **Mike Entin**. The contact window for Mike Entin's contact record appears with the word *Mike* selected.

8. Type **Michael**. *Mike* is replaced with *Michael*.

9. Press Tab. The next field is selected. Each time you press Tab, the next field in the contact window is selected.

10. Click the **+** button beside **Internet** to display a menu of Internet-related fields.

11. Click **Home Web Page**. The Home Web Page field appears.

12. Replace the placeholder text (www.example.com) with **www.mikeentin.com**, and then press Return.

13. Beneath the contact record header, click the **Notes** tab.

14. Click in the empty area beneath the tabs. A blinking cursor appears.

15. Type **Does excellent work and is a really great guy.** The note appears in the box. You can enter as much information as you like in this box.

16. On the **Contact** tab, click the **Save & Close** button. All of your changes are saved to the contact record.

    Tip When you edit a contact record in the main Outlook window, changes are automatically saved. When you edit a contact record in the contact window, you must manually save changes when you are finished editing. If you close a contact window without saving changes, Outlook displays a dialog sheet that prompts you to save or discard changes.

17. In the item list, make sure **Michael Entin** is selected.

18. Press the Delete key. A dialog sheet appears, asking if you're sure you want to permanently delete the selected item.

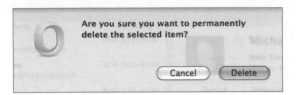

19. If you wanted to delete the record, you'd click **Delete**; for now, click **Cancel**.

20. In the item list, double-click **Michael Entin** to open his contact record window again.

Delete

21. On the **Contact** tab, click the **Delete** button. A dialog sheet appears, asking if you're sure you want to permanently delete the selected item and warning you that the operation can't be undone.

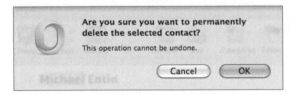

22. If you wanted to delete the record, you'd click **OK**; for now, click **Cancel**.

23. In the contact window title bar, click the close button. If a dialog sheet asks to save changes, click **Don't Save**.

 **CLEAN UP** No clean-up steps are required. You are ready to continue to the next exercise.

Working with Contact Groups

If you often send email messages or meeting invitations to the same group of contacts over and over, you can create a *contact group* and address messages or invitations to the group. This automatically sends the message or invitation to each person in the group.

For example, suppose you're working on a project with four coworkers, an outside contractor, and a client. Every project-related message or meeting that you create needs to be sent to all six contacts. By creating a group that includes the six contacts, you can quickly address communications to all of them by entering just the group name. Not only does this save time, but it prevents you from accidentally omitting one or more recipients.

In this exercise, you'll learn how to create and modify a contact group. You'll also see how you can use a group to quickly address messages and meeting invitations.

SET UP If you did not import the six vCard files as instructed in Chapter 3, "Composing and Sending Email Messages" (or have deleted them since then), drag the six vCard (.vcf) files from the vCards folder in the Chapter09 folder into the Contacts view window to add them to your address book. When you're finished, you should have, at a minimum, seven contact records. Then follow these steps.

Contact Group

1. On the **Home** tab, click the **Contact Group** button. An Untitled Group window appears with its name field selected.

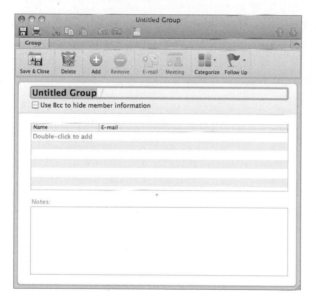

2. Type **Project X**, and then press Return. The name of the group appears in the window's title bar.

3. In the list area, click on the words *Double-click to add*. A line is inserted and the name field is selected.

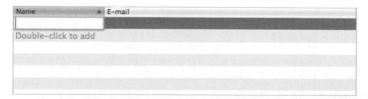

4. Start typing **Kim**. As you type, the Contacts And Recent Addresses menu appears.

5. Click **Kim Akers**. Kim Akers is added to the list and another blank line is inserted.

6. Repeat this process to add **Ben Andrews**, **Michael Entin**, and **Josh Bailey**.

   Tip Extra empty lines may be created as you perform this step. Ignore them; Outlook will remove them when you save the group.

7. On the **Group** tab, click the **Save & Close** button. The Project X group appears in the item list.

8. In the item list, select the **Project X** group. A list of its members appears in the reading pane.

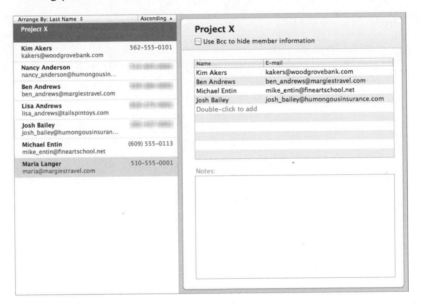

9. In the reading pane, select **Ben Andrews**, and then press Delete. Ben Andrews is removed from the list.

10. To make sure Outlook records this change, press Command+S.

11. In the reading pane, click in the **Notes** box. A cursor appears in the box.

12. Type **Contact list for Project X**. This text appears in the box. You can enter any notes you like for a group.

13. In the view switcher, click the **Mail** button to switch to **Mail View**.

Email

14. On the **Home** tab, click the **Email** button to open a message composition window.

15. In the **To** field, start to type **Project X**. The Contacts And Recent Addresses menu appears. It shows that Project X has 3 members.

16. With **Project X** selected in the menu, press Return. *Project X* appears in the To field. Sending the message would send it to all three recipients.

> **Tip** You could also address an email message to group members by selecting the group in the Contacts view item list and clicking the Email button on the Home tab.

17. In the title bar, click the close button, and then click **Discard Changes** in the dialog sheet that appears.

18. In the view switcher, click the **Contacts** button to switch back to **Contacts view**.

19. In the item list, make sure **Project X** is selected.

Meeting

20. On the **Home** tab, click the **Meeting** button. A meeting window appears. It's automatically addressed to all three members of the group.

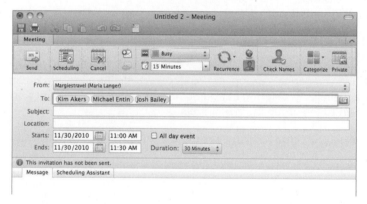

> **Tip** You could also invite group members to a meeting by creating a meeting in Calendar view and then entering the group name in the To field of the meeting window.

21. In the title bar, click the close button, and then click **Discard Invitation** in the dialog sheet that appears.

22. In the item list, make sure **Project X** is still selected.

23. In the reading pane, select the **Use Bcc to hide member information** check box.

24. To make sure Outlook records this change, press Command+S.

25. On the **Home** tab, click the **Email** button. A message composition window appears with *Project X* entered in the Bcc field.

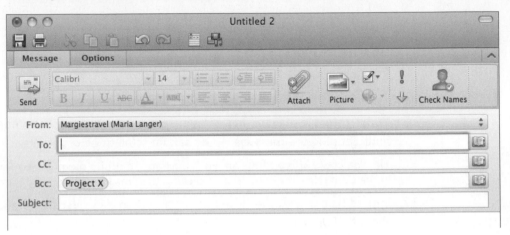

Tip You can use the Bcc option for a group to create private mailing lists.

26. In the title bar, click the close button, and then click **Discard Changes** in the dialog sheet that appears.

27. In the item list, make sure **Project X** is selected.

28. Press the Delete key. A dialog sheet appears, asking if you're sure you want to delete the selected item.

29. Click **Delete**. The group is deleted.

Tip When you delete a group, the contact records for people in the group are not removed. Similarly, deleting a group does not delete any messages or meetings addressed to the group or its members.

CLEAN UP No clean-up steps are required. You can continue to the next chapter.

Key Points

- You can create contact records for specific people or for companies.

- A contact record can contain virtually any information you want to store about the contact.

- Contact records can be modified to add, remove, or change information.

- You can delete a contact record at any time.

- Contact groups make it quick and easy to send messages or meeting invitations to multiple contacts at once.

Chapter at a Glance

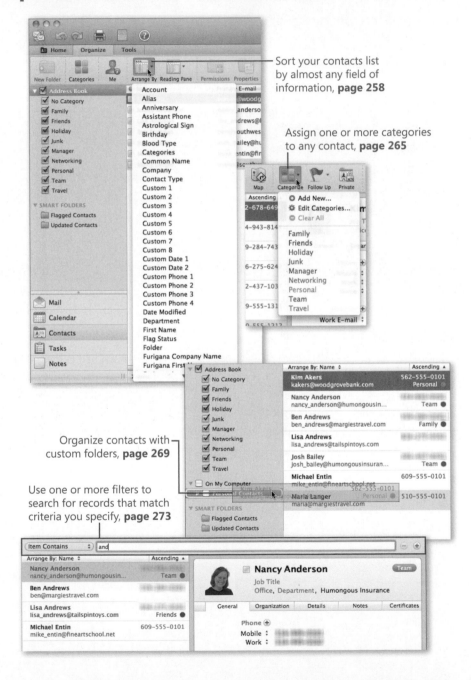

Sort your contacts list by almost any field of information, **page 258**

Assign one or more categories to any contact, **page 265**

Organize contacts with custom folders, **page 269**

Use one or more filters to search for records that match criteria you specify, **page 273**

10 Organizing Your Contacts List

In this chapter, you will learn how to

✔ View and sort the contacts list.

✔ Assign categories to contacts.

✔ Organize contacts with folders.

✔ Search for contacts.

✔ Use smart folders.

There's no practical limit to the number of contacts you can add to your Microsoft Outlook for Mac 2011 contacts list. Each time you add a contact record, the list grows. Before long, you may have dozens—or even *hundreds*—of contacts stored in Outlook for Mac.

Fortunately, Outlook makes it very easy to keep contacts organized. You can change the appearance of the Contacts view to sort contacts in a different order or display information in a different layout. You can assign one or more categories to contacts to put them in context. You can group contacts into folders. You can also search for contacts based on one or more fields of information and save those searches as smart folders, making it easy to find the same contacts again. This chapter looks at all of these contact organization techniques.

> **Practice Files** Before you can complete the exercises in this chapter, you need to have at least six contact records set up in Outlook. If you have not created your own contact records, you can copy the ones in the Chapter10 practice files folder. (These are the same contact records found in the Chapter09 practice files folder; if you have already copied them, do not copy them again.) A complete list of practice files is provided in "Using the Practice Files" at the beginning of this book.

Viewing and Sorting the Contacts List

The appearance of the contacts list depends on several factors:

- The appearance and position of the reading pane.
- The sort order of the contacts in the list.
- The columns displayed in the contacts list.

You can set each of these options independently, with a wide range of variables. As a result, there is almost an infinite number of ways to display the contacts list in Outlook.

Outlook offers three options for displaying the window's reading pane in Contacts view:

- **Right** This option displays the reading pane on the right. This is the default option.

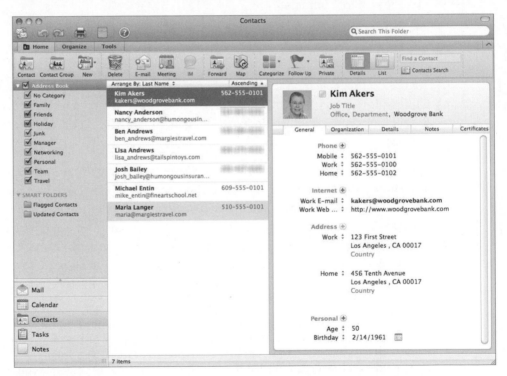

- **Below** This option displays the reading pane below the contacts list. This widens both panes.

- **Hidden** This option removes the reading pane from view. To see a contact's records, you must open its contact window.

See Also Viewing contact record details is covered in the section titled "Viewing Contact Information" in Chapter 9, "Managing Contact Information."

If you place the reading pane below the contacts list or hide it entirely, the contacts list widens and displays more columns of information. This makes it possible to see more information about each contact without having to select it in the list. You can even specify which columns you want to appear.

You can sort the contacts list by any contact field, making it easy to display contacts in the order in which you need them to appear. Outlook offers two ways to change the sort order:

- Use the Arrange By menu to choose the field you want to sort by.
- In the contacts list, click the column heading for the field you want to sort by.

See Also A complete list of contact fields can be found in the section titled "Creating Contact Records" in Chapter 9.

In this exercise, you'll explore the options on the Organize tab's Reading Pane menu to change the appearance of Contacts view. You'll also change the columns of information that appear in the contacts list with the reading pane hidden. Finally, you'll experiment with different ways to change the sort order of the contacts list.

SET UP Make sure you have at least six contacts created in Outlook. In the view switcher, click Contacts.

Reading Pane

1. On the **Organize** tab, click the **Reading Pane** button to display its menu of options.

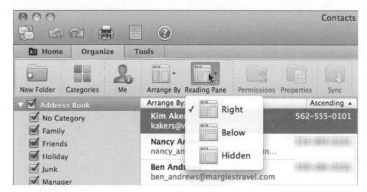

2. Click **Below**. The window's view changes to display the reading pane below the contacts list.

3. Click the **Reading Pane** button again, and then click **Hidden**. The reading pane disappears.

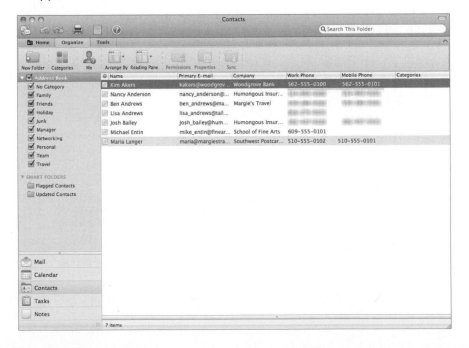

Details

List

Arrange By

4. On the **Home** tab, click the **Details** button. The view changes to display the reading pane on the right.

5. On the **Home** tab, click the **List** button. The view changes to display the reading pane beneath the contacts list.

6. Click **List** again. The view changes to remove the reading pane again.

7. On the **Organize** tab, click the **Arrange By** button to display its menu of options.

8. Click **Company**. The contacts list is sorted alphabetically by the Company field. Note that if a record does not include data in that field, that record will be sorted to the top of the list.

9. Click the **Arrange By** button again to display its menu of options.

10. Click **Work Zip**. (You will have to scroll down on the menu to find it.) The records are sorted by the work address ZIP code. Note that a field does not need to be displayed to be used as a sort field when you are using the Arrange By menu.

11. In the contacts list, click the **Primary E-mail** column heading. The list is sorted alphabetically by that field, the column heading turns blue, and an up-pointing triangle appears on its right side.

12. Click the **Primary E-mail** column heading again. The list is sorted in reverse alphabetical order by that field and the triangle on the heading's right side changes to point down.

13. On the menu bar, click the **View** menu, and then point to **Columns** to display the **Columns** submenu.

14. Click **Work Fax**. (You will have to scroll down on the menu to find it.) The Work Fax column is inserted in the contacts list between the Mobile Phone and Categories columns.

15. On the menu bar, click the **View** menu and then point to **Columns** to display the **Columns** submenu.

16. Click **Mobile Phone**. (You may have to scroll down on the menu to find it.) The Mobile Phone column is removed from the contacts list.

17. Position the mouse pointer on the line between the **Work Fax** and **Categories** column headings. The mouse pointer turns into a vertical line with an arrow pointing to the left.

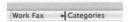

18. Press the mouse button and drag to the right. The Work Fax column gets wider so phone numbers can fit. You can use this technique to change the width of any column.

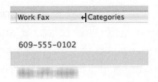

19. Position the mouse pointer on the **Company** column heading, press the mouse button, and drag to the left. As you drag, the entire column moves with the mouse pointer.

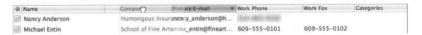

20. When the column is on to the left of the **Primary E-mail** column, release the mouse button. The two columns change place.

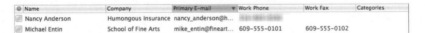

21. On the **Organize** tab, click the **Arrange By** button to display its options.

22. Scroll down to the bottom of the menu. The last command, Make This The Default View, would set the current view options as the default view for the contacts list. Do *not* choose this command now.

23. Click **Restore to Defaults**. The contacts list returns to the default settings for columns and sort order.

✖ **CLEAN UP** On the Organize tab, click Reading Pane and then Right. You are now ready to continue with the next exercise.

Assigning Categories to Contacts

The category feature makes it possible to assign one or more color-coded categories to items throughout Outlook—including contacts. When you apply a category to a contact, not only do you change the color that it appears in the item list, but you add a category tag that you can use for sorting or searching. Assigning categories to contacts also makes it easy to show or hide contacts by using the category check boxes in the navigation pane.

You apply a category to a selected contact with the Categorize button on the Home tab. Select the contact in the contacts list and then click the Categorize button to display a menu of available categories. Choose the category you want to apply, and that category tag is added to the contact. The color of the contact text in the contacts list changes to the color of the category and the category name appears beneath the phone number in the list.

You can repeat this process as much as you like to apply multiple categories to a contact. To remove a category, simply click it on the menu again to clear the check mark. To clear all categories from a message, click Clear All on the Categorize menu.

Outlook comes predefined with nine categories: Family, Friends, Holiday, Junk, Manager, Networking, Personal, Team, and Travel. But you can add, remove, or modify categories if desired to better meet your needs.

See Also Adding, removing, or modifying categories is covered in detail in the section titled "Managing Categories" in Chapter 14, "Using Shared Features."

In this exercise, you'll apply categories to a number of contacts to see how their appearance changes. You'll also work with category check boxes in the navigation pane to show or hide contacts based on categories. Finally, you'll remove individual categories and clear all categories from a contact.

SET UP Make sure the six sample contacts in the Chapter10 folder have been copied to Outlook as instructed at the beginning of this chapter. In the view switcher, click Contacts.

1. In the contacts list, click **Kim Akers** to select her record.

2. On the **Home** tab, click the **Categorize** button to display its menu of options. This menu will include all categories set up in Outlook.

Categorize

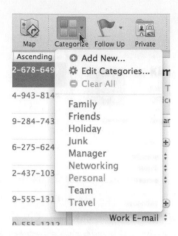

3. Click **Friends**. The Friends category is applied to Kim's record. It appears in the contacts list as well as at the top of the reading pane with her record selected.

4. Click the **Categorize** button again to display its menu of options. Note that the Friends category appears with a check mark beside it, because it is applied to Kim's record.

5. Click **Personal**. The Personal category is also applied to Kim's record. It appears in the contacts list as well as at the top of the reading pane beside the Friends category with her record selected.

6. In the contacts list, select any other record. Note that Kim's name and email address appear in the same color as the Personal category—green, unless you've changed it—and the Personal category appears beneath the phone number. Only the last category name appears in the contacts list, even with multiple categories applied.

7. In the contacts list, select the **Ben Andrews** record.

8. Using the **Categorize** button's menu, apply the **Personal** and **Family** categories to his record in that order. Note that only the Family category name appears in the contacts list.

9. In the contacts list, select the **Josh Bailey** record.

10. Hold down the Command key and, in the contacts list, click **Nancy Anderson**. Both records are now selected. You can use this technique to select any number of records.

11. Using the **Categorize** button's menu, apply the **Team** category to the selected records.

12. If necessary, in the navigation pane, click the disclosure triangle beside **Address Book** or **My Contacts** to display contact categories. (If you have more than one contacts list, also click the disclosure triangle beside the one you copied the sample contacts to to display its categories list.)

13. In the navigation pane, clear all displayed check boxes. (A quick way to do this is to clear the top level check box; all check boxes below it are also cleared.) All contacts disappear from the contacts list.

14. In the navigation pane, select the **Team** check box. The two records you applied the Team category to (Nancy Anderson and Josh Bailey) appear in the contacts list.

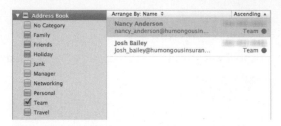

15. In the navigation pane, select the **Personal** check box. The two records you applied the Personal category to (Kim Akers and Ben Andrews) appear in the contacts list, even though both of them also have another category applied and that category is not selected.

16. In the navigation pane, select the **Family** check box. The contacts list does not change because the only contact with the Family category applied (Ben Andrews) is already displayed because of its Personal category.

17. In the navigation pane, clear the **Personal** check box. The record that has the Personal category and another unchecked category (Friends; Kim Akers) is removed from the list.

18. In the navigation pane, select the **No Category** check box. All contacts that have no category applied are added to the contacts list.

19. In the contacts list, select **Lisa Andrews** and, using the **Categorize** button's menu, apply the **Friends** category to her record. Lisa's record disappears from the contacts list because it has an undisplayed category applied to it.

20. In the navigation pane, select the check box beside **Address Book** or **My Contacts** to display all contacts lists (if you have more than one), categories, and contacts.

21. In the contacts list, select **Kim Akers**.

22. On the **Home** tab, click the **Categorize** button, and then click **Friends**. The Friends category is removed from Kim's record. Selecting a selected category removes that category.

23. In the contacts list, select **Ben Andrews**.

24. On the **Home** tab, click the **Categorize** button and then click **Clear All**. All categories are removed from Ben's record.

✖ CLEAN UP No clean-up steps are required. You are ready to continue to the next exercise.

Organizing Contacts with Folders

With Outlook, you can create multiple folders for storing contacts. This makes it possible to keep separate contacts lists.

Why would you want to do this? Well, perhaps you use Outlook for both personal and business communications. You might want to maintain separate contacts lists for each use. This makes it easy to separate business from pleasure while making all information easily accessible in the same application.

Tip If you have a Microsoft Exchange Server account, Outlook will automatically create a separate contacts list for your Exchange contacts, which are stored on the Exchange server. You can find it listed in the navigation pane, along with an On My Computer list for locally stored contacts.

When you have multiple contacts list folders, you can move items from one folder to the other. When you create a new item, it is added to the folder that is selected when you create it. When you delete a folder, all of the items it contains are deleted.

In this exercise, you'll create a new contacts list folder and move some contacts into it. You'll then see how you can toggle the display of contacts from each list.

➡ SET UP No additional practice files are necessary. Follow these steps.

1. In the navigation pane, select **Address Book** (if you have only one address book) or **On My Computer** (if you have multiple address books).

2. On the **Home** tab, click the **New** button to display a menu of options.

New

3. Click **Folder**. An **Untitled Folder** item appears in the navigation pane with its name selected.

Tip The new untitled folder may appear under an On My Computer heading in the navigation pane, depending on your Outlook account configurations.

4. Type **Personal Contacts**, and then press Return. The folder is renamed.

Tip You can rename a folder at any time by double-clicking its name, typing a new name, and pressing Return.

5. In the navigation pane, make sure the check box beside the name of your original contacts list is selected so all categories of contacts appear in the contacts list.

6. In the navigation pane, make sure the check box beside **Personal Contacts** is cleared.

7. Drag the contact record for **Kim Akers** from the contacts list to **Personal Contacts** in the navigation pane.

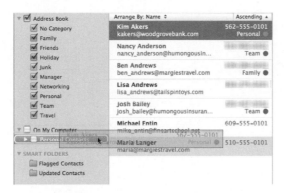

8. When **Personal Contacts** becomes selected, release the mouse button. Kim's record disappears from the contacts list because you have moved it to a folder that is not displayed.

9. In the navigation pane, select the check box for **Personal Contacts**. Kim's record reappears in the contacts list because you are now displaying the folder into which her record has been moved.

10. In the navigation pane, clear the check box for your original contacts list. All records other than Kim's disappear from the contacts list because Kim's record is the only one in the displayed folder.

11. In the navigation pane, select all check boxes to display all contacts lists, folders, and categories.

12. If necessary, in the navigation pane, click the disclosure triangle beside **Personal Contacts** to display all categories within it. As you can see, the categories in a new folder are the same as they are for all other contacts lists and folders.

13. In the contacts list, drag the contact record for **Lisa Andrews** to **Personal Contacts**. When you release the mouse button, nothing seems to happen.

14. In the navigation pane, clear the check box beside **Personal Contacts**. The contact records for Kim and Lisa disappear from the contacts list, because they are both in Personal Contacts.

15. In the navigation pane, select the check box beside **Personal Contacts**. All records reappear in the contacts list.

16. In the contacts list, click **Kim Akers** to select her record.

17. Hold down the Command key and click **Lisa Andrews**. Both records are now selected.

18. Drag either record from the contacts list to the name of your original contacts list in the navigation pane. An icon indicates that you are dragging two records.

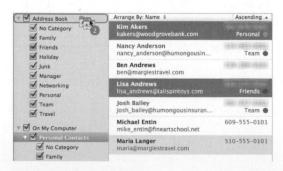

19. When your original contacts list is selected, release the mouse button to move the records back to where they were at the start of this exercise.

20. In the navigation pane, click **Personal Contacts** to select it.

Delete

21. On the **Home** tab, click the **Delete** button. A confirmation dialog box appears to ask if you're sure you want to delete the selected folder.

22. Click **Delete**. The Personal Contacts folder is deleted.

 CLEAN UP No clean-up steps are required. You are ready to continue to the next exercise.

Searching for Contacts

When you have many contact records stored in Outlook, scrolling through them all to find a specific one can be time consuming. It can also be nearly impossible if you can't remember the contact's name.

That's when the contact search feature of Outlook can come in handy. It enables you to search through your contacts lists to find records that match the search word or phrase you specify. If you can't remember a contact's name or which contacts list he's in, no problem—you can search globally, though all fields and lists. Search results appear in their own window. You can select a contact in the window and use buttons beneath the contact name to create a new email message or schedule a new meeting, right from that window.

Outlook also offers an advanced search feature that you can use to set up multiple search filters. For example, suppose you want to find all contacts with companies based in California. You can set up multiple filters and Outlook will attempt to match the criteria in all filters to list just the contacts you're looking for.

In this exercise, you'll experiment with both simple and advanced search features that you can use with your contacts lists.

➡ **SET UP** No additional practice files are necessary to complete this exercise. In the navigation pane of Contacts view, make sure all contacts list and category check boxes are selected. Then follow these steps.

1. In the **Find a Contact** box on the **Home** tab, type **andr**.

2. Press Return. The Contacts Search window appears with search results displayed.

3. In the search box at the top of the **Contacts Search** window, click the **X** button to clear the search characters. Then type **hum**.

4. If no search results appear, click the menu on the left beneath the search box and click **Search All Fields**. If there are still no search results, click the menu on the right beneath the search box and click **All Folders**. Outlook should display two contacts who work for Humongous Insurance.

5. In the search box at the top of the **Contacts Search** window, click the **X** button to clear the search characters. Then type **Friends**. No search results appear. Even though the Friend category has been applied to at least one contact record, you cannot use this simple search feature to search based on category.

6. Close the **Contacts Search** window.

7. On the menu bar, click **Edit**, and then click **Find** and **Advanced Find** or press Shift+Command+F. The Search contextual tab appears, along with a line for entering filtering criteria.

All Contacts

8. On the **Search** tab, click the **All Contacts** button.

9. In the search box above the contacts list and reading pane, type **and**. After a moment, the contacts list is filtered to show only those contact records that contain the text string *and*.

10. On the filter line, click the **Item Contains** pop-up menu to display its options. Then click **Last Name**. The contact list is filtered to show only those records with the characters *and* in the Last Name field.

11. On the filter line, click the **Contains** pop-up menu to display its options. Then click **Does Not Contain**. The contacts list is filtered again to show all records that do not contain the characters *and* in the Last Name field.

12. On the filter line, click the **Last Name** pop-up menu to display its options. Note that it includes most fields.

13. On the filter line, click the **Does Not Contain** pop-up menu to display its options. Note that the options that appear on this menu vary depending on the field that is selected in the menu beside it. When this menu isn't needed, it does not appear at all.

Name

14. On the **Search** tab, click the **Name** button. Another filter line appears with the Display Name option chosen from the first pop-up menu. This offers a quick way to filter contact records by name.

Email

15. On the **Search** tab, click the **Email** button. Another filter line appears, this time with E-Mail Address chosen from the first pop-up menu. This offers a quick way to filter contact records by email address.

Company

16. On the **Search** tab, click the **Company** button. Another filter line appears, this time with Company chosen from the first pop-up menu. This offers a quick way to filter contact records by company name.

17. On the **Search** tab, click the **Has Phone** button. Another filter line appears, this time with Phone chosen from the first pop-up menu and Exists chosen from the second pop-up menu. This offers a quick way to display only contacts with at least one phone number in their contact record.

18. On the **Search** tab, click the **Has Address** button. Another filter line appears, this time with Street Address chosen from the first pop-up menu and Exists chosen

from the second pop-up menu. This offers a quick way to display only contacts with at least one address in their contact record.

19. On the **Search** tab, click the **Flagged** button. Another filter line appears, this time with Follow Up Flag chosen from the first pop-up menu and Not Completed chosen from the second pop-up menu. The contacts list is cleared out because no records match the current filtering criteria.

20. Beneath the **Search** tab, click the **–** button on the right end of each filter line except the one for **Display Name**. As the filter lines are removed, the contacts list items should reappear.

21. On the **Search** tab, click the **Modified** button to display its options.

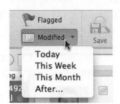

22. Click **This Week** on the **Modified** button. Another filter line appears, this time with Date Modified chosen from the first pop-up menu and This Week chosen from the second pop-up menu. The contacts list is filtered to show only those contacts modified in the past week.

23. Click the **This Week** menu, and then click **Today**. The contacts list is filtered to show only those contacts modified today.

24. On the far-right end of the **Date Modified** filter line, click the **–** button. The line and its filtering are removed.

25. On the remaining filter line, choose **State/Province** from the first pop-up menu, and **Is** from the second pop-up menu. Then type **CA** in the text box. The list is filtered to show only contacts with addresses in California.

26. On the **Search** tab, click the **Company** button to add a **Company** filter line. Then click **Exists** on the second pop-up menu. The list is filtered to show only contacts with addresses in California and the company name included in the contact record.

✖ CLEAN UP No clean-up steps are required. Leave the Advanced Search filters set as is; you will work with them in the next exercise.

Using Smart Folders

Smart folders make it possible to save advanced search filters so they can be used again and again. When you open a smart folder, Outlook applies the saved filters to your contacts and displays the results in the contacts list.

By default, two smart folders are preconfigured for Contacts view:

- **Flagged Contacts** This smart folder uses the Follow Up Flag filter to display all contact records that are flagged as not completed.

- **Updated Contacts** This smart folder uses the Date Modified filter to display all contact records that have been modified within the past week.

In this exercise, you'll learn how to create your own smart folders, modify existing smart folders to change their settings, and delete smart folders you no longer need.

SET UP No additional practice files are necessary to complete this exercise. This exercise assumes you have just completed the previous exercise and have filters set. Follow these steps.

Save

1. On the **Search** contextual tab, click the **Save** button. An Untitled smart folder appears in the navigation pane under the Smart Folders heading.

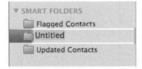

2. Type **CA Businesses**, and then press Return. The smart folder is renamed and it shifts to the top of the Smart Folders list in the navigation pane.

3. In the **Smart Folders** area of the navigation pane, click the **Updated Contacts** smart folder. The contacts list changes to display only contact records that have been modified within the past week.

Advanced

4. If necessary, on the **Search** tab, click the **Advanced** button to display the search filter for the currently selected smart folder.

5. On the search filter line, click the **Within Last Week** menu, and then click **Since Yesterday**. The contacts list displays only those contact records modified since yesterday.

6. On the **Search** tab, click the **Save** button. The change you made to the filter is saved to the smart folder, thus modifying it to reflect the current settings.

7. In the **Smart Folders** area of the navigation pane, click the **CA Businesses** smart folder. The contacts list changes to display only contacts with addresses in California and the company name included in the contact record.

8. If necessary, on the **Search** tab, click the **Advanced** button to display the search filters for the currently selected smart folder.

9. On the search filter line, edit *CA* to read **NJ**. The contacts list changes to display only contacts with addresses in New Jersey and the company name included in the contact record.

10. At the top of the navigation pane, select the name of your contacts list or the **On My Computer** heading. A dialog box appears, asking if you want to save the changes that you made to your smart folder. Outlook makes it impossible to forget to save changes.

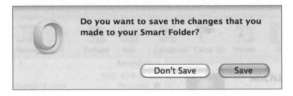

11. Click **Don't Save** to dismiss the dialog box without saving changes to the smart folder.

12. In the **Smart Folders** area of the navigation pane, click the **CA Businesses** smart folder again.

13. On the **Home** tab, click the **Delete** button. A dialog box appears and asks if you're sure you want to permanently delete the smart folder.

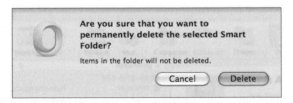

14. Click **Delete**. The smart folder is removed.

   Tip Deleting a smart folder does not delete any contact records.

15. In the **Smart Folders** area of the navigation pane, right click the **Updated Contacts** smart folder to display a contextual menu of options.

16. Click **Edit**. The search filter line appears beneath the ribbon.

17. Click the **Since Yesterday** pop-up menu, and then click **Within Last Week**.

18. On the **Search** tab, click the **Save** button. This smart folder is now reset to its original configuration.

19. At the top of the navigation pane, select the name of your contacts list or the **On My Computer** heading. The advanced search feature is turned off and all contact records are displayed in the contacts list again.

✕ CLEAN UP No clean-up steps are required. You are ready to continue to the next chapter.

Key Points

- You can change the appearance of Contacts view to show the reading pane beneath the contacts list or hide it completely.

- When the contacts list is wide, you can display different columns of information.

- You can sort the contacts list by almost any field of information.

- You can assign one or more categories to each contact to help organize them by context.

- You can organize your contacts into multiple folders.

- You can search your contacts list for specific contact records based on contact name or other criteria.

- Advanced contact searching enables you to set up multiple filters for narrowing down your contacts list.

- Smart folders make it possible to save search filters for future use.

Chapter at a Glance

Initiate basic communication tasks from within a contact record, **page 286**

Assign categories while importing vCards, **page 290**

Import vCards into Outlook with drag and drop, **page 290**

Use the Print dialog box to print contact records in two styles, **page 295**

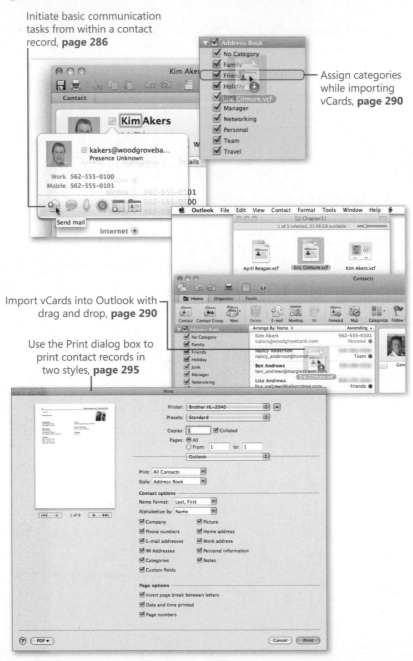

11 Working with Contact Records

In this chapter, you will learn how to

- ✔ Set contact options.
- ✔ Work with contact information.
- ✔ Create and share vCards.
- ✔ Print contact records.
- ✔ Synchronize contacts.

How the Contacts view features in Microsoft Outlook for Mac 2011 work are determined, in part, by settings that you can modify in Outlook for Mac preferences. For example, you can control the format of a contact's address and phone number and specify how contacts should be sorted in the Contact Search pane. These options enable you to fine-tune Outlook so its Contacts view features work the way you want them to.

You can also use Outlook features to work with individual contact records or groups of records. For example, you can import or export records, share records with others via email, and print records using two different layouts. You can also create a personal vCard file that you can share with others, making it easy for them to include your contact information in their address book. And if you have multiple computing devices, you might find the contact synchronization feature handy for duplicating your Outlook contacts list on the MobileMe service and other compatible devices.

In this chapter, you will take a look at contacts list customization options in Outlook preferences. You will then explore how you can print or work with contact records to share them with others, and synchronize them among your devices.

> **Practice Files** Before you can complete the exercises in this chapter, you need to copy the book's practice files to your computer. The practice files you'll use to complete the exercises in this chapter are in the Chapter11 practice files folder. A complete list of practice files is provided in "Using the Practice Files" at the beginning of this book.

Setting Contact Options

Outlook offers four basic options for configuring its contacts list. They can be found in the Contacts preferences pane.

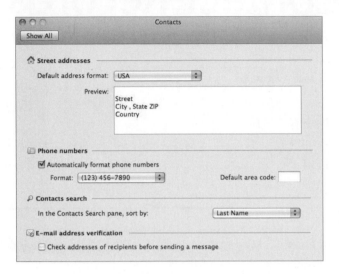

- **Street addresses** The Default Address Format pop-up menu enables you to choose from among 20 different predefined address formats. Each format is named for the country it's most likely to be used in. If you're using Outlook in the United States, this option will most likely be set to USA. However, if you have more contacts in another country, you can use this pop-up menu to choose the country you prefer. The Preview area shows how each contact's address information will be laid out.

- **Phone numbers** There are two different Phone Numbers options:

  - **Automatically format phone numbers** When selected, this option tells Outlook to format phone numbers by using the option you specify with the Format pop-up menu. There are many formats to choose from, including several that include the country code.

  - **Default area code** This option can be used to specify an area code for most new records you create. With this text box filled in, you can enter just the seven-digit phone number for a contact and Outlook will automatically enter the area code you specified. You might find this useful if most of your contacts are in the same area code.

- **Contacts search** This option enables you to use a pop-up menu to specify how you want search results sorted in the Contacts Search pane. Your options are simple: First Name or Last Name.

● **Email address verification** If you have one or more LDAP servers configured in Outlook for your contacts, you can select this check box to have Outlook automatically verify the email addresses of the contacts you send messages to.

> **Important** The email address verification feature cannot check addresses for contacts that are not listed in Microsoft Exchange Server or LDAP directories you access. As a result, you should not rely on this feature to determine whether the email addresses you use for those contacts outside your organization are accurate.

In this exercise, you'll open Outlook preferences and display the Contacts preferences pane. You'll then explore the options to see how they might apply to the way you use Outlook.

 SET UP You don't need any practice files to complete this exercise. In the view switcher, click the Contacts button and then follow these steps.

1. On the menu bar, click **Outlook**, and then click **Preferences**.

   Keyboard Shortcut Press Command+, (comma) to open the Outlook Preferences window.

2. In the **Outlook Preferences** window, click the **Contacts** button to display the **Contacts** preferences pane.

3. Under **Street addresses**, note the appearance of the **Preview** area. It displays the standard layout for the selected Default Address Format.

4. Under **Street addresses**, click the **Default address format** pop-up menu to display its options.

5. Click **Germany**. The Preview area changes to display a format consistent with addresses in Germany.

6. Experiment with the **Default address format** pop-up menu to try other countries. Note how the **Preview** area changes accordingly.

7. On the **Default address format** pop-up menu, click the country you use most to set this option for how you use Outlook.

8. Under **Phone numbers**, if necessary, select the **Automatically format phone numbers** check box.

9. Click the **Format** pop-up menu to display its options.

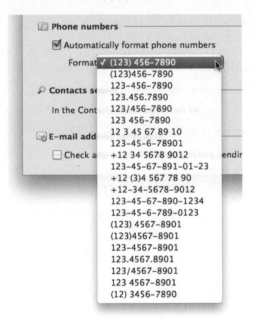

10. On the **Format** pop-up menu, click the format you prefer.

    Tip If many of your contacts reside outside your country, you may want to choose a format that includes the country code as the first digit.

11. In the **Default area code** box, type your local area code.

12. Switch to the main Outlook window, create a new contact record, and type just a seven-digit phone number in one of the phone number fields.

13. Press Tab to move to another field. Outlook automatically inserts the area code you specified in step 11.

14. Close the new contact record without saving changes.

15. Switch back to the **Contacts** preferences pane.

> **Tip** If you can't see the Contacts preferences pane to click it, you can choose Outlook Preferences from the Window menu and then click the Contacts button in the Outlook Preferences window to reopen it.

16. Under **Contacts search**, click the pop-up menu to display its options.

17. On the pop-up menu, click the option you prefer.

18. If you have an Exchange account or at least one LDAP server configured within Outlook, select the **Check addresses of recipients before sending a message** check box. This enables this feature to help ensure that your messages are properly addressed whenever possible.

19. In the **Contacts** preferences pane, click the close button to dismiss the window.

 CLEAN UP No clean-up steps are required. You are ready to continue to the next exercise.

Working with Contact Information

The contact window for a contact record offers access to a number of features you can use to work with contact information. In most cases, to access these features, all you have to do is point to the information you want to work with.

For example, pointing to the button to the left of the contact's name displays a pop-up window with some basic information about the contact, as well as buttons and links for using Outlook, Messenger, or Communicator to get in touch. You can point to a button or link to see a ScreenTip with more information or click it to perform a task.

Tip Microsoft Messenger for Mac and Microsoft Communicator for Mac are two components of Microsoft Office that enable you to establish live direct communications with contacts over the Internet. Messenger requires a Windows Live ID account, which you can set up for free, and offers chat and video chat features. Communicator, which ships only in volume license versions of Office, requires an account on a Microsoft Office Communications Server, and offers chat, video chat, telephone, and video calling features. A discussion of Messenger and Communicator is beyond the scope of this book.

In this exercise, you'll examine some of the features available within the contact window for working with a contact's information.

 SET UP You need at least one contact record created in Outlook to complete this exercise. If you want to follow along with the sample record shown in this chapter, copy the Kim Akers record to Outlook. If you have already completed exercises in Chapters 9 and 10, it should already be available.

1. In **Contacts** view, double-click the record you want to work with to open its contact window.

2. In the contact window, point to the button to the left of the contact name. A pop-up menu appears with information about the contact and a series of buttons.

3. In the pop-up window, point to the contact's phone number. An underline appears beneath it. This phone number is a link; clicking it launches Microsoft Communicator, which you may be able to use to call the contact.

4. In the pop-up window, point to each of the buttons along the bottom of the window. A ScreenTip explains what each one does.

   Important You must be logged into a Messenger or Communicator account to send an instant message, call, or start a video call with a contact.

Send mail

5. In the pop-up window, click the **Send mail** button. Outlook opens an untitled message composition window, preaddressed with the contact's email address.

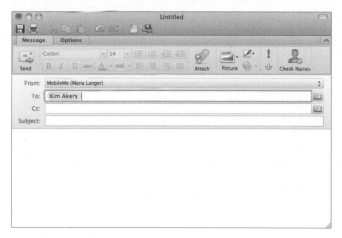

   See Also You can learn more about creating email messages in the section titled "Creating Messages" in Chapter 3, "Composing and Sending Email Messages."

6. On the message composition window title bar, click the close button and discard changes to dismiss the window.

7. In the contact window, point to the button to the left of the contact name to display the pop-up window again.

Schedule a meeting

8. In the pop-up window, click the **Schedule a meeting** button. Outlook opens an untitled meeting window, preaddressed with the contact's email address.

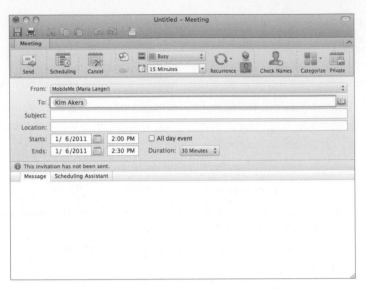

See Also You can learn more about scheduling meetings in the section titled "Scheduling Meetings" in Chapter 7, "Scheduling Appointments and Meetings."

9. On the meeting window title bar, click the close button and discard the invitation to dismiss the window.

10. In the contact window, point to one of the contact's phone numbers. A magnifying glass icon appears to the right of the number.

11. Click the magnifying glass icon. A dark gray window appears with the phone number enlarged within it, making it easier to see—even from a distance.

12. Click the phone number window's close button to dismiss it.

13. In the contact window, point to one of the contact's email addresses. An envelope icon appears to the right of the email address.

Clicking this button opens an untitled, pre-addressed message composition window so you can send the contact a message.

14. In the contact window, point to one of the contact's Web addresses. A link icon appears to the right of the Web address.

15. Click the link icon. Outlook opens your default Web browser and displays the Web page in that field.

16. Quit your Web browser and return to Outlook.

17. In the contact window, point to one of the contact's street addresses. A globe icon appears to the right of the first line of the address.

18. Click the globe icon to display a menu of options.

19. Click **Open in Bing**. Outlook opens your default Web browser and displays the address in Bing Maps.

Important The sample address shown here is not real and will not display an accurate location on Bing.

20. Quit your Web browser and return to Outlook.

21. In the contact window, point to the contact's birthday. An Add Reminder button appears to the right of the calendar icon. Clicking this button adds the contact's birthday to the calendar as an annually recurring event.

22. In the contact window title bar, click the close button and don't save any changes you might have made to dismiss the window.

✖ **CLEAN UP** No clean-up steps are required. You are ready to continue to the next exercise.

Creating and Sharing vCards

Like most contact management applications, Outlook supports the *vCard* format, a standard file format for electronic business cards. vCard files, which usually have the .vcf or .vcard file extension, contain all the contact information stored in a contact's record, including name, company, title, addresses, email addresses, Web sites, birthday—everything.

In Outlook, you can create a vCard file in two different ways:

- Use the Forward As vCard command or Forward button to forward one or more selected contact records to someone via email. Outlook automatically creates and attaches the vCard file(s).

- Drag a contact record from the contacts list to the desktop or an open Finder window. Outlook automatically creates the vCard file and saves it to the destination location.

Creating a Personal vCard

Your Outlook contacts list should include a contact record with your information. This record is created automatically by Outlook when you install and configure Outlook. It's also modified by Outlook when you add or remove email addresses. And, as you probably guessed, you can manually modify your vCard to include whatever information you like.

You can display your personal vCard by clicking the Me button on the Organize tab in Contacts view or by choosing Me Contact from the View menu. If someone else's card appears, you can set Outlook straight by selecting your card in the contacts list and then choosing This Contact Is Me from the Contact menu.

If you plan to share your contact record with others as a vCard, make sure it has only the information you want to share. For example, if you plan to share your vCard with business associates, you may want to omit your home phone number, home address, or birthday. Likewise, if you think you might share it mostly with friends, you might want to omit your work phone number and company Web site. You could also do what I do: create two contact records for yourself—one for business use and one for personal use—and choose the one to share based on who you will share it with. Remember, however: you can only have one "me" record.

When you receive a vCard file from another computer user, you can add it to your contacts list three different ways:

● Double-click the file icon. This imports the vCard data into whatever contacts list folder is selected in Outlook and opens the contact record in a contact window.

● Drag the file icon into the Outlook Contacts view navigation pane. If you drag it onto a specific contacts list folder, it is imported into that folder in Outlook. If you drag it onto a specific category, it is imported into the category's folder in Outlook and that category is assigned to it.

● Drag the file icon into the Outlook Contacts view contacts list. This imports the vCard data into whatever contacts list folder is selected in Outlook.

Important Importing a vCard for a contact that already exists in Outlook will add a new record for that contact. This could result in duplicate information within Outlook.

vCards are widely supported by contact management software for Mac OS, Windows, iOS, and even Unix. That means you can use vCards to exchange contact record information with users of Outlook for Mac or Windows, Entourage for Mac, Apple Address book, or countless other applications with contact management capabilities.

In this exercise, you'll use a variety of techniques to create vCards based on your Outlook data and add new contacts to Outlook from vCard files.

SET UP You need the vCard files for April Reagan and Eric Gilmore, both of which can be found in the Chapter11 exercise files folder. In the Outlook view switcher, click the Contacts button to switch to Contacts view if necessary. Then follow these instructions.

1. In the contacts list, select your contact record.

Forward

2. On the **Home** tab, click the **Forward** button. Outlook opens a message composition window, enters FW: followed by the name of the contact record in the Subject field, and attaches the .vcf file for your contact record.

![Screenshot of a message composition window titled "FW: Maria Langer" with From field showing "MobileMe (Maria Langer)", empty To and Cc fields, Subject field showing "FW: Maria Langer", and attachment "Maria Langer.vcf (45.5 KB)"]

3. Enter a friend's or coworker's email address in the **To** field and a brief note in the message body. Then click **Send** to send your vCard to that person.

   Tip If you prefer not to share your contact record with someone at this time, just close the message composition window without saving changes.

4. Arrange and, if necessary, resize the main Outlook window so you can see the **Finder** desktop behind it.

5. Drag your contact record from the contacts list to the desktop. A green plus symbol should appear when the mouse pointer and record are over the desktop.

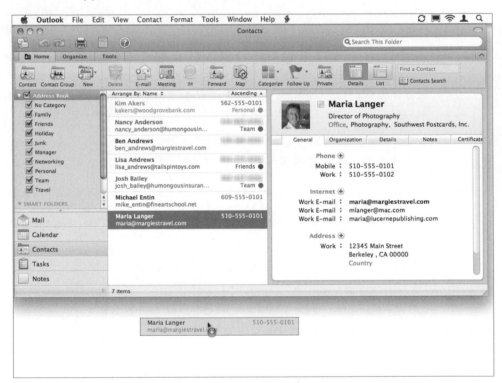

6. Release the mouse button. Although your record remains in the Outlook contacts list, a vCard icon with your name appears on the desktop.

   Tip You can share this file with anyone via email attachment, shared network folder, FTP, or any other method of exchanging files.

7. In the **Finder**, locate and open the folder containing the Chapter 11 exercise files. It should contain three vCard files.

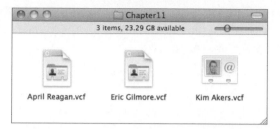

8. Double-click the **April Reagan** vCard file icon. April Reagan's vCard file opens in an Outlook contact window.

9. Close the contact window. You'll see that April Reagan's record has been added to the contacts list.

10. Arrange and, if necessary, resize the main Outlook window so you can see both it and the open **Chapter11** window in the **Finder**.

11. Drag the **Eric Gilmore** vCard file from the **Chapter11** window to the contacts list in the Outlook window. A green plus symbol should appear when the mouse pointer and record are over the contacts list.

12. Release the mouse button. Eric Gilmore appears in the contacts list.

13. Repeat step 11, but this time, drag the **Eric Gilmore** vCard file onto the **Friends** category in the navigation pane.

14. Release the mouse button. There are now two Eric Gilmore records in the contacts list. These records are duplicates except that one of them is categorized as Friends.

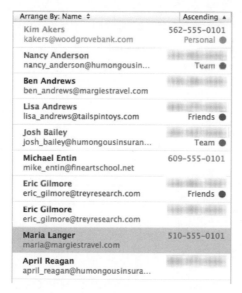

15. Delete the uncategorized **Eric Gilmore** record.

    See Also Deleting contact records is covered in the section titled "Modifying and Deleting Contact Records" in Chapter 9, "Managing Contact Information."

 **CLEAN UP** No clean-up steps are required. You are ready to continue to the next exercise.

Printing Contact Records

Although Outlook makes it easy to find and get information about your contacts, you might occasionally need to print them. Perhaps you need a printed phone list that you can consult when you're away from your computer. Or maybe you just like having a printout of important contact information handy at your desk.

Outlook enables you to print your address book in two styles: Address Book and Phone List. You can print all contacts, selected contacts, or flagged contacts. If you print in the address book style, you can specify which fields of information should print. You can also set a number of basic page options. You do all this in the Print dialog box.

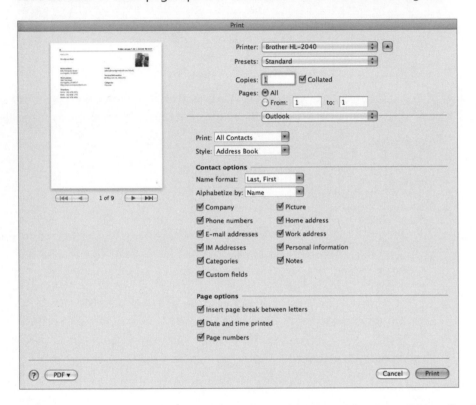

You open the Print dialog box just as you would in any other Mac OS application: by choosing Print from the File menu or by pressing Command+P. In Outlook, you can also click the print icon on the toolbar.

The Print dialog box has two different appearances: a collapsed version that shows only the Printer and Presets pop-up menus and a handful of buttons or the expanded version that shows all options, as well as a print preview. To switch from one to the other, click the disclosure triangle beside the Printer pop-up menu.

Exact printer options vary based on your printer, but the Outlook options in the lower half of the dialog box should be the same no matter what printer you have:

- **Print** Use the Print drop-down list to specify which contacts you want to print: Selected Contacts, All Contacts, or Flagged Contacts.

Tip To print all contacts in one category, in the navigation pane, clear the check boxes for every category other than the one you want to print so only those contacts are displayed. In the contacts list, select any one of the contacts and press Command+A to select all of them. Then, in the Print dialog box's Print drop-down list, choose Selected Contacts.

- **Style** Use the Style drop-down list to specify whether you want to print an Address Book or a Phone List. The Address Book style can include almost any combination of fields for a contact. The Phone list includes only the contact's name and phone numbers.

- **Contact options** This area of the dialog box includes options for the Address Book style printout. (Although you can change them even if Phone List is selected from the Style drop-down list, changes do not affect the printout.) There are two drop-down lists and a handful of check boxes:

  - ○ **Name format** Use this drop-down list to indicate whether you want the name to print as *Last, First*; *Last First* (without a comma); or *First Last*.

  - ○ **Alphabetize by** Use this drop-down list to specify whether you want contacts sorted by Name or Company.

  - ○ **Field check boxes** You can use the check boxes in this area to deter-mine which pieces of contact information will be included in the printout: Company, Phone Numbers, E-mail Addresses, IM Addresses, Categories, Custom Fields, Picture, Home Address, Work Address, Personal Information, and Notes.

- **Page options** The last three check boxes control pagination as well as the informa-tion that appears in page headers and footers:

  - ○ **Insert page break between letters** Select this check box to have each letter of the alphabet start on its own page; clear it to break pages anywhere.

    Tip For shorter printouts and to save paper, clear the Insert Page Break Between Letters check box.

  - ○ **Date and time printed** Select this check box to print the date and time that the printout was created at the upper-right of each page; clear it to omit this information.

  - ○ **Page numbers** Select this check box to print page numbers on the lower-right of each page; clear it to omit page numbers.

Tip If Outlook options are not displayed, you can show them by choosing Outlook from the pop-up menu beneath the Pages boxes near the top of the dialog box.

If Address Book is selected from the Style drop-down list, each time you make a change in one of the settings, the preview area may change accordingly. If your printout will be more than one page, you can use the arrow buttons beneath the preview to see what each page will look like when printed.

When you're ready to print, click the Print button at the lower-right corner of the dialog box. The document is sent to the printer.

Tip You can use options under the PDF menu at the bottom of the Print dialog box to create, email, or fax a PDF of your document. You might find this handy to share a "hard copy" of your contacts list without actually printing it. You can learn more about this Mac OS X feature in Mac OS Help.

In this exercise, you'll open the Print dialog box and explore some of its printing options.

  SET UP In the contacts list, select any three contacts. (Click one and then hold down the Command key while clicking two others.) Then follow these steps.

Print

1. On the toolbar, click the **Print** button. The Print dialog box appears.

2. If the dialog box does not include options and a preview area, click the disclosure triangle beside the **Printer** pop-up menu.

3. If necessary, display the **Print** drop-down list, and then click **All Contacts**.

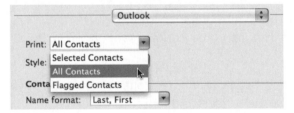

4. If necessary, display the **Style** drop-down list, and then click **Address Book**.

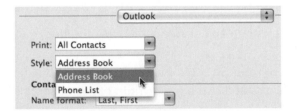

5. If necessary, in the **Page options** area, clear the **Insert page break between letters** check box.

6. Experiment with the options under **Contact options** to change the sort order and display different combinations of fields. You should see the effects of your changes in the Preview area.

7. Use the arrows under the **Preview** area to scroll forward and then backward through the pages.

8. Experiment with the options under **Page options** to change pagination and the contents of the header and footer. You should see your changes in the Preview area. When you're finished, make sure the **Insert page break between letters** check box is cleared again.

9. In the **Contact options** area, select all of the check boxes to show all fields of information.

10. Display the **Print** drop-down list, and then click **Selected Contacts**. The Preview area changes to display just the three contacts you selected before beginning this exercise.

11. Display the **Style** drop-down list, and then click **Phone List**. The Preview area changes to display the three contacts in phone list layout.

12. Display the **Print** drop-down list, and then click **All Contacts**. The Preview area changes to display all contacts; if you have many contacts, the preview might go to multiple pages.

13. Experiment with the options under **Contact options** to toggle check box settings. The Preview area should not change; you cannot customize the fields that display in a Phone List printout.

14. Display the **Alphabetize by** drop-down list, and then click whichever option is not currently selected. If you watch the Preview area closely, you should see a change in the sort order.

15. (Optional) Click **Print**. The phone list is sent to your printer and the Print dialog box disappears.

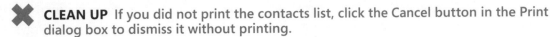 **CLEAN UP** If you did not print the contacts list, click the Cancel button in the Print dialog box to dismiss it without printing.

Synchronizing Contacts

Nowadays, it isn't uncommon for people to own more than one computer. Perhaps you have a computer on your desktop at the office and a laptop you take on the road. Or maybe you have a mobile computing device such as an iPhone, iPad, or other smart-phone or tablet.

In a perfect world, you'd have just one contacts database that you could access and modify from any device. Outlook offers the next best thing: the ability to synchronize contacts between Outlook, Apple Address Book, MobileMe, and iSync-compatible de-vices like many mobile phones.

Synching contact data in Outlook is easy. Simply enable Sync Services for contacts and follow the instructions in any prompts that appear on the screen. Your data will be synced to Apple's Address Book application, so changes in either Outlook or Address Book will be copied to the other application's database. If your Mac is set up to use a MobileMe account, your contact information will also be copied to MobileMe, where it can be accessed from any Web browser. And if you have another mobile computing de-vice that's compatible with Apple's iSync application, you can set up iSync to synchronize the data to that device, too.

Tip A discussion of iSync is beyond the scope of this book. You can learn more about setting up a device with iSync in Apple Help.

In this exercise, you'll enable Sync Services for contacts and see how it affects Address Book and MobileMe accounts.

Tip As this book was going to press, Microsoft was working on an update to Outlook that would allow syncing of calendar, task, and note data. Don't be surprised if the screenshots in this section look different when you follow these instructions with an updated version of Outlook.

SET UP No setup is required. Just follow these steps.

1. In the view switcher, click the **Contacts** button to switch to **Contacts** view, if necessary.

2. On the ribbon's **Tools** tab, click the **Sync Services** button. The Sync Services preferences pane opens.

Sync Services

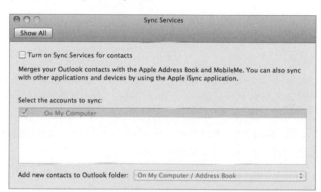

3. Select the **Turn on Sync Services for contacts** check box.

4. In the list of accounts in the bottom half of the window, select the check boxes for each account you want to enable Sync Services for.

5. If you have more than one contacts folder in Outlook, use the pop-up menu to select the folder you want to add new contacts to. (This option determines where contacts created in other applications or on other devices will be added to Outlook on synchronization.)

6. Click the **Sync Services** preferences pane close button to dismiss it. A dialog box appears to inform you that you have enabled Sync Services for contacts.

7. Click **OK**. Outlook and Mac OS immediately perform a sync. If there are any conflicts—for example, if one contact appears in both Address Book and Outlook—the Conflict Resolver dialog box appears.

8. Click the **Review Now** button to review the conflicts. When the conflicts are re-solved, the sync is completed and the updated information is copied to Outlook and Address Book.

   See Also You can learn more about using the Conflict Resolver dialog box to resolve conflicts between Address Book and Outlook data in Mac OS Help. Click the Help button in the Conflict Resolver dialog box to get started.

9. In the **Finder**, open **Address Book**. You'll see that all of your Outlook contacts have been copied to the Address Book database.

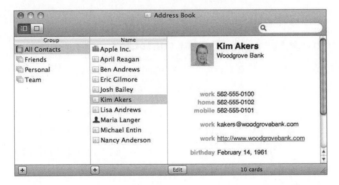

10. If you have a MobileMe account that is configured in Mac OS System Preferences, you can check to see if your contacts have been synced to MobileMe. Use your Web browser to log in to MobileMe and navigate to the **Contacts** page. The contacts should appear in the list.

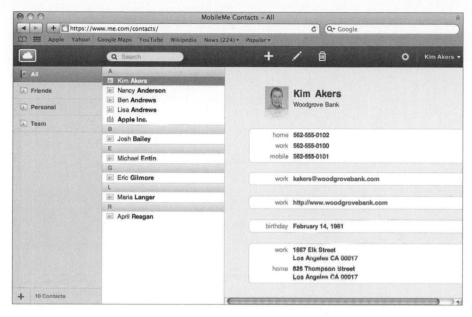

Tip MobileMe is an online service available for an annual fee from Apple, Inc. For synchronization to occur, your MobileMe account name and password must be entered into MobileMe preferences and synchronization must be enabled. Choose System Preferences from the Apple menu and then click the MobileMe icon in the System Preferences window that appears to get started.

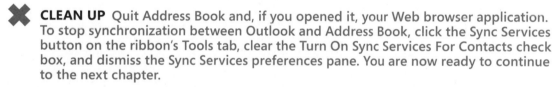

CLEAN UP Quit Address Book and, if you opened it, your Web browser application. To stop synchronization between Outlook and Address Book, click the Sync Services button on the ribbon's Tools tab, clear the Turn On Sync Services For Contacts check box, and dismiss the Sync Services preferences pane. You are now ready to continue to the next chapter.

Key Points

- You can set Contact preferences to determine default address and phone number formats and sort options.

- Buttons and commands within the contact window let you perform a variety of tasks for a selected contact.

- You can share contact information through the use of standard vCard format files.

- You can print all or selected contact records in a number of formats.

- You can synchronize your contacts between computers or devices.

Part 5

Tasks and Notes

Chapter at a Glance

Use an intuitive form to enter information about each task, **page 308**

Set custom recurrences for any event, **page 308**

Flag items for follow-up, **page 314**

Filter the tasks list to show only the tasks that interest you, **page 321**

Specify which columns should appear in the tasks list, **page 317**

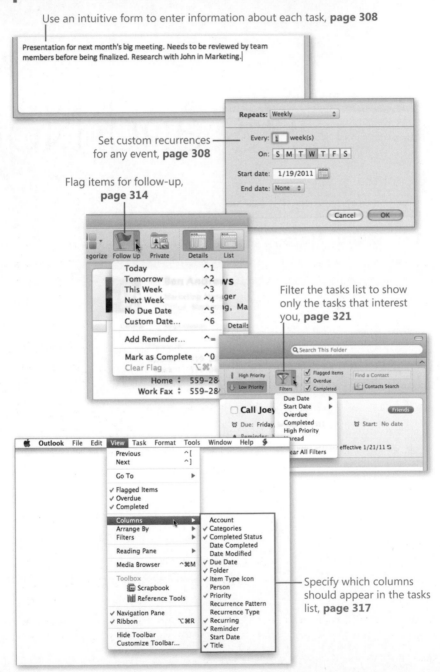

12 Tracking Tasks

In this chapter, you will learn how to

- ✔ Create tasks.
- ✔ Flag items for follow up.
- ✔ View tasks.
- ✔ Filter tasks.
- ✔ Search for tasks.
- ✔ Modify and remove tasks.
- ✔ Print tasks.

During the course of your day, you likely perform many tasks. Some are work related, such as contacting coworkers and business associates and preparing reports. Others are personal, such as taking your son to buy new sneakers or planning for a birthday party.

Some are routine tasks that you complete every day without even thinking about them: having breakfast, driving to work, checking your email Inbox. Others might be less routine and require additional thought or effort: researching a topic for a presentation, organizing a lunch meeting, planning a weekend getaway.

Projects are often made up of a series of tasks. For example, perhaps a new project requires you to build a Microsoft PowerPoint presentation, update a database of contacts in Microsoft Outlook for Mac 2011, create a form letter in Microsoft Word, and schedule a handful of meetings. You must perform these tasks—sometimes in a specific order or after a certain date—to get the job done.

In some instances, tasks may have deadlines for completion. Tasks may also be triggered by the receipt of an email message or meeting invitation. The completion of one task could lead to the need to complete another.

No matter what tasks you need to perform, good time management practices make it helpful to list your tasks. The result is a to-do list—or perhaps several of them. Listing the tasks you need to complete not only helps you remember to complete them, but it takes them off your mind until you can focus on them. This clears your mind for whatever you need to do now.

The Tasks view in Outlook for Mac makes it easy to keep track of the tasks you need to complete for work or your personal life—or both. You can enter tasks by using an intuitive form that prompts you for all the information you need to remember about the task. You can then organize tasks by category, priority, due date, or other criteria. You can see at a glance what needs to be done and check off tasks as you complete them.

In this chapter, you'll explore Tasks view in Outlook. You'll learn how to create tasks from scratch and by flagging Outlook or Microsoft Office items for follow up. You'll see how to organize and filter tasks to see just the ones you need to. You'll also learn how to modify tasks, mark them as completed, print them, and delete them.

> **Practice Files** Before you can complete the exercises in this chapter, you need to copy the book's practice files to your computer. The practice file you'll use to complete the exercises in this chapter is in the Chapter12 practice files folder. A complete list of practice files is provided in "Using the Practice Files" at the beginning of this book.

Creating Tasks

Outlook offers two ways to create a task. The most basic is with the task window. This window is a form with fields that you can fill in with task information.

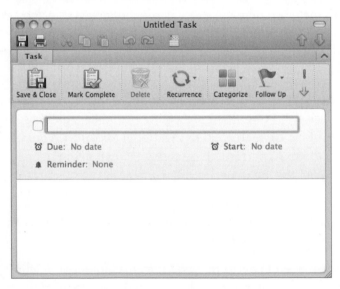

Think of a task as a to-do list item. To create it, you need to provide information about what needs to be done and when. You do this by filling in fields in the form:

- **Title** The task title is a name for the task that appears in the Tasks view window. This is the only piece of information that is required to create a task.

- **Due date** If a task is due on a certain date, you can set a due date for it. This due date will appear in lists and can be used to sort tasks.

- **Start date** If a task must be started on or after a date, you can set a start date for it.

- **Reminder** To be reminded to complete a task, you can set a date and time to be reminded.

- **Description** You can include a detailed description of a task if you need to. This is a good way to include notes or other important information you might need to complete the task.

In addition, you can include other information that helps you manage your tasks:

- **Recurrence** If a task must be completed regularly, you can set recurrence options for it. For example, suppose you create a monthly report; you can add the report as a task with the current due date and then set recurring options for the task to repeat monthly. Then, when you mark the current task as completed, a new task for the following month's report appears in the tasks list.

- **Categorize** You can use the Categorize option to set one or more categories for a task. This makes it easy to organize tasks by project or other identifying criteria you use throughout Outlook.

- **Priority** A task can be set as high, normal, or low priority. If you sort tasks by priority, you can easily see which ones are most important.

In this exercise, you'll create two tasks from scratch using the task window. You'll also set additional options for each task to help organize them within your tasks list in a later exercise.

SET UP If necessary, in the view switcher, click Tasks to switch to Tasks view. Then follow these steps.

Task

1. On the **Home** tab, click the **Task** button. An untitled task window appears.

2. In the title field (which should be selected), enter **Create Presentation**. This text appears in the title of the task window.

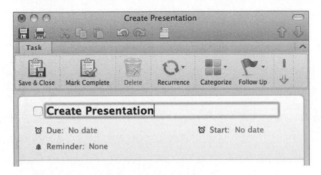

3. In the task window, click the **Due** field. A date picker appears.

4. Click a date sometime next week. The date is entered into the Due field.

5. In the task window, click the **Reminder** field. Another date picker appears.

6. Click a date two days before the **Due** date to enter it into the field. Note that the reminder time is set to midnight, which might not be practical.

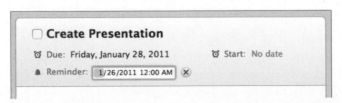

7. In the **Reminder** field, click the **12** in the hours place to select it. Then type **10** to change the time to 10:00 AM.

Categorize

8. On the **Task** tab, click the **Categorize** button to display a menu of categories.

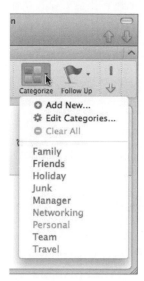

9. On the **Categorize** menu, click **Team**. The Team category is applied to the task.

10. Repeat steps 8 and 9 to also apply the **Manager** category to the task.

High Priority

11. On the **Task** tab, click the **High Priority** button. The button becomes selected and a note about the priority appears beneath the header in the task window.

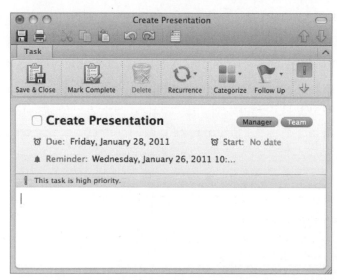

12. In the description field of the task window, enter the following descriptive text for the task: **Presentation for next month's big meeting. Needs to be reviewed by team members before being finalized. Research with John in Marketing.** The text appears in the field as you typed it. You can put as much text as you like in this field; it will scroll if it needs to.

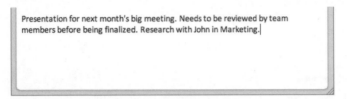

Save & Close

13. On the **Task** tab, click the **Save & Close** button. The task window closes and the task appears in the tasks list.

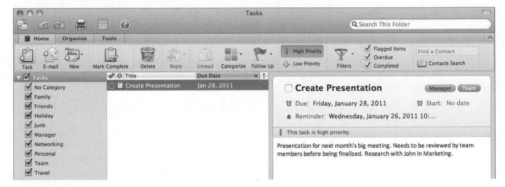

14. On the **Home** tab, click the **Task** button to open another untitled task window.

15. In the title field, type **Call Joey**. This text appears in the title of the task window.

16. Click the **Due** field, and use the date picker to enter next Friday's date.

17. On the **Task** tab, click the **Categorize** button, and then click **Friends** to assign the Friends category to the task.

18. On the **Task** tab, click the **Recurrence** button. A menu of options appears.

Recurrence

19. Click **Custom**. A dialog sheet with custom recurrence options appears.

20. On the **Repeats** menu, make sure **Weekly** is selected.

21. Enter **2** in the **Every** box.

22. Click the **F** button to select it. If any other button in that row is selected, click it to deselect it so only the F button is selected.

23. Click **OK**. The dialog sheet closes and the recurrence setting appears in the task window's header.

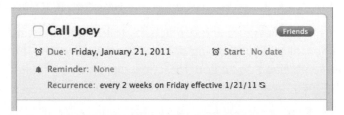

24. On the **Task** tab, click the **Low Priority** button.

25. Click the task window's close button. A dialog sheet prompts you to save changes.

26. Click **Save**. The task window closes and the new task is added to the tasks list.

Low Priority

✖ **CLEAN UP** No clean-up steps are required. You are ready to continue to the next exercise.

Project Management, Outlook Style

If you're upgrading from Entourage to Outlook, you may have noticed that the project management features that were part of Office 2008 (and earlier versions of Office for Macintosh) are not included in Office 2011. This does not mean you don't have project management capabilities. It just means that you'll need to track projects differently.

In most cases, the categorization features in Outlook should meet your needs. Create a new category for a project and assign that category to the contacts, meetings, appointments, tasks, and follow up items that you create for the project. Then, when you need to focus on the project, simply view just that category in Outlook.

See Also You can learn more about creating custom categories in the section titled "Managing Categories" in Chapter 14, "Using Shared Features."

Flagging Items for Follow Up

Often, an email message, contact, or file might be the basis for a task. If so, you can flag that item for follow up, thus creating a new task.

For example, suppose you receive an email message from your boss asking you to provide some information that you need to look up. You're busy with something else when you get the message and, fortunately, your boss doesn't need the information right away. You can flag the message for follow up, creating a task with a reminder so you don't forget.

Or maybe a coworker has sent you a file that needs your input. You get the file and spend some time working on it, then get called away to a meeting. Before you go, you can flag the document for follow up, creating a task based on that document.

In Outlook, you can flag messages and contacts for follow up. You can also flag any Office document for follow up, including documents you can open in Microsoft Excel, Word, and PowerPoint. Flagging an item for follow up attaches that item to the task, making it easy to open the original item from the task window.

In this exercise, you'll flag a contact and a Word document for follow up. As you'll see, the process is similar and can easily be applied to other Outlook and Office items.

 SET UP You need the Report document located in the Chapter12 practice files folder to complete this exercise.

1. In the view switcher in Outlook, click the **Contacts** button to switch to **Contacts** view.

2. In the contacts list, select any one of the sample contacts created or imported for a previous chapter's exercise.

Follow Up

3. On the **Home** tab, click the arrow on the **Follow Up** button to display a menu of follow up options.

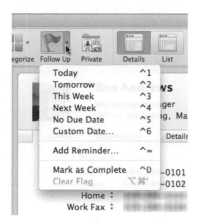

4. Click **Next Week**. A follow up flag appears beneath the contact's name in the reading pane.

5. In the view switcher, click **Tasks** to switch to **Tasks** view. The contact you flagged appears in the Tasks list.

6. In the **Finder**, open the **Report** document. This is a sample file containing some corporate-sounding gibberish.

7. On the Word menu bar, click **Tools**, and then click **Flag for Follow Up**. The Flag For Follow Up dialog box appears. If Office Reminders is turned off, it will look like the figure at the top of the next page.

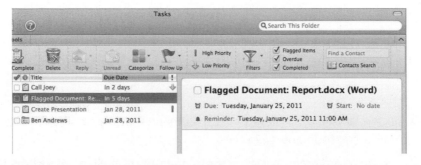

If Office Reminders is turned on, it will look like this:

8. In the **Remind me on** field, enter a date sometime next week.

9. In the **at** field, enter **11:00 AM**.

10. If the dialog box informs you that Office Reminders is turned off (as shown earlier), select the **Turn on Office Reminders** check box.

   Tip When you turn on Office Reminders, the Office Reminders window may appear and display reminders for past and future events and tasks. You can click its Dismiss button as necessary to close selected reminders for past items.

11. Click **OK** to save your settings.

12. Quit Word and switch back to Outlook. The flagged document appears in the tasks list in Tasks view.

 CLEAN UP No clean-up steps are required. You are ready to continue to the next exercise.

Viewing Tasks

Tasks appear in the Tasks view of Outlook. The Tasks view window is normally split into three panes: the navigation pane (with the view switcher beneath it), the tasks list, and the reading pane, which provides details about a selected task.

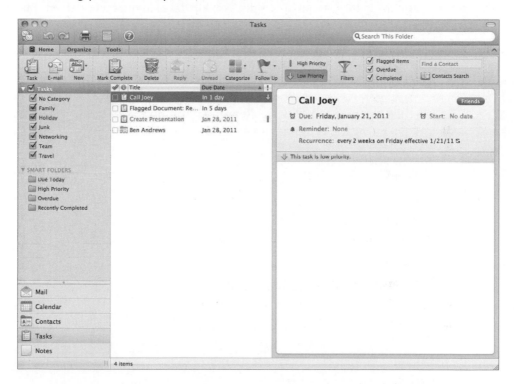

You can change this view by using the Reading Pane menu on the Organize tab to change the position of the reading pane or hide it completely. With the reading pane below the tasks list or hidden, you can also specify which columns of information should appear in the tasks list.

You can also change the sort order of the tasks list by either clicking the column heading you want to sort by or by choosing a field from the Arrange By menu on the Organize tab.

To see the details for a task in its own task window, just double-click it in the tasks list. You can then make changes to the task and save them.

See Also As you might imagine, you can also use the navigation pane to specify which tasks appear in the tasks list based on category or folder. You can even create new folders to organize tasks. Hiding and displaying categories is covered in the section titled "Assigning Categories to Contacts" in Chapter 10, "Organizing Your Contacts List"; working with folders is covered in that same chapter in the section titled "Organizing Contacts with Folders." Although these two sections apply to contacts; these features work virtually the same for tasks. Customizing the category list is discussed in detail in the section titled "Managing Categories" in Chapter 14.

In this exercise, you'll explore different ways to view the tasks list and individual tasks.

SET UP No setup is required. In Tasks view, follow these steps.

Reading Pane

1. On the **Organize** tab, click the **Reading Pane** button to display its menu of options.

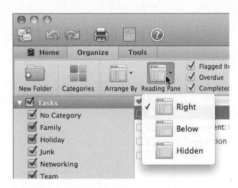

2. Click **Below**. The task pane moves to beneath the tasks list.

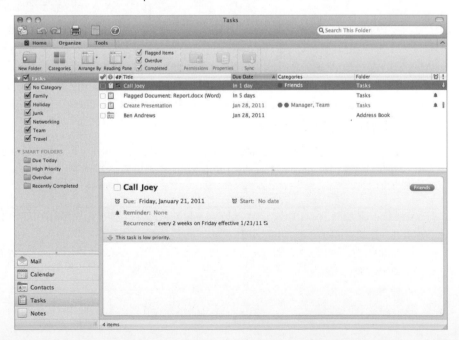

3. Click the **Reading Pane** button again, and then click **Hidden**. The reading pane disappears entirely.

4. On the menu bar, click **View**, and then select **Columns** to display a menu of columns that can appear in the tasks list.

5. Click **Categories** to clear the check box. The Categories column is removed from the tasks list. You can use this technique to hide any currently displayed column.

6. Repeat steps 4 and 5, but this time, select **Start Date** from the menu of columns. The Start Date column appears in the tasks list. You can use this technique to display any column.

7. In the tasks list, drag the right border of the **Start Date** column to the right to make it wider so the dates in the column are fully visible.

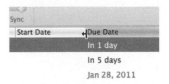

You can use this technique to change the width of any column.

8. In the tasks list, click the **Title** column heading. The tasks list is sorted in alphabetical order by task title.

9. Click the **Title** column heading again. The tasks list is sorted in reverse alphabetical order by task title.

Arrange By

10. On the **Organize** tab, click the **Arrange By** button to display its menu.

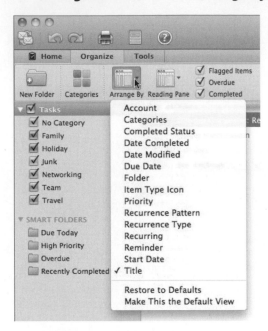

11. Click **Priority**. The tasks list is sorted in priority order: high priority, normal (or no) priority, and then low priority. You can use this menu to sort by any field, even if it is not displayed.

12. Click the **Arrange By** button again, and then click **Restore to Defaults**. The tasks list columns and sort order change to what they were before you began making changes.

13. In the tasks list, double-click the **Call Joey** item. It opens in its own task window.

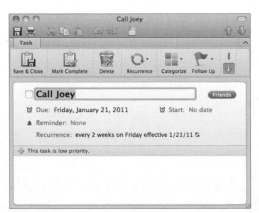

14. Click the task window's close button to dismiss the task without making any changes.

 CLEAN UP Use the Reading Pane button on the Organize tab to display the reading pane on the right again. You are now ready to continue to the next exercise.

Filtering Tasks

You can also change the display of the tasks list by filtering the tasks that are included in the list. For example:

- Toggle check boxes on the Home or Organize tab to show or hide specific types of tasks: Flagged Items, Overdue items, and Completed items.

- Use options under the Filters menu to display only those tasks that meet pre defined criteria.

- Select a smart folder in the navigation pane to display only the tasks that meet the smart folder's search criteria.

See Also Creating and working with smart folders is discussed in detail in the section titled "Using Smart Folders" in Chapter 10. Although that section applies to contacts, the smart folder feature works very much the same for tasks.

The benefit of filtering tasks is that it enables you to narrow down your tasks list. This makes it possible, for example, to focus on tasks with a high priority or tasks that are due this week.

In this exercise, you'll experiment with the task filters built into Outlook to see how they affect the tasks list.

SET UP No setup is required. In Tasks view, follow these steps.

> **Important** Keep in mind that the results of the filtering steps in this exercise will vary based on whether you have additional tasks recorded in Outlook beyond the four created earlier in this chapter. These steps assume only four tasks are created.

1. On the **Organize** tab, clear the **Flagged Items** check box. The flagged task disappears from the list.

2. On the **Organize** tab, clear the **Overdue** check box. Because all sample tasks are set for the future, the list should not change.

3. On the **Organize** tab, clear the **Completed** check box. Because none of the sample tasks have been marked as completed, the list should not change.

4. On the **Home** tab, select each of these same check boxes. For convenience, these check boxes appear on two tabs: Home and Organize. All tasks should reappear in the tasks list.

Filters

5. On the **Home** tab, click the arrow on the **Filters** button to display the **Filters** menu.

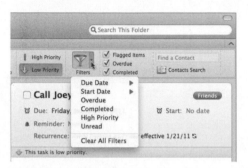

6. Display the **Due Date** submenu, and then click **This Week**. The tasks list changes to display only the single task due this week: Call Joey.

7. On the **Home** tab, click the arrow on the **Filters** button to display the **Filters** menu again.

8. Click **High Priority**. The tasks list clears. Filters are cumulative; Outlook is trying to display tasks that are due this week and have a high priority, but there are none.

9. Repeat steps 5 and 6 to clear the check mark beside **This Week**. The tasks list changes to display just the one task with a high priority: Create Presentation.

10. On the **Home** tab, click the **Filters** button. This clears all filters; all tasks should reappear in the list.

11. In the navigation pane, click each of the smart folders, one at a time:

   ○ **Due Today** This folder displays only tasks due today. There are none.

   ○ **High Priority** This folder displays only tasks set with a high priority. There is only one: Create Presentation.

   ○ **Overdue** This folder displays only tasks that are overdue. There are none.

   ○ **Recently Completed** This folder displays only tasks that have been recently marked as completed. There are none.

12. In the navigation pane, click the name of your primary tasks list. If you have only one, it will be named Tasks. This displays all tasks in that folder again, rather than the most recently selected smart folder.

 CLEAN UP No clean-up steps are required. You are ready to continue to the next exercise.

Searching for Tasks

When you have many tasks stored in Outlook, you might find it helpful to be able to search for a specific task based on information stored in one or more fields for the task. You can do this with the advanced search feature. This feature enables you to set up multiple custom filters that Outlook will use to find tasks.

See Also The section titled "Searching for Contacts" in Chapter 10 explains how to use the advanced search feature as it applies to contacts. You'll find that this feature works very much the same for tasks.

In this exercise, you'll explore the advanced search feature as it applies to tasks.

SET UP No setup is required. Simply follow these steps. Your search results may vary if you have tasks entered in Outlook in addition to those created in previous exercises in this chapter.

1. On the menu bar, click **Edit**, and then click **Find** and **Advanced Find** or press Shift+Command+F. The Search contextual tab appears, along with a line for entering filtering criteria.

All Tasks

2. On the **Search** tab, click the **All Tasks** button. This tells Outlook to only search tasks.

3. In the search box above the tasks list and reading pane, type **John**. After a moment, the tasks list is filtered to show only the task that contains the text string *John:* Create Presentation. (The name John appears in the description area if you closely followed the instructions to create this task earlier in this chapter.)

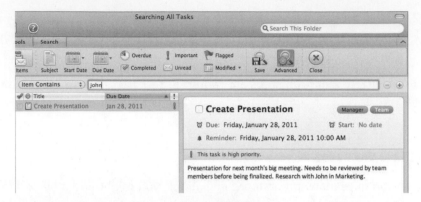

4. On the filter line, click the **Item Contains** pop-up menu to display its options.

5. Click **Title**. The tasks list clears because the search word, *John*, does not appear in the title of any task.

6. In the search box beside **Contains**, type **Joe**. The list filters to show the Call Joey record, because that record contains the word *Joe* in the title.

7. On the **Search** tab, click each of the following buttons and observe the changes above the tasks list; you'll see that each button or menu is a shortcut for adding one or more filter lines:

Subject

Start Date

○ **Subject** Adds another filter line for the Title field.

○ **Start Date** Displays a menu of options for entering a search line for the start date. Choose one of the options to see how the filter line is added.

Due Date

Modified ▼

○ **Due Date** Displays a menu of options for entering a search line for the due date. Choose one of the options to see how the filter line is added. Note that a filter line for incomplete items is also added.

○ **Overdue** Adds a filter line for overdue items and a filter line for incomplete items.

○ **Completed** Adds a filter line for completed items.

○ **Important** Adds a filter line for high priority items.

○ **Unread** Adds a filter line for unread items.

○ **Flagged** Adds a filter line for flagged items.

○ **Modified** Displays a menu of options for entering a modification time period. Choose one of the options to see how the filter line is added.

Tip Outlook will attempt to match all search criteria, so it's unlikely that you'd ever need to use this many filter lines for a search. Clicking these buttons is for illustrative purposes only.

8. On the far-right end of any filter line, click the – button. The line disappears. You can use this technique to remove any of the filter lines.

Close

9. On the **Search** tab, click the **Close** button. All filter lines and the Search tab disappear.

✖ **CLEAN UP** No clean-up steps are required. You are ready to continue with the next exercise.

Modifying and Removing Tasks

You can change the details for a task at any time. This means you can change the task title or description, set a different due or start date, create or change reminders, or modify any other field information recorded for the task.

You can also mark a task as completed. Marking a task as completed places a check mark beside it in lists to show that it's done. You can hide completed items from view by clearing the Completed check box on the Home tab. You can also view a list of recently completed tasks by selecting the Recently Completed smart folder in the navigation pane.

If you no longer need a record of a task, you can simply delete it from Outlook. Just select it in the tasks list and press the Delete key on the keyboard or click the Delete button on the Home tab. A confirmation dialog sheet appears to make sure you really do want to delete the task.

In this exercise, you'll make some changes to the tasks created in this chapter. You'll also mark two tasks as completed and delete a task you no longer need to see.

 SET UP No setup is required. Just make sure you are in Tasks view, and then follow these steps.

1. In the tasks list, select the **Create Presentation** task.

2. In the reading pane, click the **Due** date. A date picker appears.

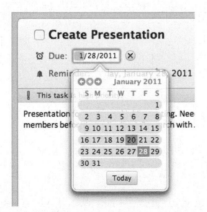

3. In the date picker, select the Monday after the currently selected date. Note that the date in the Reminder field also changes.

4. Beside the **Start** field, click **No date** to display a date picker.

5. In the date picker, click **Today**.

6. Click the **Reminder** date and time to display a date picker.

7. Clear out the reminder by clicking the X button beside the date and time.

8. In the description field, after the word *Marketing*, insert **at ext. 123**.

9. In the tasks list, click the **Flagged Document** task. Your changes to the Create Presentation task are automatically saved.

10. In the tasks list, double-click the **Flagged Document** task. It opens it in a task window.

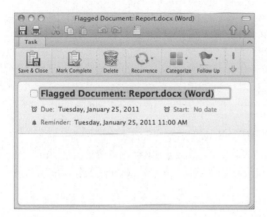

11. In the title field, replace the selected text with **Review Report.docx with John**.

12. In the title bar, click the close button. A dialog box asks if you want to save changes.

13. Click **Save** or press Return. The task's name is changed in the tasks list.

14. In the tasks list, select the check box beside the contact name you flagged for follow up. A check mark appears in the box and a Completed note appears beneath the header in the reading pane.

15. In the tasks list, double-click the **Call Joey** task to open it in a task window.

16. On the **Task** tab, click the **Mark Complete** button. A check mark appears in the check box beside the task title and a strikethrough line appears through the task title.

Mark Complete

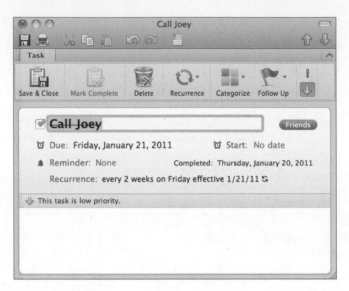

17. On the **Task** tab, click the **Save & Close** button. Although the Call Joey task is marked completed, another Call Joey task appears with a due date two weeks later.

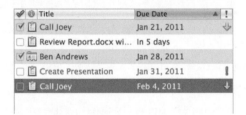

The new task appears because the original task is recurring; marking it complete once does not mark it as complete for every occurrence. Instead, a new occurrence is added to the tasks list.

18. On the **Home** tab, clear the **Completed** check box. The two tasks you marked as completed disappear.

19. In the navigation pane, select the **Recently Completed** smart folder. The tasks list clears out completely with the message No Results.

20. On the **Home** tab, select the **Completed** check box. The two tasks you marked as completed appear alone in the tasks list.

21. In the navigation pane, click the name of your primary tasks folder. (This will be Tasks if you only have one tasks folder.) All tasks reappear.

22. In the tasks list, select the **Review Report.docx** task.

Delete

23. On the **Home** tab, click the **Delete** button. A confirmation dialog sheet appears.

24. Click **Delete** to delete the task. (The file you flagged is not deleted.)

25. In the tasks list, select the contact you flagged for follow up and later marked as completed.

26. On the **Home** tab, click the arrow on the **Follow Up** button to display a menu of options.

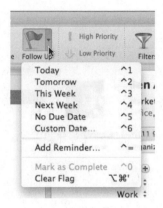

27. Click **Clear Flag**. The follow up flag is removed from the contact and the contact is removed from the Tasks list.

   Important Deleting a flagged contact from the tasks list will remove the contact from Outlook—which is probably not something you want to do. To get a contact off the tasks list without deleting it, clear the follow up flag as discussed here.

 CLEAN UP No clean-up steps are required. You are ready to continue to the next exercise.

Printing Tasks

If you need a printed list of tasks—perhaps something that's easy to consult when you're on the road—you can use the Print command to create one.

Outlook provides two styles for printing tasks: Memo and Table. You can print all tasks, selected tasks, or tasks based on due date or completion status. For either style, you can specify which fields of information should print. You can also set a number of basic page options. You do all this in the Print dialog box.

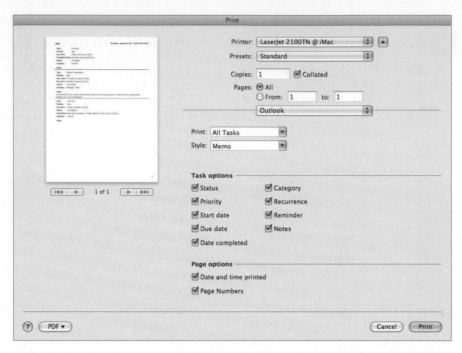

You open the Print dialog box just as you would in any other Mac OS application: by choosing Print from the File menu or by pressing Command+P. In Outlook, you can also click the print icon on the toolbar.

The Print dialog box has two different appearances: a collapsed version that shows only the Printer and Presets pop-up menus and a handful of buttons, or the expanded version that shows all options, as well as a print preview. To switch from one to the other, click the disclosure triangle beside the Printer pop-up menu.

Exact printer options vary based on your printer, but the Outlook options in the lower half of the dialog box should be the same no matter what printer you have:

- **Print** Use this list to specify which tasks you want to print: Selected Tasks, All Tasks, Tasks Due Today, Tasks Due This Week, All Incomplete Tasks, or Current Tasks List.

    Tip To print all tasks in one category, in the navigation pane, clear the check boxes for every category other than the one you want to print so only those tasks are displayed. In the tasks list, select any one of the tasks and press Command+A to select all of them. Then, in the Print dialog box's Print drop-down list, choose Selected Tasks.

- **Style** Use this list to specify whether you want to print in Memo or Table style. Either style can include almost any combination of fields for a task.

● **Task options** This area of the dialog box enables you to select the fields you want to include in the printed tasks list: Status, Priority, Start Date, Due Date, Date Completed, Category, Recurrence, Reminder, and Notes.

● **Page options** The last two check boxes control the information that appears in page headers and footers.

   ○ **Date and time printed** Select this check box to print the date and time that the printout was created at the upper-right of each page; clear it to omit this information.

   ○ **Page numbers** Select this check box to print page numbers on the lower-right of each page; clear it to omit page numbers.

Tip If Outlook options are not displayed, you can show them by choosing Outlook from the pop-up menu beneath the Pages boxes near the top of the dialog box.

Each time you make a change in one of the settings, the preview area may change accordingly. If your printout will be more than one page, you can use the arrow buttons beneath the preview to see what each page will look like when printed.

When you're ready to print, click the Print button at the bottom-right corner of the dialog box. The document is sent to the printer.

Tip You can use options under the PDF menu at the bottom of the Print dialog box to create, email, or fax a PDF of your document. You might find this handy to share a "hard copy" of your tasks list without actually printing it. You can learn more about this Mac OS X feature in Mac OS Help.

In this exercise, you'll open the Print dialog box and explore some of its printing options.

 SET UP No setup is required. Make sure you are in Tasks view and then follow these steps.

Print

1. On the toolbar, click the **Print** button. The Print dialog box appears.

2. If the dialog box does not include options and a preview area, click the disclosure triangle beside the **Printer** pop-up menu.

3. In the **Print** drop-down list, select each of the different options, one at a time, and see the results in the preview area.

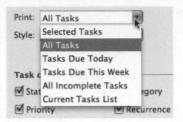

The number of tasks that appear should change depending on what option is selected.

4. In the **Print** drop-down list, select **All Tasks**.

5. If necessary, in the **Style** drop-down list, select **Memo**.

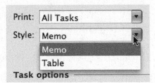

The preview area shows task details listed one above the other.

6. In the **Style** drop-down list, select **Table**. The preview area changes to show tasks in a tabular format.

7. Clear the **Wrap Text** check box. Only the first few words of the notes field appear in the table.

Note The Wrap Text check box appears when Table is chosen in the Style drop-down list, but is covered by the drop-down list when open.

8. Select the **Wrap Text** check box to display all notes for each task.

9. In the **Task options** area, toggle check boxes to see the changes in the preview area. Column widths automatically change to distribute displayed information.

10. In the **Style** drop-down list, select **Memo**.

11. In the **Task options** area, toggle check boxes to see the changes in the preview area. The number of lines of information for each task changes accordingly.

12. (Optional) Click **Print**. The tasks list is sent to your printer and the Print dialog box disappears.

✖ **CLEAN UP** If you did not print the tasks list, click the Cancel button in the Print dialog box to dismiss it without printing.

Key Points

- You can use Outlook to keep track of tasks you need to complete.
- In addition to a task name, a task can also include a due date, start date, reminder, and detailed description.
- Tasks can be categorized to help organize them by context.
- You can create recurring tasks for things you need to do regularly.
- Flagging an item for follow up creates a task for it.
- You can view tasks a number of ways.
- You can filter or search your tasks list to find specific tasks.
- You can modify a task, mark a task as completed, or remove a task at any time.
- You can print tasks lists in two formats with the fields you specify.

Chapter at a Glance

Create formatted notes in Notes view, **page 335**

Share notes with others via e-mail, **page 348**

Use the Media Browser to add photos to notes, **page 339**

Sort notes by any field of information, **page 343**

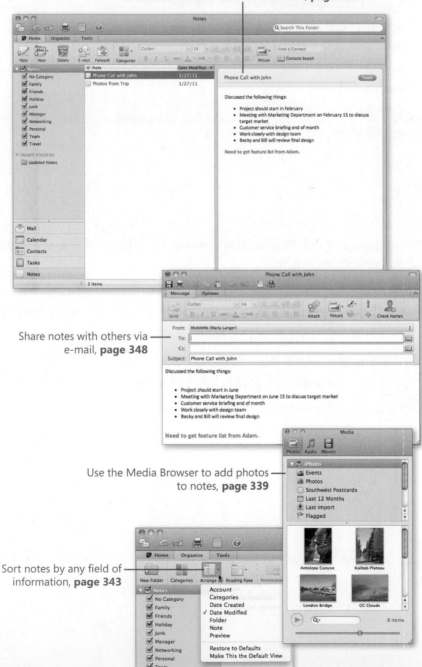

13 Taking Notes

In this chapter, you will learn how to

✔ Create notes.

✔ Format notes.

✔ View and organize notes.

✔ Share notes.

As you work, you may find a need to jot down notes in a place they can be easily saved and accessed. Perhaps it's an idea that just came to you that you don't want to forget. Or maybe it's a bunch of key points from a telephone conversation or from a report you just read. No matter what the source, you'll probably agree that it's better to file all your notes in one place rather than on scraps of paper scattered all over your desk.

The Notes feature of Microsoft Outlook for Mac 2011 might be just what you're looking for. It enables you to create formatted notes that you can organize by category or folder. The notes can include text and pictures. Once created, they can be edited, sent in an email, or forwarded to a friend or coworker.

In this chapter, you'll take a look at the Notes feature of Outlook for Mac. You'll learn how to create, format, and organize notes. You'll also see how you can share your notes with others.

> **Practice Files** Before you can complete the exercises in this chapter, you need to copy the book's practice files to your computer. The practice files you'll use to complete the exercises in this chapter are in the Chapter13 practice files folder. A complete list of practice files is provided in "Using the Practice Files" at the beginning of this book.

Creating Notes

You create a note in the Notes view of Outlook. Start by clicking the Note button on the Home tab to display a note window.

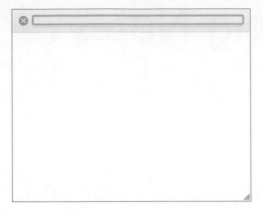

As you can see, the note window is very simple. It includes just two fields:

● **Note name or title** Use this field to enter a brief name or title for the note. This is what appears in the note list.

● **Note contents** This is the main part of the note window. The note contents can include formatted text and pictures.

After you've entered the name and content for a note, you can use the Save command or Command+S shortcut key to save it. Or simply close the window and click Save in the dialog sheet that appears. The note appears in the notes list in Notes view.

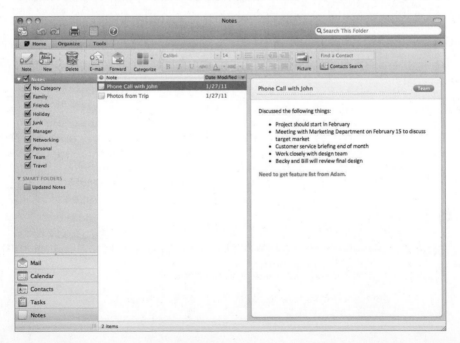

In this exercise, you'll create and save two simple notes that consist of a note name and some brief text.

SET UP You need the Phone Call Note text document located in the Chapter13 practice files folder to complete this exercise. Double-click the text document to open it in TextEdit (or your default text editing application). You'll use the text in this document in the body of one of the notes you create. Leave the document open and switch to Outlook. In the view switcher, click Notes to switch to Notes view. Then follow these steps.

Note

1. On the **Home** tab, click the **Note** button. A blank note window appears.

2. In the note name field (which should be selected), type **Photos from Trip**.

3. Press the Tab key to move the cursor to the note contents field.

4. Type **We visited the Grand Canyon on our trip.** Then press Return twice.

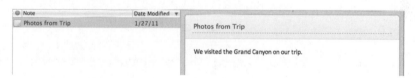

5. Press Command+S. Behind the note window, a new note appears in the notes list in the main Outlook window.

You'll insert some photos in an exercise later in this chapter.

6. In the note window, click the close button, which looks like a large X. The note window disappears.

7. On the **Home** tab, click the **Note** button to open a new note window.

8. In the note name field, type **Phone Call with John.**

9. Press the Tab key to move the cursor to the note contents field.

10. Type **Discussed the following things:**. Then press Return twice.

11. Switch to the **Phone Call Note** text document.

12. Press Command+A to select all text in the document.

13. Press Command+C to copy all selected text.

14. Press Command+Q to quit **TextEdit** (or the application in which the document was opened).

15. If necessary, switch to Outlook and display the **Phone Call with John** note.

16. With the blinking cursor after the text typed in the body of the note, press Command+V to paste in the copied text.

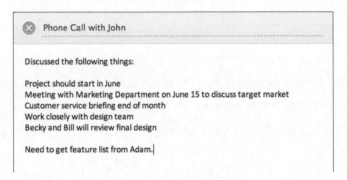

You'll format this text in an exercise later in this chapter.

17. In the note window, click the close button. A dialog sheet appears, asking if you want to save changes.

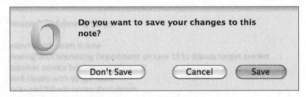

Outlook won't let you close the window without reminding you to save changes.

18. Click **Save**. The dialog sheet and note window disappear and the new note appears in the notes list.

 **CLEAN UP** No clean-up steps are required. You are ready to continue to the next exercise.

Formatting Notes

Outlook offers the same kind of formatting for notes as it does for email messages. You can change the font and font size of text; make text bold, italic, or underlined; and even change text color. You can also create bulleted or numbered lists, modify paragraph alignment, and adjust indentation. All of these options are easily accessible using buttons and menus on the Home tab.

See Also For more information about formatting text in Outlook, consult the section titled "Formatting Message Text" in Chapter 3, "Composing and Sending Email Messages."

You can also include images within notes. Outlook offers two ways to insert images: with the Photo Browser that's part of the Media Browser window and by selecting an image from a standard Mac OS Open dialog box. You can even drag an image from the Finder into a note window or paste a copied image into a note.

See Also For more information about inserting pictures into Outlook items, consult the section titled "Inserting Media in Messages" in Chapter 3.

In this exercise, you'll format one of the notes you created in the previous exercise and add photos to the other one. This will give you a good chance to explore note formatting options.

SET UP You need the images located in the Chapter13/Images folder to complete this exercise. Copy the image files to iPhoto (if it is installed on your computer). These images were used in exercises for Chapter 3, so if you've already copied them to iPhoto, you can skip this step to avoid duplicates. (Note that if you do not have iPhoto installed, you will not be able to complete steps 12 through 17.) Make sure you're in Notes view and follow these steps.

1. In the notes list, select the **Phone Call with John** note. The note text appears in the reading pane.

2. In the reading pane, select the five lines in the middle of the note.

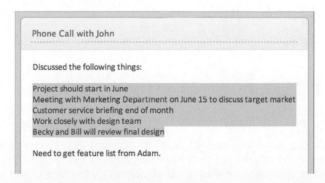

Bulleted List

3. On the **Home** tab, click the **Bulleted List** button. The selected lines are formatted as a bulleted list.

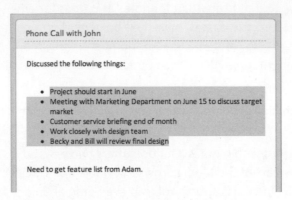

Phone Call with John

Discussed the following things:

- Project should start in June
- Meeting with Marketing Department on June 15 to discuss target market
- Customer service briefing end of month
- Work closely with design team
- Becky and Bill will review final design

Need to get feature list from Adam.

4. In the reading pane, select the line *Need to get feature list from Adam.*

Font Size

5. On the **Home** tab, enter **16** in the **Font Size** box, and then press Return. The selected text becomes larger.

Tip You could also click the arrow beside the Font Size box to choose one of several predefined sizes.

Bold

6. On the **Home** tab, click the **Bold** button. The selected text becomes bold.

Font Color

7. On the **Home** tab, click the arrow on the **Font Color** button to display a menu of colors.

8. Click **Red**. The selected text turns red.

Tip If red already appears on the Font Color button, you don't need to display the menu to apply the red color to selected text. Instead, just click the button. Display the menu when you want to apply a color that is not displayed on the face of the button.

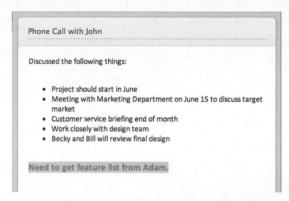

9. In the notes list, click the **Photos from Trip** note. Outlook does not prompt you to save changes to the other note. Changes are saved automatically.

10. In the reading pane, click to place the cursor on one of the blank lines after the note text.

Picture

11. On the **Home** tab, click the **Picture** button to display a menu of options.

12. Click **Photo Browser**. The Photos pane of the Media Browser window appears.

13. Locate the image called **GC Clouds** and select it.

Tip If you have many images, you can type the name *GC Clouds* into the Spotlight search box at the bottom of the browser window to find it.

14. Drag the **GC Clouds** image from the browser window into the reading pane. When you release the mouse button, the image appears in the note.

15. Click the **Media Browser** window's close button to dismiss it.

16. In the reading pane, position the blinking cursor after the image, and then press Return twice.

17. On the **Home** tab, click the **Picture** button to display its menu.

18. Click **Picture from File**. A standard Open dialog sheet appears.

19. Navigate to the **Chapter13/Images** folder, and then select the image named **GC Trees**.

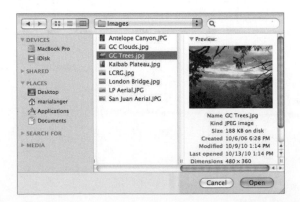

20. Click **Open**. The image is inserted into the note.

 CLEAN UP No clean-up steps are required. You are ready to continue to the next exercise.

Viewing and Organizing Notes

Outlook offers a number of ways to view and organize notes:

- Use the Reading Pane menu on the Organize tab to change the layout of the reading pane in Notes view.
- Sort notes by a specific note field.
- Assign one or more categories to a note to view notes by category.
- File notes into folders, including custom folders you create.
- Search for notes that match criteria you specify.
- Create and view the contents of smart folders that display notes matching saved criteria.

If these techniques sound familiar, it's because they also apply to items in most other Outlook views. Rather than read through the techniques again here, you can review them in previous chapters.

See Also Working with reading pane options is discussed in detail in the section titled "Viewing Tasks" in Chapter 12, "Tracking Tasks"; searching for items is covered in the section titled "Searching for Tasks." Hiding and displaying categories is covered in the section titled "Assigning Categories to Contacts" in Chapter 10, "Organizing Your Contacts List"; working with folders is covered in the section titled "Organizing Contacts with Folders." Although these sections apply to other views, these features work virtually the same for tasks. Customizing the category list is discussed in detail in the section titled "Managing Categories" in Chapter 14, "Using Shared Features."

In this exercise, you'll review some of the viewing and organization features of Outlook as they apply to notes.

 SET UP No setup is required. Just follow these steps.

Reading Pane

1. On the **Organize** tab, click the **Reading Pane** button to display a menu of options.

2. Click **Below**. The reading pane shifts into position below the notes list.

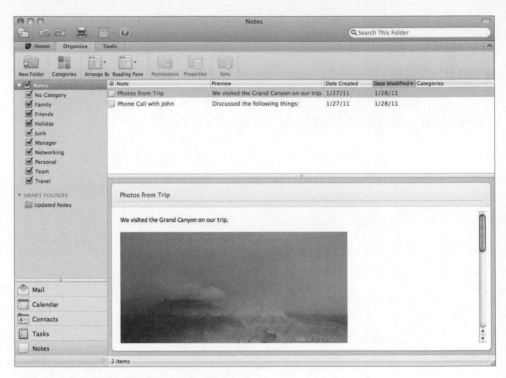

Arrange By

3. On the **Organize** tab, click the **Arrange By** button to display a menu of options.

4. Click **Note**. The notes are sorted by name.

5. In the notes pane, click the **Date Modified** column. The notes are sorted by the modification date and time. (You may not notice a change with only two notes.)

6. Click the **Date Modified** column again. The notes are sorted in descending order by the modification date and time. (The two notes should switch position.)

7. In the notes list, select the **Phone Call with John** note.

8. On the **Home** or **Organize** tab, click the **Categorize** button to display a menu of categories.

Categorize

9. Click **Team**. The Team category is assigned to the note. Team appears in the Categories column beside the note in the notes list and on the right side of the note title area in the reading pane.

10. In the notes list, select the **Photos from Trip** note.

11. On the **Home** or **Organize** tab, click the **Categorize** button, and then click **Family** from the menu that appears. The Family category is applied to the note.

12. Repeat step 11, but this time, click **Friends**. The Friends category is also applied to the note.

13. In the navigation pane, clear the top-level check box for **Notes**. This should clear all the other check boxes. The notes list clears.

    Tip If you have more than one folder of notes, clear the top-level check boxes for all folders.

14. In the navigation pane, select the check box beside **Friends**. The Photos From Trip note reappears. You can use these check boxes to display only certain categories of notes.

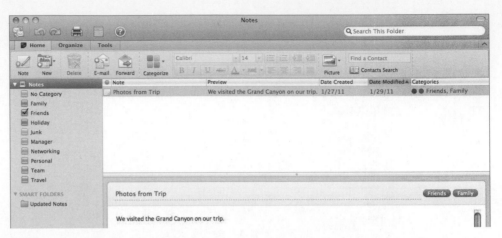

15. In the navigation pane, select the top-level check box for **Notes**. All check boxes become selected again and both notes are displayed.

New

16. On the **Home** tab, click the **New** button to display a menu of options.

17. Click **Folder**. An untitled folder appears under On My Computer in the navigation pane.

18. While the folder name is still selected, type **Photos**, and then press Return.

19. If necessary, click the disclosure triangle beside **Photos** to display a list of categories.

20. Drag the **Photos from Trip** note from the notes list to the **Photos** folder in the navigation pane. The Photos from Trip note disappears from the notes list.

21. In the navigation pane, select the **Photos** check box. All category check boxes beneath it are selected and the Photos From Trip note reappears.

22. Drag the **Photos from Trip** note from the notes list to the **Personal** category under **Notes**. This moves the note out of the Photos folder and back into the Notes folder. It also adds the Personal category.

23. In the navigation pane, select the **Photos** folder.

24. On the **Home** tab, click the **Delete** button. A confirmation dialog box appears.

25. Click **Delete**. The Photos folder is removed from the navigation pane.

Delete

 CLEAN UP On the Organize tab, click the Arrange By button, and then click Restore To Defaults to restore the notes to the default sort order. Then on the Organize tab, click the Reading Pane button, and click Right to restore the window to the usual reading pane arrangement. You are now ready to continue to the next exercise.

Sharing Notes

Outlook offers three buttons for sharing your notes with others:

- **Email** This button enables you to email your note to someone else. Clicking this button creates an email message with your note in the message body. You address the note, make changes to the subject and contents as necessary, and send it.

    See Also Composing and sending email messages is covered in detail in Chapter 3.

- **Forward** The Forward button enables you to forward your note to someone else. Clicking this button creates an email message with an HTML version of your note attached. The recipient can open the note in his or her Web browser or any other application able to open and read HTML files.

    See Also File attachments are discussed in the section titled "Attaching Files to Messages" in Chapter 3.

- **Print** This button enables you to print one or more notes. Clicking this button opens the Print dialog box, which you can use to set options for printing notes:

    - ○ **Print** Use this drop-down list to specify whether you want to print selected notes or all notes.

    - ○ **Note options** Use check boxes to determine whether printed notes should include pictures in the notes and note backgrounds.

    - ○ **Page options** Use check boxes to specify whether printed notes should include the date and time printed and page numbers.

    When you click Print, the notes document is sent to your printer and printed.

In this exercise, you'll explore each of these three options to learn how you can share your notes with others.

 SET UP No setup is required. Just follow these steps.

1. In the notes list, select the **Phone Call with John** note.

Email

2. On the **Home** tab, click the **Email** button. Outlook opens a new message composition window with the contents of the note inserted into the message body. The note's formatting is retained.

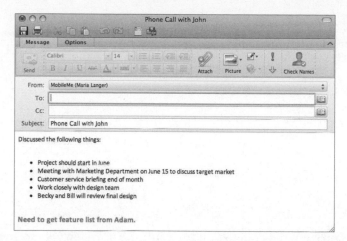

Send

3. To send the message to someone, enter a valid email address or contact name in the **To** field, and then click the **Send** button. Otherwise, close the window without saving changes.

4. On the **Home** tab, click the **Forward** button. Outlook opens a new message composition window with an HTML file attachment named for the note. The message body is empty.

Forward

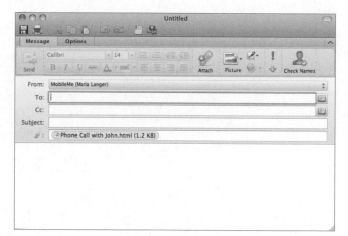

5. To see what the attachment looks like, double-click it. If a warning dialog box appears telling you that the document is a Web application downloaded from the Internet, click **Open**. Your default Web browser opens and displays the message as formatted text in a Web browser window. When you're finished looking at it, **Quit** your Web browser and return to Outlook.

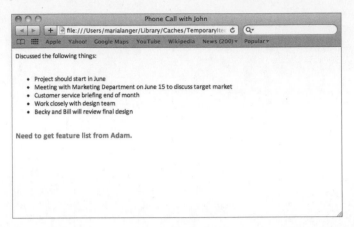

> **Tip** This step is not required to forward a note. It's provided only so you can see what a note you forward might look like to the recipient when he or she opens it.

6. To send the message to someone, enter a valid email address or contact name in the **To** field, and then click the **Send** button. Otherwise, close the window without saving changes.

7. On the toolbar, click the **Print** button. The Print dialog box appears.

Print

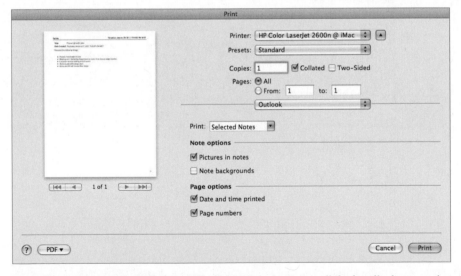

> **Tip** If a smaller version of the Print dialog box appears, click the disclosure triangle to the right of the Printer menu to expand it.

8. Make sure **Outlook** is selected from the menu beneath the **Pages** options near the top of the dialog box.

9. On the **Print** drop-down list, click **All Notes**.

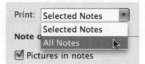

The preview area should change to display the Photos From Trip note.

10. Clear the **Pictures in notes** check box. The photos disappear from the note in the preview area.

11. Select the **Pictures in notes** check box to display the pictures again.

12. Clear the two check boxes in the **Page options** area while watching the preview area. The two items disappear from the preview.

13. (Optional) Click **Print**. The notes are sent to your printer and the Print dialog box disappears.

✖ **CLEAN UP** If you did not print the notes list, click the Cancel button in the Print dialog box to dismiss it without printing.

Key Points

- You can use the notes feature of Outlook to create and save notes.

- Notes can include formatted text and photos.

- Notes view supports the same viewing, sorting, categorization, and organization features found in other Outlook views.

Part 6

Program Management

Chapter at a Glance

Use Spotlight searching to search throughout Outlook, **page 366**

Look up words in a Thesaurus and Dictionary, **page 362**

Use the Categories preferences pane to manage Outlook categories, **page 356**

Configure the AutoCorrect feature to correct text as you type, **page 377**

14 Using Shared Features

In this chapter, you will learn how to

✔ Manage categories.

✔ Use the Toolbox.

✔ Search with Spotlight.

✔ Check spelling and grammar.

✔ Use AutoCorrect and AutoFormat.

✔ Use the My Day application.

✔ Import and export data.

Many features and interface elements in Microsoft Outlook for Mac 2011 are shared among its different views. For example, all views use categories to help organize information and put it in context. The ribbon's Home or Organize tab in each view has the same Categorize button with a menu of the same categories that can be assigned to items.

The Toolbox is another example of an Outlook for Mac feature that is available in all views. You can use its two panes—Scrapbook and Reference—to store and look up items no matter what view you're working with. Other shared features include Spotlight searching, spelling check, and AutoCorrect.

A handful of other features work with multiple Outlook views. For example, the My Day window combines calendar events with tasks in one window. With the Import and Export features, you can import data from other applications into Outlook and export data from Outlook to be used in other applications.

In this chapter, you'll learn about using shared features, such as managing categories, using the Toolbox, searching with Spotlight, and checking spelling. You'll see how you can configure and use the AutoCorrect feature and My Day window. You'll also explore the Import and Export windows to learn how to move data between Outlook and other applications.

> **Practice Files** Before you can complete the exercises in this chapter, you need to copy the book's practice files to your computer. The practice file you'll use to complete the exercises in this chapter is in the Chapter14 practice files folder. A complete list of practice files is provided in "Using the Practice Files" at the beginning of this book.

Managing Categories

As discussed throughout this book, with the category feature of Outlook, you can assign various categories to Outlook items. This gives you a way to organize them by context. Former Microsoft Entourage users might also find the category feature handy for managing the items related to specific categories.

By default, Outlook comes preconfigured with nine color-coded categories: Family, Friends, Holiday, Junk, Manager, Networking, Personal, Team, and Travel. Although you might find these useful for your needs, you can also make changes to the category list to add, rename, delete, or change the color of categories. This helps you customize Outlook so it works the way you need it to.

You manage Outlook categories in the Categories preferences pane, which lists all categories. For each category, there's a menu of colors and a check box to determine whether the category should appear in the navigation pane. You can use the buttons at the bottom of the list to add a new category or remove a selected one.

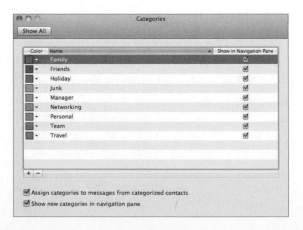

You can also add a category on the fly when you use the Categorize menu on the Home or Organize tab of the ribbon. Choosing the Add New command from the menu displays a dialog sheet you can use to enter a name and choose a color for the new category. Clicking OK adds the category to the category list.

When you make changes to the category list, your changes are automatically reflected on the Categorize menu and in the navigation pane in each view.

The Categories preferences pane also offers two options that control how categories are used by Outlook:

- **Assign categories to messages from categorized contacts** When this check box is selected, incoming and outgoing email messages will automatically be categorized based on the categories assigned to the contacts they are to or from. For example, if you receive a message from a contact categorized as Friends, that message will automatically be assigned to the Friends category. This option is enabled by default.

- **Show new categories in navigation pane** When this check box is selected, every time you create a new category, the category automatically appears in the navigation pane for all views except Mail view. This option is also turned on by default.

After you've assigned categories to your Outlook items, you can specify which items should appear in Calendar, Contacts, Tasks, and Notes view by toggling check boxes in the navigation pane. When a category check box is selected, all items with that category applied appear in the item list. When a check box is cleared, items with only that category applied are hidden from the items list. If an item has more than one category applied to it, it will appear in the item list if any of its category check boxes are selected. In addition, if every category in a navigation pane folder is selected, all items in that folder will be displayed, regardless of category.

In this exercise, you'll use the Categories preferences pane to make changes to the category list and the categories that appear in Outlook.

SET UP In Outlook, switch to Mail view. Then follow these steps.

Categorize

1. Click the **Categorize** button to display its menu of options.

2. Click **Add New**. A dialog sheet for creating a new category appears.

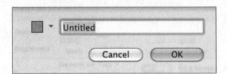

3. In the edit box, type **Project X**. The word *Untitled* is replaced with *Project X*.

4. Click the triangle between the colored square and edit box to display a menu of colors.

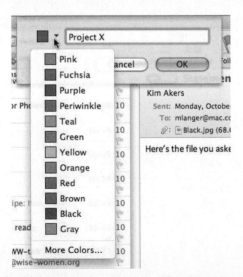

5. Click **More Colors**. A standard Mac OS Colors panel appears.

6. Use the color picker of your choice to select a color you like, and then click the **Colors** panel's close button to dismiss it. The color you selected appears in the dialog sheet.

   See Also For more information about using standard Mac OS X interface elements such as the Colors panel, consult Mac OS Help.

7. Click **OK**. The new category is created with the name and color you specified and is assigned to the currently selected email message.

8. On the ribbon's **Home** tab, click the **Categorize** button to display its menu again. The new category appears on the menu.

9. Click **Project X**. The category is removed from the currently selected email message.

10. On the **Home** tab, click the **Categorize** button to display its menu again, and then click **Edit Categories**. The Categories preferences pane appears.

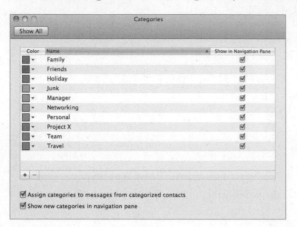

11. Double-click the **Project X** category name. An edit box appears around it.

12. Type **Product Q**, and then press Return. The category is renamed.

13. Click the triangle to the left of the **Product Q** category name to display a menu of colors. Note that none of the colors is selected because you created this category with a custom color.

14. Click **Yellow**. The category's color changes.

15. Click the **+** button at the bottom of the category list. A new category dialog sheet like the one you saw earlier appears.

16. Name the new category **Test**, choose **Black** for its color, and then click **OK**. The Test category is added to the list.

17. In the main Outlook window, switch to **Calendar** view.

18. If necessary, click the disclosure triangle(s) in the navigation pane to see a list of categories. Both Product Q and Test are listed.

These categories appear in all views as well as on the Categorize menu.

19. On the menu bar, click the **Window** menu, and then click **Categories**. The Categories preferences pane appears atop the main Outlook window.

20. In the **Categories** preferences pane, clear the check boxes beside the **Family**, **Friends**, and **Personal** categories. As you clear each check box, the associated category is removed from the navigation pane.

This change applies to all Outlook views except Mail.

21. In the **Categories** preferences pane, select the **Product Q** category.

22. At the bottom of the category list, click the **–** button. A dialog sheet appears, asking if you're sure you want to delete the category.

23. Click **Delete**. The Product Q category is removed from Outlook.

> **Tip** When you delete a category, it is deleted throughout Outlook. Only the category is deleted, however. Outlook items that have been assigned to that category are not removed; instead, the deleted category is removed from the item.

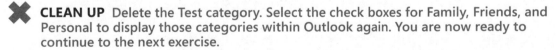 **CLEAN UP** Delete the Test category. Select the check boxes for Family, Friends, and Personal to display those categories within Outlook again. You are now ready to continue to the next exercise.

Using the Toolbox

The Toolbox is a part of Microsoft Office that is available in all Office applications. In Outlook, however, it offers just two panels:

- **Scrapbook** This panel enables you to store text, graphics, or other content that you use again and again throughout Office. You might use this to store your company logo, some boilerplate text, or your scanned signature. After an item is stored in the Scrapbook, it remains there, accessible to all Office applications, until you delete it. So even if you've never used the Scrapbook in Outlook, if you've stored content in the Scrapbook while working with Microsoft Word or Microsoft Excel, that content will appear in Outlook.

- **Reference Tools** This panel gives you access to five different reference tools: Thesaurus, Dictionary, Bilingual Dictionary, Translation, and Web Search. Some of these tools require you to be connected to the Internet to use them.

The Toolbox works the same way in Outlook as it does in any other Office application. Use commands on the View menu to open the Toolbox panel you want. Then use options within the panel to get the content or information you need.

In this exercise, you'll open each of the two Toolbox panels and take a closer look at the features each offers.

SET UP Switch to Notes view. If you completed the exercises in Chapter 13, "Taking Notes," and have not deleted the two sample notes, select the Phone Call With John note. If you do not have that note, select any existing note that includes text; you can create a new note if you need to. Then follow these steps.

1. On the menu bar, click the **View** menu to display it.

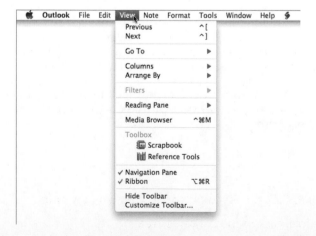

2. Click **Scrapbook**. The Toolbox window opens with the Scrapbook panel displayed.

> **Tip** If you have already added content to the Scrapbook in Microsoft PowerPoint, Word, Excel, or Outlook, that content will appear in the top part of the Scrapbook panel.

3. In the reading pane, select some text from the note.

4. In the **Scrapbook**, click the **Add** button. The selected text is added to the Scrapbook as a clipping.

5. On the **Home** tab, click the **Note** button to create a new note.

6. In the note window, click in the contents area.

Note

Paste

7. In the **Scrapbook**, select the text clipping you added earlier.

8. Click the **Paste** button. The clipping text is pasted into the note.

9. Click the note's close button. When prompted to save changes, click **Don't Save**.

10. At the top of the **Scrapbook** panel, click the **Reference Tools** button to display the **Reference Tools** panel.

11. One by one, click the disclosure triangles beside each tool heading to display and then hide them. You must display a tool to use it.

12. Click the disclosure triangles to display both the **Thesaurus** and **Dictionary** tools.

13. In the **Word or Phrase** box at the top of the panel, type **business**, and then press Return. The Meanings, Synonyms, and Dictionary areas fill with information.

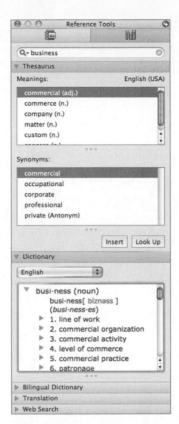

Troubleshooting If a message in the Dictionary area tells you that access to online Reference Tools is turned off, click the Here link to allow access.

14. Explore these features by double-clicking meanings and synonyms to look up words. You can get details for a definition by clicking the disclosure triangle beside the brief definition that interests you in the Dictionary area. Keep in mind that clicking the Insert button will insert the currently selected synonym into the active Outlook item—email message, calendar event, note, and so on.

15. Click the disclosure triangle beside **Dictionary** to hide the Dictionary and, instead, display the **Bilingual Dictionary**. Meanings and translations for the selected word appear in the To language.

16. Experiment with other tools and options to get an idea of how the Reference Tools work.

CLEAN UP Close the Toolbox by clicking the close button in the References Tools panel. You are ready to continue to the next exercise.

Searching with Spotlight

The Spotlight search box at the top of the main Outlook window performs two related functions:

- It initiates a search for the word or phrase you type in the currently selected folder, the folder and subfolders, the current view, or throughout Outlook.
- It displays the ribbon's Search contextual tab, which gives you access to the filters and advanced search options for the view you are in.

See Also Using filters and advanced search features is covered in the chapters related to specific Outlook views. For email, consult the section titled "Searching for Messages with Filters" in Chapter 5, "Organizing Your Inbox." For contacts, consult the section titled "Searching for Contacts" in Chapter 10, "Organizing Your Contacts List." For tasks, consult "Filtering Tasks" and "Searching for Tasks" in Chapter 12, "Tracking Tasks."

Using Spotlight to find a specific type of item in Outlook is easy. Switch to the view containing the item you want to find. For example, if you're looking for an email message, you'd switch to Mail view. Then, in the navigation pane, select the folder you want to search. In Mail view, that might be your Inbox or a specific mail folder. Click in the Spotlight search box and begin typing the word or phrase you want to search for. Outlook quickly begins matching what you type and lists the search results in the item list. You can then view the details of an item in the reading pane.

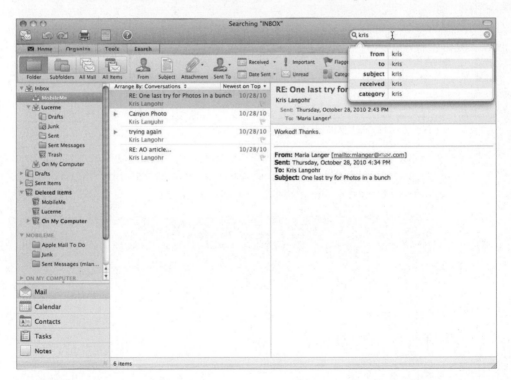

You can also use Spotlight searching to search specific locations in a view or throughout Outlook. With the Search tab displayed, click the button for the option you want.

Folder

- **Folder** Searches the folder currently selected in the navigation pane.

Subfolder

- **Subfolders** Searches the folder currently selected in the navigation pane and its subfolders.

All Mail

- **All Mail** Searches all Mail view items. This option only appears if you are in Mail view.

All Events

- **All Events** Searches all Calendar view items. This option only appears if you are in Calendar view.

All Contacts

- **All Contacts** Searches all Contacts view items. This option only appears if you are in Contacts view.

All Tasks

- **All Tasks** Searches all Tasks view items. This option only appears if you are in Tasks view.

All Notes

- **All Notes** Searches all Notes view items. This option only appears if you are in Notes view.

All Items

- **All Items** Searches throughout Outlook.

When you use the All Items option, the item list displays a mix of item types: email messages, appointments, meetings, contacts, tasks, and notes. You can click any item in the list to see its details in the reading pane.

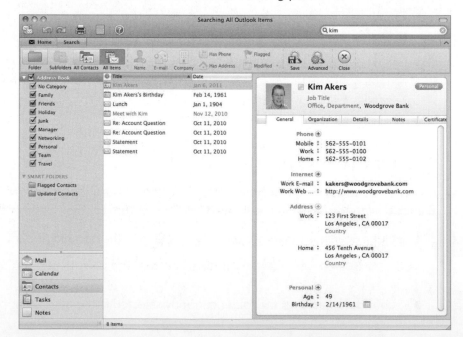

Tip Spotlight searching is a good way to start your search for content in Outlook. After you begin a search with Spotlight, you can fine-tune your search criteria by using other options on the Search tab for the current Outlook view.

In this exercise, you'll experiment with the Spotlight search feature in Outlook by searching for items in specific views and throughout Outlook.

SET UP This exercise assumes you have either sample data created throughout this book or your own data in Outlook. If you have no data, you can follow along with these instructions, but search results will be empty. In the view switcher, click Contact to switch to Contacts view.

1. In the **Spotlight** search box in the upper-right corner of the Outlook window, type all or part of the first name of any contact. As you type, three things happen:

   ○ The Outlook ribbon switches to the Search contextual tab.

   ○ A menu of options appears under the Spotlight search box.

   ○ A list of possible matches appears in the item list.

2. On the menu under the Spotlight search box, click **name**. The contents of the Spotlight search box change to include *name:* before your search string. This narrows down the search to only contacts with that search string in a Name field.

3. In the **Spotlight** search box, click the **X** to clear the search criteria. Then type the same thing you typed in step 1.

4. On the menu under the Spotlight search box, click **company**. The contents of the Spotlight search box change to include *company:* before your search string. This narrows down the search to include contacts with that search string in the Company field. (You may have no results.)

5. On the **Search** tab, click the **All Items** button. The item list remains unchanged.

6. Edit the contents of the **Spotlight** search box so only your original search criteria appears. This time, the menu beneath the search box shows different options. In addition, more items may appear in the item list.

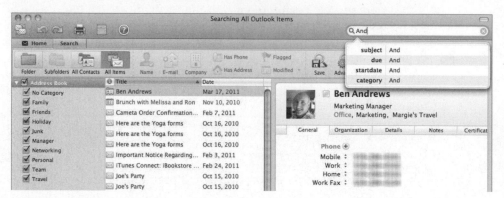

7. On the **Search** tab, click the **All Contacts** button. The item list displays only contacts that match the search criteria.

8. In the view switcher, click **Calendar** to switch to **Calendar** view.

9. In the **Spotlight** search box, type **meeting** or some other word you often use in calendar item names or descriptions. Outlook hides the reading pane and displays a list of items that meet your criteria.

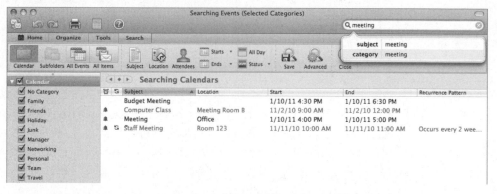

10. On the **Search** tab, click **All Items**. The window changes to display a list of matches in the item list and details about the selected item in the reading pane.

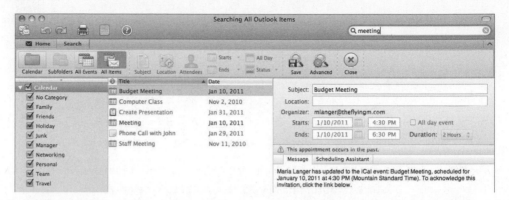

11. In the **Spotlight** search box, click the **X** to clear the search criteria. The Search tab disappears and Calendar view returns to its default appearance.

✖ **CLEAN UP** No clean-up steps are required. You are ready to continue to the next exercise.

Checking Spelling and Grammar

Outlook, like all other Office applications, has built-in spelling and grammar checking capabilities. You can use options under the Edit menu's Spelling And Grammar submenu to configure these features to work a number of ways:

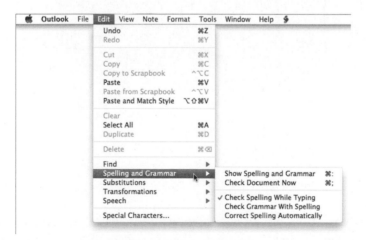

- **Check Spelling While Typing** This command tells Outlook to automatically check spelling in the background, as you type. When it finds a potential error, it displays a red dashed underline beneath it.

- **Check Grammar With Spelling** This command tells Outlook to check grammar as it checks spelling. This works with automatic spelling check or a manual spelling check. During an automatic spelling and grammar check, when Outlook finds a potential error, it displays a green dashed underline beneath it.

- **Correct Spelling Automatically** This command enables the Outlook AutoCorrect feature to automatically correct potential spelling errors. When enabled, this feature automatically replaces what Outlook believes is a misspelled word with the most likely correct spelling.

  See Also The AutoCorrect feature of Outlook is discussed in greater detail in the section titled "Using AutoCorrect and AutoFormat," later in this chapter.

With automatic spelling check turned on, correcting a spelling (or grammar) error is easy. Simply right-click on the problem word or phrase and use the contextual menu that appears to resolve the problem. In most cases, the contextual menu will offer at least one possible correction for the misspelled word. You can select it, and Outlook makes the correction.

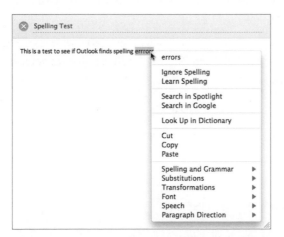

Outlook flags all words it does not recognize, even if those words are correctly spelled. For example, it may flag a proper noun such as a name or company name that it does not recognize. If you don't want Outlook to bother you about that word again, you can use one of two options on the contextual menu:

- **Ignore Spelling** This option ignores all occurrences of that word in the Outlook item.

- **Learn Spelling** This option adds the word to the Mac OS X dictionary shared by applications that use Mac OS spelling tools, such as TextEdit.

The grammar checking feature works much the same way, offering corrections based on grammar rules.

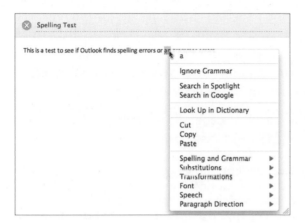

Outlook also offers the ability to manually check spelling and grammar in an Outlook item. This requires that you use one of two commands on the Spelling And Grammar submenu under the Edit menu:

- **Show Spelling and Grammar** This command displays the Spelling And Grammar window, which you can use to check for and review possible errors in your document, one at a time. Using this command immediately begins a check of the active Outlook item, starting at the cursor.

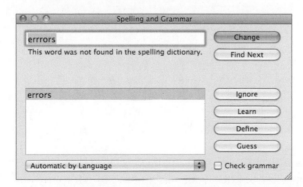

Tip Another way to open the Spelling And Grammar window while composing an email is to click the Spelling button on the Options tab in the message composition window.

- **Check Document Now** This command starts checking the active Outlook item immediately. If Outlook does not find any errors, it does not display the Spelling And Grammar window.

Tip Generally speaking, if you enabled automatic spelling or spelling and grammar check in Outlook, you would not need to use either of the manual spelling and grammar check commands.

The most important thing to remember about any spelling or grammar checker is that it is not foolproof. If you spell a word incorrectly and that word spells another word, Outlook will not flag it as a possible spelling error. Similarly, the grammar checker isn't programmed with all grammar rules, so it can't be relied upon to make sure your grammar is perfect. It's vital that you manually proofread any important document—such as an email message—before sharing it with others. This is true for all applications and all spelling and grammar checkers—not just Outlook and Office.

In this exercise, you'll create an email message with a number of errors, and experiment with the spelling and grammar checkers to see how they work.

SET UP In Outlook, display the Spelling And Grammar submenu under the Edit menu. Make sure check marks appear beside Check Spelling While Typing and Check Grammar With Spelling only. (You can choose a menu item to toggle its check box.) In Word or a favorite text editor, open the Message Text text document located in the Chapter14 folder. Select all text and use the Copy command to copy it to the Clipboard. Then switch to Outlook and, in the view switcher, click the Mail button to switch to Mail view. You're now ready to follow these steps.

Email

1. On the **Home** tab, click the **Email** button to open a message composition window.

2. Click to position the cursor in the message body.

3. On the **Edit** menu, click **Paste**, or press Command+V. The text you copied into the Clipboard is pasted into the body of the message composition window.

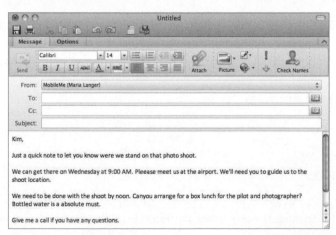

4. Click to position the cursor at the beginning of the pasted text. (This is not necessary to perform a spelling check, but it will ensure that your results match these instructions.)

Spelling

5. On the ribbon's **Options** tab, click the **Spelling** button. Outlook begins to check the spelling and grammar in the document. It should select the first unknown word, *Pleease*, and display the Spelling And Grammar window.

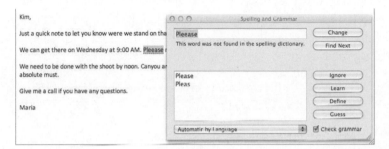

6. In the **Spelling and Grammar** window, select the correct spelling (*Please*), and then click **Change**. The misspelled word is replaced and the spelling check continues.

7. When the spelling and grammar checker stops at *Canyou*, select *Can you* in the **Spelling and Grammar** window, and then click **Change**.

8. When the spelling and grammar checker stops at *a*, select *an* in the **Spelling and Grammar** window, and then click **Change**.

9. The spelling and grammar checker does not find any other problems. Click its close button to dismiss it.

10. Read the message text carefully. Did the spelling and grammar checker find all problems? Note that the first sentence, *Just a quick note to let you know were we stand on that photo shoot*, has an error. The word *were* should be *where*. This error was not found because *were* is not a misspelled word.

11. Close the message composition window without saving changes.

12. In the view switcher, click the **Notes** button.

13. On the **Home** tab, click the **Note** button to open a note window.

14. Click to position the cursor in the note text area.

15. Type **Don't forget to check for mispelled words.** The word *mispelled* is misspelled. The spelling checker places a dotted red line beneath it.

16. Right-click on the word *mispelled*. The word is selected and a contextual menu of options appears.

17. Click *misspelled*. The selected word is replaced.

18. Click at the end of the sentence, and then press Return twice.

19. Type **Proseware, Inc**. The spelling checker marks *Proseware* as a possible misspelling.

20. Right-click on *Proseware*. The word is selected and a contextual menu of options appears. Suppose *Proseware* is the name of a real software company and is spelled correctly. If you often use this word in your documents and never want to be bothered about spelling again, click Learn Spelling. This tells the spelling checker that the word is correctly spelled and adds it to the Dictionary. If, however, you seldom use this word and just don't want to be bothered about it in this document, click Ignore Spelling. Either way, the red dotted underline beneath the word disappears. For now, click **Ignore Spelling**.

21. Close the note window without saving changes.

✖ **CLEAN UP** No clean-up steps are required. You are ready to continue to the next exercise.

Using AutoCorrect and AutoFormat

The AutoCorrect and AutoFormat features of Outlook can automatically correct and format text as you type it. This can make it quicker and easier to compose and format Outlook items.

You configure and enable the AutoCorrect and AutoFormat features in the AutoCorrect preferences pane. Each feature has its own panel of options.

AutoCorrect options control how Outlook makes changes to text. The AutoCorrect feature can make changes to text as you type it, replace text that you type with other text, and correct capitalization.

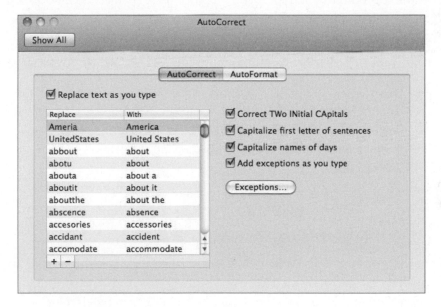

- **Replace text as you type** When this option is enabled, if you type a word that appears in the Replace column of the list, Outlook replaces it with the corresponding word in the With column of the list. As you can see by scrolling through the list, most of the words in the Replace column are common typos or misspellings. Thus, enabling this option can automatically correct some spelling errors as you type. You can add other word pairs by clicking the + button at the bottom of the list; you can remove a word pair by selecting it in the list and clicking the − button.

- **Correct TWo INitial CApitals** When this option is enabled, Outlook will automatically correct capitalization if you type two uppercase characters in a row, by converting the second character to lowercase.

- **Capitalize first letter of sentences** When this option is enabled, Outlook will automatically capitalize the first letter of the first word of a sentence. Outlook recognizes a new sentence by the presence of a period, question mark, exclamation mark, or Return character before the sentence.

- **Capitalize names of days** When this option is enabled, Outlook will automatically capitalize the first letter of weekday names: Sunday, Monday, Tuesday, and so on.

- **Add exceptions as you type** When this option is enabled, if Outlook makes a capitalization change and you immediately undo it, Outlook will add the word it changed to its exception list so it doesn't change it again.

- **Exceptions** Clicking the Exceptions button displays a dialog sheet with two panels:

  ○ **First Letter** This panel lists abbreviations ending with a period that Outlook should not recognize as the end of a sentence. Capitalization of words following these abbreviations will not be changed by Outlook. This list contains many entries; you can modify it by clicking the + and − buttons at the bottom of the list.

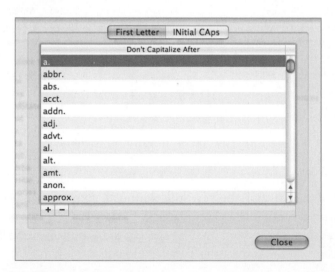

  ○ **INitial CAps** This panel lists words with two or more capital letters at the beginning of the word. Outlook will not change capitalization for any of the words on this list. The list starts out empty, but you can modify it by clicking the + and − buttons at the bottom of the list.

AutoFormat options control how Outlook formats text. The AutoFormat feature can automatically create bulleted and numbered lists, replace dashes, enter ellipsis characters, apply bold and italic formatting, and format Internet and network paths as hyperlinks.

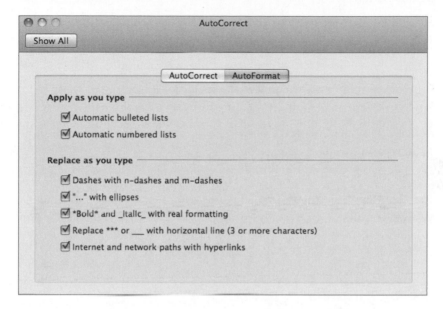

- **Apply as you type** These options will automatically apply bulleted or numbered list format when you type list items that include bullets, asterisks, or numbers. List formats include hanging indentation and are generally more attractive than plain lists.

- **Replace as you type** These options replace certain character strings with other strings or with formatting. For example, Dashes With N-Dashes And M-Dashes will replace a single dash character with an en-dash and a pair of dash characters with an em-dash. *Bold* And _Italic_ With Real Formatting applies bold or italic formatting to character strings surrounded by asterisks or underscore characters. Internet And Network Paths With Hyperlinks converts URLs into clickable links.

In this exercise, you'll check the settings for the AutoCorrect and AutoFormat features and then experiment with them to see how they work.

SET UP If necessary, in the view switcher, click the Notes button. Then click the Note button on the Home tab, position the cursor in the text area of the note, and follow these steps.

1. On the **Outlook** menu, click **Preferences**, or press Command+, (comma). The Outlook Preferences pane appears.

2. Click the **AutoCorrect** button to display the **AutoCorrect** preferences pane.

3. If necessary, click the **AutoCorrect** button to display its options.

4. For the purposes of this exercise, make sure all check boxes are selected. (This is the default setup.)

5. Scroll the replace text list so you can see the first bunch of entries.

6. Arrange the note window and **AutoCorrect** preferences pane so you can see this list and the note window at the same time, with the note window active.

7. Type **accomodate an abscence of accesories**. Because the three misspelled words are in the Replace column of the list, Outlook corrects each word as you type it.

8. Activate the **AutoCorrect** window.

9. At the bottom of the word list, click the **+** button. A new line appears at the bottom of the list.

10. Type your initials in the **Replace** box, press Tab, and type your full name in the **With** box. Then click on any other word pair in the list to save your entry.

11. Switch back to the note window, and then press Return once or twice to create a new line.

12. Type your initials and a space. Outlook replaces your initials with your name.

   Important If your initials spell a word, such as *at* or *top*, it's probably not a good idea to add this AutoCorrect shortcut to Outlook. Doing so would enter your name every time you typed that word!

13. Switch back to the **AutoCorrect** preferences pane.

14. Select the entry you created, and click the **–** button at the bottom of the list to remove it.

15. Switch back to the note window, and then press Return once or twice to create a new line.

16. Type **sunday** and a space. Outlook capitalizes the *S*.

17. Type **MIcrosoft** and a space. Outlook converts the *I* to lowercase.

18. Type **GEnie** and a space. Outlook converts the *E* to lowercase.

19. Press Command+Z to undo the correction.

20. Switch back to the **AutoCorrect** preferences pane, and then click the **Exceptions** button.

21. In the **Exceptions** dialog sheet, click the **INitial CAps** button. The word *GEnie* appears in the list. Outlook automatically added this exception when you undid its change.

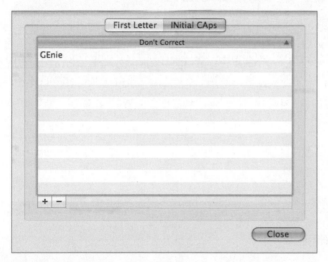

22. Select this entry and click the − button at the bottom of the list to remove it.

23. Click the **Close** button to dismiss the **Exceptions** dialog sheet.

24. In the **AutoCorrect** preferences pane, click the **AutoFormat** button to display **AutoFormat** options.

25. For the purposes of this exercise, make sure all check boxes are selected. (This is the default setup.)

26. Switch back to the note window, and then press Return once or twice to create a new line.

27. Type * **Today**, and then press Return. Outlook converts the asterisk into a bullet and creates an indented bulleted list. It even enters the next bullet for you.

28. Beside the next bullet, type **Tomorrow**, and then press Return. The list can be as long as you need it to be.

29. Press Return again. Outlook ends the list.

30. Type **http://microsoft.com**, and then press Return. Outlook formats the URL as a blue, underlined, clickable link.

✖ **CLEAN UP** Close the note window without saving changes. Click the close button at the top of the AutoCorrect preferences pane to dismiss it.

Using the My Day Application

My Day is a simple application that works with Outlook to display the calendar items and tasks for a single day. The My Day window, which is small, is perfect for leaving open on your desktop to remind you about your appointments, meetings, and tasks. Outlook does not need to be running for this window to be displayed, making it a great way to stay focused on the things you need to do without the distraction of incoming email messages.

Using My Day is easy. In Outlook, simply click the My Day button on the toolbar or choose My Day from the Window menu. The My Day window opens, displaying the current date's activities. A green arrow and horizontal line indicate the current time of day. You can use the scroll bar to scroll through the day's events and arrow buttons at the top of the window to move from day to day; the diamond-shaped button will get you right back to the current date and time. Use the buttons at the top of the Tasks pane to display unfinished or completed tasks at the bottom of the window.

Tip If Outlook is not running, you can open My Day by opening its application icon. You can find it in the Office folder inside the Microsoft Office 2011 folder in your Applications folder. If you often use My Day, consider dragging its icon to the Dock so it's quick and easy to launch any time.

Buttons at the bottom of the My Day window offer access to other features and information:

Create a Task

- **Create a task** This button displays a pop-up window you can use to enter information about a new task. The only field that is required is the Task Title field; the others are optional. When you click Save, the task is added to the Outlook Tasks list; if you set a due date to the current date, it also appears in the My Day window.

Tasks

- **Tasks** This button toggles the display of the Tasks pane at the bottom of the My Day window.

Contacts

- **Contacts** This button hides the Tasks pane (if displayed) and displays a search box you can use to search Outlook contacts. When you enter a search word or phrase and set search options, search results appear in the top of the window.

Settings

- **Settings** This button displays the My Day Preferences window, which you can use to set options for how My Day looks and works. There are three separate panes of options: General, Calendars, and Tasks.

In this exercise, you'll open the My Day window, navigate through its information, add a new task, and search for a contact.

SET UP No setup is required. Just follow these steps.

My Day

1. On the Outlook toolbar, click the **My Day** button. The My Day window opens.

2. Use the scroll bar to scroll through the day's events. Note the green arrow and line that indicate the current date and time.

3. At the top of the window, click the **Previous Day** button (the left arrow) to view the previous day's activities.

4. At the top of the window, click the **Today** button (the diamond) to return to the current day's activities.

5. At the bottom of the window, look at the **Tasks** button. If it is blue, tasks are displayed in a pane at the bottom of the window. Click the button to toggle the display. Be sure to toggle the Tasks pane back on when you're finished.

6. Click the **Completed** button. The Tasks pane displays only the current day's completed events (if any). Click the **Tasks** button again to display uncompleted tasks (if any).

7. At the bottom of the window, click the **Create a task** button to display a form for entering task details.

8. In the **Task title** field, type **Write up meeting summary.**

9. Click **Save**. The task does not appear in the My Day window because it does not have a due date of today.

10. Switch to Outlook and, if necessary, click the **Tasks** button in the view switcher to display **Tasks** view. The task you created in My Day appears in the tasks list.

11. Click the **Write up meeting summary** task to select it.

12. In the reading pane, click the **Due** field to display a date picker, and then click **Today**.

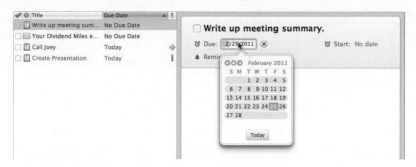

13. On the **Outlook** menu, choose **Quit Outlook**. Outlook quits, but the My Day application and its window remain open.

14. Look in the Tasks pane of the **My Day** window. The *Write up meeting summary* task now appears because it has a due date of today.

15. At the bottom of the **My Day** window, click the **Contacts** button. The Tasks pane closes and the Contacts pane appears in its place.

16. Type all or part of a contact name. (If you have the sample contacts for this book in your Outlook file, try typing **AND**.) Outlook searches through contacts and immediately displays matches in the top pane of the My Day window.

17. At the bottom of the **My Day** window, click the **Tasks** button to display calendar items and tasks again.

18. In the Tasks pane, select the **Write up meeting summary** task, and then press the Delete key.

19. In the dialog sheet that opens, click the **Delete** button. The task is removed.

20. In the top half of the **My Day** window, double-click any calendar item. Outlook opens and displays the appointment or meeting window for that event.

✖ CLEAN UP Close the appointment or meeting window without saving changes. Use the Dock to switch back to My Day. On the My Day menu, click Quit My Day. Switch back to Outlook. You are now ready to continue to the next exercise.

Importing and Exporting Data

Outlook makes it possible to import and export data in a number of formats. This makes it easy to bring information created in another application into Outlook and share Outlook information with other applications.

The import feature supports a number of formats:

- **Outlook Data File** Includes Outlook data in a file with a .pst or .olm file extension

- **Entourage information from an archive or earlier version** Includes Entourage archive files with an .rge file extension, Entourage 2008 (including the Web Services Edition), and Entourage 2004

- **Information from another application** Includes Apple Mail, most versions of Eudora, contacts saved in a comma-separated values (CSV) or tab-separated values text file, or messages saved as an MBOX format text file

- **Contacts or messages from a text file** Includes contacts saved in CSV or tab-separated values text file or messages saved as an MBOX format text file

- **Holidays** Imports holidays for one or more countries from a special Holidays file installed with Office on your computer

The export feature lets you export a variety of data types to different formats:

- **Contacts to a list** Exports contacts to a tab-delimited text file. This is a standard format text file that can be opened and read by any application able to read text.

- **Outlook for Mac Data File** Creates a file with an .olm file extension that can be read by Outlook for Mac. This makes it possible to export all or part of your Outlook data so you can import it into another copy of Outlook on another computer. You might find this useful to share Outlook data with a coworker or family member or to help speed the setup of Outlook on a new computer.

You can initiate an import or export by clicking the appropriate button on the ribbon's Tools tab. Outlook displays an Import or Export wizard that guides you, step by step, through the process of importing or exporting data.

In this exercise, you'll import holidays into Outlook and export a tab-delimited text file containing your contacts. These examples should give you a good idea of how the import and export features work.

SET UP No setup is required. Just follow these steps.

Import

1. On the ribbon's **Tools** tab, click the **Import** button to display the **Import** window.

2. Select **Holidays**, and then click the right arrow button at the bottom of the window. The Import Holidays screen appears.

3. Scroll through the list and select the check boxes for each country you want to import holidays for. Normally, this will be just your country, but if you often work with people in other countries, you can include those countries, too.

4. Click the right arrow button at the bottom of the window. Outlook imports the holidays for the countries you selected.

5. Click **OK** in the confirmation dialog box that appears.

6. Click **Finish** in the **Import** window to return to the Outlook main window.

7. If necessary, in the view switcher, click **Calendar** to switch to **Calendar** view.

8. Navigate to a month with one or more holidays. The holidays you imported appear on the calendar. In addition, Outlook may have created a new category for each country for which holidays were added and assigned that category to the imported holidays.

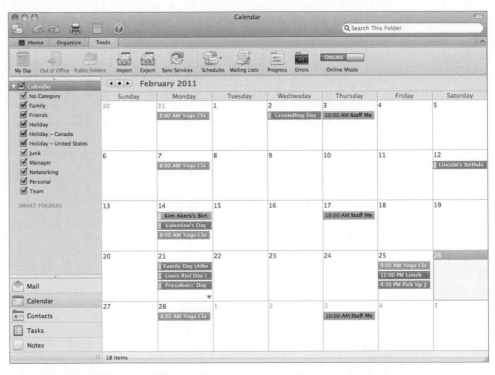

9. On the **Tools** tab, click **Export**. Outlook displays the Export window.

Export

10. Select **Contacts to a list (tab-delimited text)**, and then click the right arrow at the bottom of the window.

11. Use the **Save** dialog box that appears to navigate to the disk location where you want to save the exported data, and then click **Save**.

12. Click **Done** in the **Export** window to return to the Outlook main window.

13. In the **Finder**, navigate to the location where you saved the file, and double-click it to open it in your default text editing application. The file includes all possible field names followed by one paragraph for each contact record.

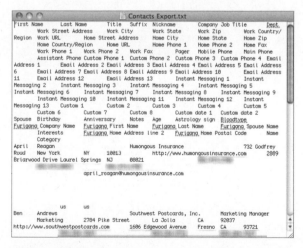

Tip This tab-delimited format can easily be imported into any database or contact management software.

 CLEAN UP Quit the text editing application you used to open the exported text file. Switch back to Outlook.

Key Points

- You can modify the default list of categories to customize it for your own needs.

- The Scrapbook makes it possible to save and reuse text, images, and other items in all Microsoft Office applications, including Outlook.

- The Toolbox contains handy reference tools such as a Dictionary and Thesaurus, as well as Web-based translation and searching.

- You can use Spotlight searching features to search throughout Outlook for items that match criteria you specify.

- You can use a spelling and grammar checker to help proofread items you create in Outlook.

- The AutoCorrect feature can correct typos and some misspellings as you type.

- The AutoFormat feature can format text as you type based on predetermined for-matting rules.

- The My Day application offers a simple interface for viewing a single day's calendar events and tasks.

- You can import and export a wide variety of Outlook data.

Glossary

address book See *contacts list*.

appointment A block of time you schedule on your calendar that has a defined start time and end time, and to which you do not invite other attendees. See also *meeting*.

appointment window The application window displaying the form in which you enter information about an appointment. See also *meeting window*.

arrangement A predefined combination of grouped and sorted messages in the item list.

AutoCorrect The feature that automatically corrects errors as you type based on your selection of predefined correction rules.

AutoFormat The feature that automatically formats text as you type based on your selection of predefined formatting rules.

calendar item An appointment or meeting.

Calendar view The application view displaying calendar items and the tools to create and manage them.

category A color-coded label that can be applied to an Outlook item to help organize, locate, or establish relationships between items.

Clipboard A Mac OS feature that enables you to copy and paste content among documents in the same or different applications.

contact A person inside or outside of a user's organization, for whom the user can save several types of information, such as street and email addresses, telephone and fax numbers, and Web page URLs.

contact card An interactive informational box that appears when you point to the presence icon of a message sender or recipient. The contact card contains contact information as well as options for contacting the person by email,

instant message, or telephone; for scheduling a meeting; and for working with the person's contact record. The expanded contact card also contains information about the person's position within the organization and distribution list memberships.

contact record A body of information you collect about a contact and store as an Outlook item.

contact window The application window displaying the form in which you enter information about a contact.

contacts list The center pane that displays content in Contacts view. Also, a group of all contacts organized by account or folder.

Contacts view The application view displaying contact records and the tools to create and manage them.

conversations A means of organizing and viewing email messages that have the same subject line.

date picker A pop-up window displaying a calendar with buttons that can be clicked to select and enter a date.

Day view A calendar view that shows the events for one day at a time.

delimited text file See *separated text file*.

Dictionary A component of the Toolbox that enables you to look up the definition of a word.

digital signature Data that binds a sender's identity to the information being sent. A digital signature can be bundled with any message, file or other digitally encoded information, or transmitted separately. Digital signatures are used in public key environments and provide authentication and integrity services.

disclosure triangle An interface element that, when clicked, expands or collapses a list of sub-items beneath an item.

distribution list A group of recipients addressed as a single recipient. Administrators can create distribution lists that are available in the contacts list. Users can create distribution lists and add them to their personal contacts lists.

domain On the Internet and other networks, the highest subdivision of a domain name in a network address, which identifies the type of entity owning the address (for example, .com for commercial users or .edu for educational institutions) or the geographical location of the address (for example, .fr for France or .sg for Singapore).

draft A temporary copy of a message that has not yet been sent, located in the Drafts folder.

email Short for *electronic mail*. The exchange of electronic text messages and computer file attachments between computers over a communications network, such as a local area network or the Internet.

email account A password-protected login on an email server that enables the account holder to send and receive email messages.

email message A message that is sent over a communications network such as a local area network or the Internet.

email server A computer that stores email messages that can be retrieved by email account holders.

encryption The process of disguising a message or data in such a way as to hide its substance.

event A calendar item, such as an appointment or meeting.

Fonts panel The interface element that offers options for setting the font, font size, font style, and other font-related options for selected text.

Global Address List (GAL) The address book that contains all user, group, and distribution list email addresses in your organization. The administrator creates and maintains this address book. It might also contain public folder email addresses.

grammar checker A feature that helps proofread text by identifying possible grammar errors based on an internal set of rules.

group An area of a ribbon tab containing buttons related to a specific document element or function.

Hypertext Markup Language (HTML) In Outlook, an email message format that supports paragraph styles, character styles, and backgrounds. Most email applications support the HTML format.

Hypertext Transfer Protocol (HTTP) A protocol used to access Web pages from the Internet.

Inbox The default location for incoming email. Each email account has its own Inbox; selecting the top-level Inbox item displays Inbox messages for all accounts.

Information Rights Management (IRM) A policy tool that gives authors control over how recipients use the documents and email messages they send.

instant messaging (IM) The ability to exchange messages in real time over the Internet. Most exchanges are text-only; however, some services allow attachments.

Internet Message Access Protocol (IMAP) A popular protocol for receiving email messages. It allows an email client to access and manipulate an email message without downloading it to the local computer. It is useful for accessing email from multiple devices or locations.

item list The center application pane that lists email messages, contacts, tasks, or notes depending on the current view.

junk email Unsolicited commercial email (UCE). Also known as *spam*.

keyboard shortcut Any combination of keystrokes that can be used to perform a task that would otherwise require a mouse or other pointing device.

Mail view The application view displaying email items and the tools to create and manage them.

meeting A block of time you schedule on your calendar that has a defined start time and end time, and to which you invite other attendees. See also *appointment*.

meeting request A message form linked to an Outlook calendar item. Meeting requests are generated by Outlook to manage meeting attendance.

meeting window The application window displaying the form in which you enter information to place a meeting on your calendar.

message body The portion of an email message containing the message text.

message composition window The application window displaying the form in which you create or respond to an email message.

message header Summary information for an email message that includes these fields: Subject, From, Received, Importance, Attachment, and Size.

message reading window The application window displaying the contents of a received email message.

MobileMe A fee-based service offered by Apple, Inc. that includes an IMAP email account, online data storage, and other features.

Month view A calendar view that shows the events for one month at a time.

My Day An application that is part of Microsoft Outlook; it displays the calendar items and tasks associated with the current day.

navigation pane The column on the left side of the Outlook window that includes a list of accounts, folders, and categories. Click an item folder to show its contents.

Notes view The application view displaying notes and the tools to create and manage them.

offline address book A copy of an address book that has been downloaded so that an Outlook user can access the information it contains while disconnected from the server. Exchange administrators can choose which address books are made available to users who work offline, and they can also configure the method by which the address books are distributed.

Outbox An email folder containing email messages to be sent. The Outbox is created automatically by Outlook when the user is working offline and disappears as soon as its contents are sent.

Outlook Help button The button located on the toolbar, labeled with a question mark (?), that provides access to the Outlook Help system.

permissions Rules associated with a shared resource on a network, such as a file, directory, or printer. Permissions provide authorization to perform operations associated with these objects. Permissions can typically be assigned to groups, global groups, or individual users.

phishing message A technique used to trick computer users into revealing personal or financial information. A common online phishing scam starts with an email message that appears to come from a trusted source but actually directs recipients to provide information to a fraudulent Web site.

phishing site A Web site that prompts users to update personal information, such as bank accounts and passwords, which might be used for identity theft.

Plain Text An email message format that does not support character or paragraph formatting. All email applications support Plain Text.

plain text files Files that contain no formatting elements. Plain text files can be opened and edited with all text editing applications, including TextEdit, and can be accessed on all operating systems.

plain text messages Messages that don't support character or paragraph formatting in the message content.

point to To pause the cursor over a button or other area of the display.

Post Office Protocol (POP) A standard method that computers use to send and receive email messages. POP messages are typically held on an email server until you download them to your computer, and then they are deleted from the server.

presence icon A colored icon that indicates the online presence and status of a contact.

Quick Look A Mac OS feature that enables you to see the content of a file attachment without opening the attachment in another application. Quick Look works within Outlook for certain types of files.

reading pane The right pane in the Outlook window that displays the details of an item selected in the item list.

recurring item An appointment, meeting, or task that occurs repeatedly on a specific schedule. For example, a weekly status meeting or a monthly haircut can be designated as recurring. You can specify a calendar item or task as recurring, and set the frequency of recurrence. Outlook then creates a series of items based on your specifications.

Reference Tools A Toolbox window pane that offers access to Thesaurus, Dictionary, Bilingual Dictionary, Translation, and Web Search features.

reminder A message that appears at a specified interval before an appointment, meeting, or task that announces when the activity is set to occur. Reminders appear any time Outlook is running, even if it isn't your active application.

resend Create a new version of an original message with none of the extra information that might be attached to a forwarded message.

resolving The process of matching a user name to the information on a network server, resulting in the user name being replaced by a display name and the name underlined.

ribbon A user interface element that organizes commands into logical groups, which appear on separate tabs.

rules Sets of criteria defining specific actions that Outlook takes when the criteria are fulfilled.

Scrapbook A Toolbox feature that enables you to store text, images, and other contents that can be pasted into documents created with any Microsoft Office for Mac application.

ScreenTip A note that appears on the screen to provide information about a toolbar button, tracked change, or comment, or to display a footnote or endnote. ScreenTips also display the text that will appear if you choose to insert a date or AutoText entry.

Secure Multipurpose Internet Mail Extensions (S/MIME) A protocol that supports secure mail features such as digital signatures and message encryption.

separated text file A file containing unformatted text organized into fields and records. Records are separated by carriage returns; fields are separated by a specific character such as a comma, tab, colon, or semicolon. Separated text files might have the file name extension .txt or .csv.

shared attachment An attachment saved on a SharePoint document workspace Web site, where a group can collaborate to work on files and discuss a project.

shortcut menu A menu that shows a list of commands relevant to a particular item. Sometimes referred to as a *context menu*.

smart folder A special folder created using the search feature that displays current search results whenever selected. Smart folders appear in the navigation pane.

spam Unsolicited commercial email (UCE). Also known as *junk email*.

spelling checker A feature that helps proofread text by identifying possible spelling errors based on internal and user dictionaries.

Spotlight A Mac OS search feature implemented in Outlook through the use of a search box in the toolbar. Entering any search criteria in the Spotlight search box immediately displays search results in the Outlook window and offers additional searching options on the Search tab.

status bar A line of information related to the current application. The status bar is usually located at the bottom of a window. Not all windows have a status bar.

tab A tabbed page on the ribbon that contains buttons organized in groups.

task window The application window displaying the form in which you enter information to create or manage a task.

tasks list The center pane that displays content in Tasks view.

Tasks view The application view displaying tasks and the tools to create and manage them.

thread In email conversations, a series of messages and replies that are all related to a specific topic.

title bar The horizontal bar at the top of a window that contains the name of the window. On many windows, the title bar also contains the Close, Minimize, and Zoom buttons.

toolbar The row of buttons beneath the main window's title bar.

Toolbox A floating window that offers access to the Scrapbook and Reference Tools features of Outlook.

Uniform Resource Locator (URL) An address that uniquely identifies a location on the Internet. A URL is usually preceded by http://, as in http://www.microsoft.com. A URL can contain more detail, such as the name of a page of hypertext, often with the file name extension .html or .htm.

view switcher A series of buttons located on the left side of the window beneath the navigation pane; it is used to switch between the five Outlook views and access their data and features.

views Function-based collections of interface elements for accessing Outlook features. Outlook has five views: Mail, Calendar, Contacts, Tasks, and Notes.

virtual private network (VPN) The extension of a private network that encompasses encapsulated, encrypted, and authenticated links across shared or public networks. VPN connections typically provide remote access and router-to-router connections to private networks over the Internet.

Week view A calendar view that shows the events for one week at a time.

work week The days and times you define within Outlook as available for work-related activities.

Work Week view A calendar view that shows the events for one work week at a time.

Index

A

About the Author

Maria Langer has written more than 70 books about business and productivity software (Microsoft Office, FileMaker Pro), web publishing software (WordPress), social networking services (Twitter), financial software (QuickBooks, Quicken), and operating system software (Mac OS).

Read more from Maria on her blog at http://www.aneclecticmind.com. You can also follow Maria on Twitter at http://twitter.com/mlanger.

What do you think of this book?

We want to hear from you!

To participate in a brief online survey, please visit:

microsoft.com/learning/booksurvey

Tell us how well this book meets your needs—what works effectively, and what we can do better. Your feedback will help us continually improve our books and learning resources for you.

Thank you in advance for your input!

Microsoft®
Press

Stay in touch!

To subscribe to the *Microsoft Press® Book Connection Newsletter*—for news on upcoming books, events, and special offers—please visit:

microsoft.com/learning/books/newsletter